CHILDREN, WELFARE
AND THE STATE

CHILDREN, WELFARE
AND THE STATE

Edited by Barry Goldson
Michael Lavalette and Jim McKechnie

SAGE Publications
London • Thousand Oaks • New Delhi

SAGE Publications Ltd
6 Bonhill Street
London EC2A 4PU

SAGE Publications Inc.
2455 Teller Road
Thousand Oaks, California 91320

SAGE Publications India Pvt. Ltd
32, M-Block Market
Greater Kailash – I
New Delhi 110 048

British Library Cataloguing in Publication data
A catalogue record for this book is available from the British
Library

ISBN 0 7619 7232 3
      0 7619 7233 1 (pbk)

Library of Congress control number 2002101996

Typeset by Mayhew Typesetting, Rhayader, Powys
Printed in India at Gopsons Papers Ltd, Noida

Contents

Acknowledgements

We would like to thank each of the contributors for the help, advice and patience that they offered during the writing and editorial process in the course of preparing this book. At Sage Karen Phillips has been very supportive of the project as has the production team, including in particular Louise Wise and Lauren McAllister. The comments that we received from the appointed external referees were helpful and thought-provoking and we have tried to take account of their advice, guidance and concerns, although only they can judge the extent to which we have succeeded in this respect. Finally, many of the ideas that inform this book have been 'tried and tested' on our students in various childhood studies courses that we run at our universities. Their contributions, insight, feedback and queries have helped to clarify our ideas and they have hopefully served to assist our students of the future by making this a better book.

Barry Goldson, Michael Lavalette and Jim McKechnie
January 2002

Contributors

Brian Corby is Professor of Social Work at the University of Central Lancashire.

Stephen Cunningham is a lecturer in Social Policy at the University of Central Lancashire.

Barry Goldson is a senior lecturer in the Department of Sociology, Social Policy and Social Work Studies at the University of Liverpool.

Deena Haydon is a Principal Officer for Research and Development with Barnardos and Research Fellow at the Centre for Studies in Crime and Social Justice at Edge Hill University College.

Sandy Hobbs is a Reader in Psychology at the University of Paisley.

Chris Jones is Professor of Social Work and Social Policy at the University of Liverpool.

Michael Lavalette is a senior lecturer in the Department of Sociology, Social Policy and Social Work Studies at the University of Liverpool.

Henry Maitles is a lecturer in Education at the University of Strathclyde, Jordanhill Campus.

Jim McKechnie is a senior lecturer in Psychology at the University of Paisley.

Tony Novak is a lecturer in the Department of Sociology, Social Policy and Social Work Studies at the University of Liverpool.

Phil Scraton is Professor of Criminology and Director of the Centre for Studies in Crime and Social Justice at Edge Hill University College.

Niamh Stack is a lecturer in Psychology at the University of Paisley.

ONE

Children, Welfare and the State: An Introduction

BARRY GOLDSON

This book is primarily intended for undergraduate students engaged in the broad area of childhood and youth studies. Increasing numbers of students and academics alike are developing interests in this area of scholarship across a wide disciplinary spectrum. Furthermore, in addition to taught courses there is a thriving research agenda in the field, together with sustained interest in policy analysis and the impact of state policy formation specific to children and young people. Such developments are not confined to the UK and are being replicated elsewhere. Indeed, in many important respects international standards, treaties and rules – perhaps most notably the United Nations Convention on the Rights of the Child – have served to energise such academic study and research across a global context.

Set against this backdrop there is also a relatively far-reaching sense of unease in the UK in relation to children and young people, or with regard to certain constituencies of children and young people to be more precise. Such concern takes various forms. Many commentators have argued that children's rights are unduly limited and their opportunities to actively participate in civic life is unnecessarily circumscribed. Others have suggested that children have too many rights and claim that this has led to indiscipline and a diminishing sense of respect within the young. On the one hand there is an increasing awareness of extensive child poverty in the UK despite relative national prosperity, and this has served to mobilise action and raise fundamental questions with regard to social justice and child welfare. On the other hand, Jeffs and Smith (1996) have suggested that adult anxieties have rumbled uncomfortably in recent years in tandem with the 'widespread belief' that children and young people 'are in some way turning feral' and this has led to calls for greater controls, stricter discipline and ultimately harsher punishment. Indeed, the populist notion that a 'crisis' besets contemporary childhood, necessitating firm action, is not uncommon (Scraton, 1997).

This book addresses many of the complex and competing issues that increasingly exercise the minds of students, academics, policy-makers, professional practitioners, parents, members of the public and children and young people alike, questions, that is, that relate directly to children, welfare and the state.

In Chapter 2 Lavalette and Cunningham engage with some of the most pressing contemporary sociological debates in relation to children and childhood. They begin with two primary questions: *who are children* and *what is childhood*, questions which can serve to unsettle and disturb otherwise fixed ideas and domain assumptions. The chapter identifies polarised conceptualisations of childhood: from the idealised notion of a carefree period of protected insulation from the harshness of the adult world, to a decidedly more austere abstraction which portrays children as an oppressed people subject to adult domination and coercion. Lavalette and Cunningham proceed to distinguish universalistic conceptualisations from those which emphasise spatial and temporal specificities and the 'moving image' of childhood. Moreover, the determining contexts of class, 'race' and gender are examined and the differentiated experiences of children, contingent upon structural relations, are illustrated and discussed. The chapter summarises the principal arguments that have been developed within classical historical accounts of childhood before assessing the divergent theoretical priorities characteristic of the 'new sociology'. In this latter endeavour Lavalette and Cunningham critically assess the different theoretical strains that are rooted in, and informed by, relations between *socio-economic structure* and *individual agency* on the one hand, and *post-modernist* paradigms on the other. The authors conclude by re-stating the primacy of social class in determining children's experiences of childhood, a theme which features both implicitly and explicitly throughout the book.

In Chapter 3 Hobbs too engages in debate with the 'new' sociologists of childhood, particularly in respect to the contribution that psychology has made, and can make, to comprehending children and childhood. Indeed, Hobbs argues that some of the 'new sociologists' have tended to essentialise and over-simplify psychology and have neglected to recognise the diversity of psychological perspectives and approaches. Furthermore, Hobbs contends that such apparent reductionism has served to misrepresent the work of prominent psychologists including Piaget and Freud, and to misunderstand the psychologists' appreciation of the significance of children's agency. Hobbs analyses examples of applied psychological research which have directly benefited certain constituencies of children. In this respect the argument returns to the problems associated with an homogenised conceptualisation of childhood, as previously raised by Lavalette and Cunningham. Indeed, the importance of recognising the differentiated nature of childhood experience is illustrated by reference to children with autism, and Hobbs sets out a persuasive case with regard to the contribution of psychology in this respect. Ultimately Hobbs appeals for a more integrated, and less fragmented and mono-discipline-oriented social science in relation to the development of childhood studies.

In Chapter 4 McKechnie traces a convergence of developments which have combined to shape and influence the direction of contemporary empirical research into children and childhood. In this sense it is argued that international standards, treaties and rules (perhaps most notably the United Nations Convention on the Rights of the Child), together with the provisions of domestic statute, increasingly emphasise the child's right to express an opinion. More importantly, however, the same legal instruments provide that children's opinions should be taken into account in any matter of procedure that might affect them. McKechnie observes that the policies, procedures and practices of many non-governmental organisations have been particularly influenced by such developments, and so too have academic researchers (including the 'new sociologists' of childhood) in their quest to seek the 'voice of the child'. McKechnie welcomes the new emphasis on children's agency and the 'actor-status' of the child, together with the overall methodological priority to engage with the child as *subject* as distinct from mere *object* of inquiry. However, he also explicitly recognises the practical and methodological complexities of actually reaching, understanding, interpreting and applying 'children's voices' to the development of knowledge in ways that are robust and defensible. In considering such issues McKechnie critically assesses the respective merits and deficits of qualitative and quantitative research approaches, illustrating both by reference to practical examples. He also explores the technical, epistemological and ideological imperatives that influence methodological preferences and specific research designs, and he makes a case for a synthesis of methods (and academic disciplines) which most appropriately suit the specificities of circumstance in researching children and childhood.

Taken together, Chapters 2–4 therefore address and critically examine some of the 'big' questions in relation to the study of children and childhood: contemporary developments in sociological and psychological theorisation and research, together with an assessment of qualitative and quantitative research approaches. The remaining chapters serve to narrow the focus and identify the significance of major aspects of social policy and state agency responses with regard to specific elements of childhood experience and/or particular constituencies of children. Here the emphasis is placed on rich children, poor children, those in school and subject to formal education, those engaged in work and labour, those 'looked after' by the state, those in conflict with the law, those who endure violation and abuse from adults, those whose sexuality and sexual identity are circumscribed and regulated, and finally those who mobilise particular forms of resistance.

In Chapter 5 therefore, Novak re-engages with the notion of differentiated childhood by addressing the primacy of social class and the contrasting experiences of children living in a grossly unequal and deeply divided Britain. Whereas child poverty and social exclusion feature prominently on the respective agendas of government departments, state agencies and the panoply of non-governmental organisations, Novak argues that the analytic, policy and practice emphasis tends to treat poor children in isolation. This chapter rectifies such partiality by examining the relation between poverty and wealth and by starkly juxtaposing the respective fortunes of poor children and rich children. Novak contends that although the post-war period of reconstruction and the emergence of the welfare state offered some relief from the excesses of inequality and injustice, the consolidation of neo-liberalism and the social consequences of a completely unbridled free-market economy have re-established patterns of acute social and economic polarisation over the past two decades. Within this context childhood is divided and compartmentalised along class lines and by focusing upon health and education in particular, Novak examines the disadvantages of poor children with the contrasting privileges of their rich counterparts. The analysis exposes both the limitations of monolithic conceptualisations of childhood together with the profound impediments of the New Labour government's approach to eradicating child poverty.

In Chapter 6 Maitles further develops the theme of class-based inequality with specific regard to children's education. Here it is argued that the relation between poverty and disadvantage on the one hand, and educational under-achievement on the other, is well-established within social scientific research and education practice experience. Notwithstanding this, however, Maitles contends that the primary implications of such a relation are being neglected within contemporary education policy and practice which has been witness to significant shifts in emphasis in recent years. He argues that in this respect earlier (and to a certain extent effective) efforts to address educational inequalities by means of comprehensive schools, reduced class sizes and improved staff–pupil ratios, have been supplanted by increasingly managerialist and market-oriented techniques ostensibly targeted at improving efficiency and effectiveness. Consequently children are being subjected to increasing assessment and tests, schools are having to contend with crude performance inspections which gauge their success or otherwise in meeting externally imposed targets, and the educational system is facing burgeoning deregulation as private business interests steadily assert their influence. Not unlike Novak, Maitles contrasts the generous educational resources and privileges that are available to certain constituencies of children with the hardships and rations that are endured by others. Furthermore, despite the rhetoric of the New Labour government and its associated pro-education claims, Maitles detects little evidence to suggest that access to educational opportunities is a right that the children of the poor can expect to enjoy.

There is a certain irony in the observation that state education, which Novak and Maitles each regard as failing significant proportions of working-class children at the beginning of the twenty-first century, essentially served to 'rescue' such children from exploitative employment relations during the 19th century. Indeed, in Chapter 7 Stack and McKechnie trace the historical processes and key policy developments which have effectively re-situated children's 'place' from work and wage labour to school and state education. This re-situating resonates with the social constructionist concepts that Lavalette and Cunningham introduced in Chapter 2 and it reveals the means by which conceptualisations of children and childhood change over time and space. Notwithstanding this, however, Stack and McKechnie argue that child employment legislation and associated regulatory policies and practices have largely been ineffective. Indeed, by referring to various research studies they demonstrate that work is neither a marginal nor a particularly safe activity for children. Children are engaged in a wide variety of work practices within which they are largely under-paid and under-protected. Stack and McKechnie begin to unravel many of the complex issues relating to child employment including its relation to children's educational performance. They conclude the chapter by suggesting that notwithstanding the methodological complexities (as considered by McKechnie in Chapter 4), the processes of gleaning greater understanding of working children necessitates engaging with the 'voice' of such children themselves.

In Chapter 8 Jones traces the key policy milestones that have shaped the development of state responses to the welfare needs of the most disadvantaged children and young people. In common with previous chapters social class is central to the analysis and it is argued that state social work in Britain has always been a class-specific activity. By initially focusing upon the Children Acts of 1908 and 1948 Jones contends that post-war policy developments can be seen to represent a departure – albeit qualified and tentative – from what he terms the 'purposeful neglect' of that which had gone before. Notwithstanding this, Jones argues that formal state welfare is ultimately driven by instrumental purpose (economic imperatives, regulation and the maintenance of order) as distinct from intrinsic human concern and compassion. As the demand for labour and a healthy and educated mass workforce has receded in recent years Jones detects that rehabilitative ideals and the ostensible rationality of therapeutic casework have equally diminished within state social work. Instead, the practices of restriction, regulation, surveillance and control have gained ascendancy. Not unlike Novak in Chapter 5, Jones contends that New Labour has determinedly refused to abandon neo-liberal priorities. Furthermore, within this macro context, and despite the best and most genuine efforts of many social work practitioners at the micro level, it is argued that the children of the poor have their rights routinely violated and their needs denied along a state social work continuum extending from indifference at one end to abject abuse at the other.

In Chapter 9 I focus attention on children in conflict with the law, and on the historical development of policy and state agency practice with regard to such children. The chapter engages with a number of key issues that are raised throughout the book. First, the means by which children who 'offend' are *socially constructed*. Are they to be seen primarily as 'children' or as 'offenders'? How do the identities that are ascribed to them impact upon and influence the construction of policy and the formal responses of state agencies? Second, the relationship between *socio-economic structure* and *individual agency*. Are the children who come to the attention of state agencies as child offenders (most of whom are drawn from the most disadvantaged sections of the working class) to be conceptualised as 'deprived' or 'depraved'? Third, the tensions between welfare, care and supportive advocacy on the one hand, and punishment, control and subordinating regulation on the other. What political priorities, economic interests and ideological imperatives impact upon policy and practice responses to children in trouble? Not unlike Jones's analysis of contemporary developments within state social work, the concluding observations of this chapter identify a burgeoning mood of impatience and intolerance in relation to children in trouble and a corresponding proclivity to subject them to increasingly repressive modes of governance and regulation.

In Chapter 10 Corby explicitly focuses upon the abuses endured by many children together with the formal apparatus comprising the child protection system. Earlier chapters have raised a range of discomforting doubts with regard to the benign intent of state policy and the deficiencies of agency practices. Corby too engages with such concerns, and in providing a historical review of child protection policy development he critically examines the complex and competing (even contradictory) priorities that have exercised influence in this field. The relation between the state and the family is central to Corby's analysis within which the respective rights, duties and responsibilities of state agencies, parents and children are negotiated and settled. Dominant conceptualisations of the caring and protective capacities of adults with regard to children are challenged as Corby considers various forms of violation: sexual abuse; physical abuse; emotional and psychological abuse; organised and ritualised abuses; and cruelty and neglect. Moreover, the chapter considers child abuse both within and outwith families including the violation of children 'looked after' in public care, and in so doing it connects with a number of issues raised by Jones's critical analysis of state social work. Corby also addresses the structural contexts within which child abuse is located and examines gender relations together with the impact of class and poverty, further developing and applying some of the core themes which run across the book.

In Chapter 11 Haydon and Scraton further develop the critical assessment of the state–'family' relation. Here it is initially argued that moral reductionism has displaced material context in dominant contemporary analyses of the sexual behaviour of children and young people. This particularly applies to the tendency to problematise and morally scold teenage pregnancies, the 'irresponsible' sexual behaviours of children and young people, and the (working-class) families (even communities) within which they live. Haydon and Scraton provide an overview of policy developments in relation to formal sex and sexuality education within which they critically interrogate its politics and underpinning priorities. They argue that although certain progressive shifts in contemporary approaches to such education are discernible (within which crude medico-biological emphases are being replaced with a more holistic health orientation embracing personal and social education), reactionary domain assumptions continue to prevail. In this sense Haydon and Scraton identify the hegemonic symbolic presence of conjugal family forms, marriage, parenthood and 'conventional' gendered relations; the normalisation of heterosexual relations and the reproductive imperative; and the corresponding marginalisation (if not moral condemnation) of gay and lesbian sexualities. Furthermore, they argue that the omnipresent construction of childhood 'innocence' and vulnerability serves to legitimise the 'protection' of children and the regulation of their formal sex and sexuality education in ways which control and confine them and profoundly circumscribe their rights.

Chapters 5–11, therefore, essentially examine the means by which state policy, and the practices of its agencies, establish the conditions within which children (especially working-class and particularly disadvantaged children) live their childhoods. In this sense the chapters critically assess what the state does *for* children and what it does *to* them. The penultimate chapter departs from this sequence in an important respect and re-engages with the notions of 'children's voice' and 'children's agency' (discussed in Chapters 2–4) in a unique and distinctive way. Indeed, in Chapter 12 the analytical emphasis shifts from what is done *for* and *to* working-class children, to what such children can collectively do for themselves in advancing and promoting their particular interests and concerns.

In Chapter 12, then, Cunningham and Lavalette examine the concept of children's agency not on an individualised level but with regard to organised political protest and collective action. Despite frequently expressed concerns (and some evidence) that working-class children and young people increasingly show signs of 'disaffection' from, and uninterest in, the 'mainstream' political process, Cunningham and Lavalette argue that many such children and young people are actively engaged in politics in a wider context. Moreover, they contend that such engagement has a long and well-established history. By drawing on four discrete but inter-related examples, Cunningham and Lavalette examine the active role of working-class children in collective action in 1889, 1911, 1972 and 1985. Three introductory points are particularly noteworthy with regard to this analysis.

First, and especially in relation to the more contemporary examples identified by Cunningham and Lavalette, is the significance of the primary concerns that underpinned children's protest and collective action: an objection to being subjected to corporal punishment at school; a distaste for regimentation and uniformity at school; a demand for meaningful participation within school; and frustrated aspirations for a decent future within which employment is a realistic prospect. The 'ordinariness' and 'reasonableness' of such concerns is conspicuous and they resonate with many issues that prevail within contemporary academic and policy debates in relation to children and young people: child abuse and the right of the child to physical integrity and freedom from assault; children's right to free expression; citizenship, participation and school councils; and school–work transitions and youth labour markets. Second, is the extraordinary sense of class consciousness, collectivity and revulsion at social injustice expressed by the children and young people, together with their disciplined determination to make the world a better place. Third, is the reaction to the children's actions by the media and the state, a reaction characterised by hostility, impatience and contempt and accompanied by an adult determination to seek revenge through punishment. It is the stark contrast between the first two of these points and the third that is most striking. In many important respects such contrast epitomises the issues that lie at the core of this book.

The chapters that follow therefore provide an introductory overview of the diversity of experiences, the key questions within contemporary social scientific analyses and the major sites of state policy formation with regard to children and childhood. Whilst it is increasingly necessary to analyse and theorise childhood as a discrete conceptual entity, it is equally important to appreciate its diversity and to understand that not all children experience their childhood in the same way. In this book the various contributors explicitly emphasise class relations, alongside a more implicit analysis of gendered and racialised divisions, which interact with class to comprise the structural complexity within which childhood is, and has always been, located. Let us be clear in case there is any misunderstanding: we are fully aware of the range of social divisions that impact upon children's experience of childhood. We emphasise class in the belief that within the developing academic literature on childhood its central significance is increasingly marginalised.

The discussion and analyses that follow are by no means exhaustive. However, we suggest that they provide a very firm foundation which will serve to underpin further reading, research and study – research and study that will of necessity focus on the range of social divisions that interact with class and define the contours of children's lives.

TWO

The Sociology of Childhood

MICHAEL LAVALETTE AND STEPHEN CUNNINGHAM

[A] right to childhood . . . [is] the noblest duty of the Republic [of the USA]. (US Reformer Florence Kelley, in 1905, quoted in Lindenmeyer, 1997: 1)

In medieval society the idea of childhood did not exist; this is not to suggest that children were neglected, forsaken or despised. The idea of childhood is not to be confused with affection for children. (Ariès, 1962: 125)

There is nothing natural or inevitable about childhood. Childhood is culturally defined and created. (Nandy, 1992: 56)

Of the many variables concerning childhood . . . one stands out: the difference between rich and poor childhoods. (Davin, 1990: 37)

[Childhood] is a cocoon [which] can stifle and oppress as well as comfort. (Franklin, 1995: 7)

INTRODUCTION

We all have a very clear idea about what we think the concepts 'child' and 'childhood' are. After all we have all been children (though we may disagree about the age we stopped being a child, and we may question the UN Convention on the Rights of the Child which provides that childhood extends up until the age of 18). Further, most of us can remember – perhaps rather idealistically – the experiences that made up our own childhood. In general, *children* are viewed as vulnerable, in need of protection (and perhaps discipline), and in some way 'incomplete' – not yet adults, not yet fully rational, not yet fully able to participate in social life. In modern society, *childhood* is usually thought of as a natural set of experiences suitable to individuals at this early stage of human development. Childhood is protected and respected, free from (adult) worries and responsibilities, a time of learning and play, a period of happiness and relative freedom.

Yet the various quotations given at the start of this chapter pose a number of searching questions that can puncture this idealisation of childhood: Who are children? What is childhood, and has it always been the same? Is childhood the same in all cultures? How is childhood affected by class (or gender, or 'race', or indeed racism)? Does childhood bring benefits to children, or does it oppress them – is it something to be strived for and defended or castigated and abolished?

These kinds of questions are not easy to resolve. Often apparently simple solutions (for example, the claim that children are all young people under the age of 16 – the first school-leaving age in Britain) can, on further analysis, be *simplistic* – failing to grasp the complexity and range of the issues at stake. Thus with this example, we should immediately ask: *'why 16?'* Although students can leave school at 16 today, prior to 1944 the school-leaving age was 14, and was only raised to 16 in 1972. In other countries there are different school-leaving ages: thus, do age-related definitions of 'the child' vary historically and cross-culturally or is a child the same in all countries and in all eras? In Britain people cannot vote until the age of 18, thus in terms of official politics they are viewed as immature until this age – and this is the rationale adopted by the UN Convention: children become adults when they reach the age of majority. In England and Wales people cannot get married without parental permission until they are 18 (though this is not a requirement in Scotland where they can marry from 16). Children can, however, be tried for crimes – as adults, but usually in special courts – from the age of 10. Thus even an apparently simple process like defining children by reference to age is fraught with problems.

Issues like these are not new; indeed they have been around in various guises for at least the last 200 years as various social commentators have tried to come to terms with the 'problem of children'. From the early nineteenth century in Britain, for example, there have been various groups advocating the 'protection' of poor and working-class children from the harsh social consequences of the Industrial Revolution and rapid urbanisation – for some this included direct intervention by state agencies into children's lives. Amongst the protectionist advocates were both middle- and upper-class philanthropists (such as Richard Oastler or Lord Shaftesbury) as well as political radicals (such as Frederick Engels) and working-class political activists (like those active in the Workers' Short-Time Committees). Protectionist positions reflected a variety of concerns, many of them similar to social policy anxieties about children today – abhorrence at children's working and living conditions; the effects of family breakdown on young people; fear of uncontrolled and unruly groups of 'delinquents' and their involvement in crime; the economic effects of uneducated children (and hence uneducated future workers), and the imperial and social consequences of unfit and unhealthy future citizens. There was no single cause or direction to such concerns, nor was there a single solution offered. But what we can start to identify is a set of responses that were structured by both 'caring' and 'controlling' imperatives – and in terms of state-directed social policy often both these themes operated at the same time.

SOCIOLOGICAL CONCERNS

Until relatively recently sociologists tended to consider children within discrete sub-disciplinary boundaries such as 'the sociology of education' or the 'sociology of the family', and the dominant approach tended to be shaped by notions of 'socialisation' – that is, the various social processes at work *upon children* which shape them as adults.

However, from the late 1970s there has been a growing sociological interest in children and childhood as social categories, within which children themselves are active in shaping their own worlds and destinies. This is an approach that stresses the socially constructed nature of childhood as opposed to its biological 'naturalness'. It is a perspective that suggests that the present roles and activities of children are relatively recent historical and cultural creations – that in different societies children engage with social life in ways that contrast markedly with the expectations that dominate our present notion of what children should do and what childhood should be like.

Central to the sociological rethinking of childhood has been a reappraisal of the work of the French academic Philippe Ariès. In 1960 Ariès published a seminal work, *Centuries of Childhood* (first published in English in 1962), which argued that childhood had not always existed but was 'discovered'. The first tentative steps in this process were taken at the end of the thirteenth century and gradually developed and became more defined as a result of social changes from that period onwards – becoming more sharply formed at the end of the sixteenth and seventeenth centuries. Ariès' case was that the discovery of childhood coincided with the growth of the bourgeoisie as a social class in Europe and that childhood was a 'modern' phenomenon.

Over the last twenty years or so the notion that childhood is a recent creation of West European and North American societies has gained credence in a variety of policy-making and non-governmental organisation (NGO) circles. This is a partial reflection of at least four inter-related social and political developments. First, there has been an increased policy focus on children as a consequence of the *International Year of the Child* (1979) and the subsequent formulation of the *United Nations Convention on the Rights of the Child* (1989). Second, there has been an increasing focus within social theory on social roles, identities and oppression, which developed out of the growth of the social movements of the late 1960s (the women's, gay and black movements for example). Third, there has been a growing recognition that children's lives are radically different across the globe and, for some, this has led to a rejection of the notion that the 'Western ideal of childhood' is something to be strived for; this itself is a partial reflection of the fact that in 'Western' societies many children's lives do not match the 'ideal' but are scarred by sexual abuse, violence, poverty and discrimination. In these circumstances, a liberal cultural relativism – a notion that all cultures, and cultural practices and activities, are equally valid and contradictory, have their own internal logic and require understanding in their own terms – has come to dominate within NGO circles, with the consequence that a range and variety of – equally valid – childhoods have been identified. Finally, there has been the more visible involvement of children in campaigns affecting their lives (the National Union of School Students in Britain, the French pupils who took over and ran their schools during the occupations of 1968 and 1973, the black school students' boycott of lessons taught in Afrikaans in South Africa during the apartheid regime, the growth of unions for child workers in many developing countries). In these circumstances there have been increasing demands to listen to children's opinions and take account of their wants and desires, to recognise that children are legitimate social actors and not mere passive objects. For these and related reasons sociologists from the late 1970s onwards started to pay more attention to the social position and roles of children in society and what this meant for our understanding of childhood (Qvortrup, 1994).

More recently there has developed what advocates call a 'new sociology of childhood' (NSC) (James et al., 1998). The approach of the NSC is increasingly dominant within the social sciences. It is a committed and engaged approach to studying the worlds of children and emphasising children's rights, needs and interests. Nevertheless, despite its increasingly hegemonic dominance within childhood studies and in child advocacy circles later in this chapter (and in the two chapters that follow) we engage with what we see as some of its limitations.

Before this, however, we look more closely at the Ariès thesis. The importance of *Centuries of Childhood* cannot be overstated – it is a core text for anyone interested in the study of children and childhood. It is a text that poses a key question very sharply: has childhood always existed?

THE DISCOVERY OF CHILDHOOD?

Centuries of Childhood has three interlocking themes: the development of the modern privatised family, the growth of education, and the discovery and development of modern childhood. Ariès' method is to look at periods in the past and show that certain modern 'concepts' simply did not exist. When this is established he sets himself the task of tracing the processes whereby the 'old' relationships, forms of living or cultural practices gave way to 'new' or modern relationships. This is the approach he utilises to argue that childhood has not always existed but is in fact a modern 'discovery' or 'invention'.

During what he terms the *'ancien régime'* Ariès claims that there was a different pattern of age stratification to the present-day norm: unlike today, after a relatively short period of infancy children joined the adult world and were conceptualised and treated as small adults. Ariès suggests that there was an indifference to children, and that if children were ill, injured or died these events were faced with far less sentimentality than is the case today; there was a degree of coldness in parental–sibling relations that strikes us as unusual.

To justify his case Ariès draws on several sources of evidence, all of which seemed to indicate that in the past there was a different way of relating to and perceiving children. He produces evidence that suggests that young children dressed the same as adults:

> As soon as the child abandoned his swaddling-band . . . he was dressed just like the other men and women of his class. (1962: 48)

He suggests that children witnessed (and indeed participated in) various sexual activities:

> The lack of reserve with regard to children surprises us: we raise our eyebrows at the outspoken talk but even more at the bold gesture, the physical contacts, about which it is easy to imagine what a modern psychoanalyst would say. . . . Nowadays the physical contacts [typical of the early seventeenth century] . . . would strike us as bordering on sexual perversion and nobody would dare to indulge in them publicly. (1962: 101)

He claims that various games and pastimes (such as storytelling), that we tend to think of as appropriate to children, were actually activities that the entire community participated in:

> In 1600 the specialization of games and pastimes did not extend beyond infancy. After the age of three or four it decreased and disappeared. From then on the child played the same games as the adults, either with other children or with adults. (1962: 68)

And he argues that if we look at pictures of the period there is no evidence that children were seen as children: 'Artists were unable to depict a child except as a man on a smaller scale' (1962: 10).

But perhaps the source Ariès makes most use of is a diary of Heroard, the court physician during the reign of King Henri IV of France, which provides details of the life and experiences of the 'Dauphin', the future King Louis XIII.

There is no doubt that Heroard's diary portrays a childhood quite different from that ordinarily associated with the present-day norm. However, one must be aware that Heroard's descriptions of the Dauphin's experiences may be exaggerated and an idealisation of what actually took place; after all, this was no ordinary child. Ariès denies this point has any validity by claiming that: '[all] the royal children, legitimate or illegitimate, were treated in the same way as all aristocratic children and there was as yet no real difference between the king's palaces and the gentry's castles . . . young Louis XIII was brought up like his companions' (1962: 60).

Nevertheless, this is, in many ways, an admission that the childhood being described was typical of the children of the dominant classes. It certainly was quite unlike the lives led by the vast majority of children at this time who would, of course, have been the children of the peasantry.

In each of these sources Ariès notes a trend towards the 'discovery' of childhood around the beginning of the thirteenth century, but these only start to gain full significance in the late sixteenth and seventeenth centuries – a result of technological progress, the increasing hold of Christian ideas stressing child purity and the growth (numerically, as well as in terms of power and influence) of the bourgeoisie. These together created the conditions to establish the privatised family form, with the new protected and extended life-stage of childhood centrally embedded within it.

There is no doubt that Ariès' argument is powerful. The evidence he gathers clearly points to a world where children were treated differently to the norms and expectations of the modern world – indeed in places the contrast between the 'old' and the 'new' is so extreme (especially his discussion of the sexual liaisons of the young Dauphin) that it can be disconcerting for us to read and difficult for us to comprehend the ways in which children lived and were apparently treated in the past. But before we accept the Ariès case we need to look at a number of criticisms that are made of his argument before coming to a balanced assessment of the 'discovery thesis'.

THE CRITIQUE OF ARIÈS

Ariès' work has been subjected to considerable critical evaluation. In general terms it is useful to distinguish between three types of criticism: first, there are a number of writers who dispute the evidence gleaned from the historical sources used – and the meanings Ariès attaches to them; second, it is claimed there are a number of technical or conceptual difficulties in the form of explanation used by Ariès, and finally, there has been the evidence produced by a number of historians who undermine much of the 'discovery' thesis by emphasising the existence of childhood in earlier periods. We will look at each of these in turn.

As we noted, Ariès places considerable emphasis on the apparent inability of artists to paint children – depicting them as miniature adults. Yet two powerful critiques have questioned the validity of this claim. Wilson (1980) suggests that his claim rests on a simplistic theory that art directly mirrors the ways of social life. He argues:

It is to see them [the miniature adult paintings] as unconstrained reproductions, as objective documentation instead of the subjective and determinate artefacts which in fact they are. (1980: 140)

Peter Fuller argues that these paintings clearly had a social and political role – they were used as a bargaining factor in the negotiation of political marriages:

> Even when they had some other function, they were designed to express what the parents of the child hoped he or she would become. The way the child was made to appear in the present was always an appeal to a future which was projected onto the child, from the outside. . . . When we look at such pictures we should remember that what we are seeing has little, if anything, to do with the point of view of the child, or with the child's experience of the world. (1979: 78)

In other words, these pictures were an attempt to show children resplendent with the artefacts of their future power and wealth, or were an attempt to flatter wealthy parents about the beauty and social standing of their offspring.

As Fuller notes, there were artists at this period who did paint children as children (he lists, for example, Velazquez, Crivelli, Durer and Murillo) and it is also the case that today we are often confronted by images and photographs that portray children 'as adults' – what are often thought of as 'cute' images of children performing adult tasks, or dressed as adults, or rather more disturbingly, posing 'provocatively' to help sell clothes, fashion accessories or cosmetics.

Further, as both Wilson (1980) and Fuller (1979) point out, 'the miniature adult' paintings were focused on the children of the wealthy and powerful – the children of the dominant classes in society. On the whole, when children of the oppressed and exploited appeared in paintings they appeared from the perspective of the dominant class.

Similar criticisms could be made of the other evidence Ariès gathers. The notion that the discovery of childhood brought in its wake distinct clothing for children seems plausible – but then the children of the poor, whether poor peasant children or at a later date poor working-class children, did not have clothing that was obviously distinct from that of their parents. Today, designer labels and logo sportswear – which copy adult fashions – dominate children's clothing. Further, the development of the so-called 'tweeny market' has brought all variety of adult dress, cosmetic and fashion accessories to younger and younger children.

It is certainly true that there were different attitudes to sex and sexuality in the past. Crowded living conditions meant that children were much more aware of adult sexual activity, but there is little evidence of widespread sexual abuse of children in the past (Pollock, 1983). The state regulation of sexuality in its myriad forms only developed in the late nineteenth century, reflecting a variety of what we might term 'bourgeois concerns' about social order, family formation and the 'decline of the national character and stock' (Weeks, 1989; Woodward, 2001).

Games and pastimes have clearly changed and become more delineated over the last few hundred years. But it was never simply the case that adults and children always played together and nor is it the case that they never share pastimes and communal activities today – think of the many sporting activities enjoyed and played by adults and children, or going to the movies, or watching television. Children sometimes partake of these activities 'with other children and sometimes with adults' to apply Ariès' (1962: 68) claim about pastimes in the medieval era.

Finally, as we noted above, the diary of Heroard is not written about a typical child but a privileged one – whose life may have had similarities with other children in his social class but was a world away from the lives of the vast majority. In each of the sources Ariès cites, the poor and the dispossessed – and their children – simply do not appear. The sources used are class biased and, as Wilson (1980: 139) notes, 'one may ask how the illiterate would record their ideas and feelings; how the poor would commission works of art'.

The second set of criticisms relate to claimed technical and conceptual limitations with *Centuries of Childhood*. Ariès is accused of being 'chronologically vague'. For example, the beginning of the seventeenth century is variously described as both early and late in the period of discovery. His use of the imprecise concept *'ancien régime'* compounds this vagueness. Finally, the various concepts – like the significance of 'Christianisation' – are stated but never fully explained. He identifies various elements in the development of childhood – the growth of the bourgeoisie, the expansion of education, technological developments – but their links, how they reflect and impact upon each other, are never discussed leaving us with an unconnected list, the random and coincidental appearance of which created the conditions for childhood to emerge.

The final set of criticisms comes from a number of historians who, through their own research, identify a different set of parent–child relations to that suggested by Ariès from his reading of the early medieval period.

One early critic was Lloyd DeMause who edited a book called *The History of Childhood* (1974), in which he provided the theoretical case for what was termed the 'psychogenic' approach to childhood. DeMause argued that childhood had gradually evolved over thousands of years as a consequence of a closing of 'psychic' distance between parents and children. In the past parents had few parenting skills and hence treated children badly – indeed he argues that while a minority of children are abused in the world today, if we were to go back we would reach a point where most children were abused. Gradually, however, the psychic gap has been closed and we now have a more enlightened set of parent–child relations.

DeMause has been criticised for having a simplistic theory of psychological development (he assumes that personality is completely formed and unchangeable as a result of early parent–child interactions) and of producing a history of child abuse rather than childhood (Pollock, 1983). In his history, 'fragments' of evidence have been pieced together, but there is little general historical feel for each era being discussed. The collection as a whole is internally contradictory and both idealises the present and stigmatises the past.

But perhaps the reason for the various contradictions and inadequacies in the work are revealed in a footnote to the first theoretical chapter, where DeMause declares the psychogenic approach is a conscious application of methodological individualism (MI) to the history of childhood. MI is an approach that tries to explain societies and their institutions by reference to the individuals who comprise those societies or institutions, their concerns and actions. But the collection is clearly an example of theory driving historical research and interpretation with 'facts' being used to emphasise the significance of the psychogenic approach. It is also an 'anti-sociology' of childhood. For DeMause the parent–child relationship and closing psychic distance are the main determinants of historical development and any notion of social structure is deemed irrelevant.

The most powerful critique of Ariès comes from Linda Pollock in her book *Forgotten Children* (1983). Pollock's work is a devastating attack on the Ariès thesis. She is very critical of the use of indirect or secondary evidence used and suggests that when primary evidence is utilised (such as autobiographies and children's diaries) a much more familiar picture of childhood emerges. From her own research (an analysis of 500 diaries, autobiographies and related sources of British and American children) she suggests:

> Nearly all children were wanted, such development stages as weaning and teething aroused interest and concern, and parents revealed anxiety and distress at the illness or death of their children. (1983: 268)

Pollock's work itself is not without criticism (for Ariès weaning and teething were associated with infancy not childhood, so Pollock may miss her target here; the use of diary and autobiography means she relies on children of the upper classes as her main source and hence she is open to the accusation of class bias that is levelled at Ariès) but it did lead to the growth of what is sometimes called the 'new history of childhood' where the focus was on rediscovering children's accounts of their social lives – rather than adult conceptions of children and childhood. In *Growing Up in Medieval London* (1993) Barbara Hanawalt uses a variety of sources to try and capture the lives of children and young people in fourteenth- and fifteenth-century London. While noting that life was exceptionally harsh for children (and indeed for adults), and that the mortality rate for young children was high, she suggests there was no evidence of widespread abandonment or infanticide. She points to evidence suggesting that children were seen as being different from adults, that orphans were offered some degree of protection from the courts and that physical abuse of young people by adults (other than their parents) was viewed as unacceptable. Hanawalt (1993: 66) depicts a life where 'play, rather than serious work' was viewed as a central part of children's lives. Finally, she notes that in various pageants and festivals children had their own separate roles to perform – and in doing so she emphasises how children participated in, and created, their own cultures. As Corsaro points out, Hanawalt clearly challenges prior work which:

> Claimed that children were treated harshly in the medieval period and that they were forced to enter adult society at an early age with little opportunity to have or enjoy their childhoods. (1997: 56)

Hanawalt and Pollock both emphasise that children were viewed as different to adults in the 'pre-modern' era. However inarticulately expressed by those living through these earlier times, children were thought to have distinct needs and requirements, it was assumed they went through identifiable periods of development and, hence, they engaged with society and those about them in a distinct way – as children.

ARIÈS: AN ASSESSMENT

The various criticisms levelled at Ariès' work clearly leave a major question mark against the 'discovery thesis'. What kind of assessment should we come to?

The first point to re-emphasise is the importance of his work. It focused the sociological imagination on childhood and emphasised that childhood is not a static life-stage but has altered across time and space.

But Ariès' work has been shown to be inaccurate in so far as it claims that childhood was 'discovered' – rather than noting the ways it has changed in different settings and at different times. The childhoods described by, for example, Hanawalt are not the same as the supposed ideal experienced by children in modern Western societies today – childhood has changed as societies have changed. But Pollock and Hanawalt clearly show that in pre-modern societies there was a recognition that children were different from adults and that they had distinct biological and psychological needs – these were expressed and experienced through 'childhood', albeit a radically different childhood from the dominant one within Western societies today.

Thus while Ariès' work points to the *social construction* of childhood, we need to add that it is constructed within particular contexts. As the dominant social relations of production, family form and the individual's engagement with society have altered so too have the various forms of 'childhood' changed.

What Ariès identified was the development of a more recognisably 'bourgeois' childhood – a development that grew up within the feudal absolutist regimes in the sixteenth and seventeenth centuries. But this was a process that affected a minority of children at this period, for the majority of children in this era childhood was radically different. Similarly the transition to capitalism and the rise to dominance of the bourgeoisie as a class did not immediately lead to the imposition of a bourgeois family form or a bourgeois form of childhood onto the rest of society. In the seventeenth, eighteenth, nineteenth and even twentieth centuries class divisions, and differences in class experience, meant that there were still clearly distinct childhoods. In the following section we look at this contrast by looking at working-class childhoods.

WORKING-CLASS CHILDHOODS

Class location has always had a major impact on childhood. Looking at the eighteenth and nineteenth centuries the social historian Anna Davin (1990) has argued that bourgeois and working-class children had quite different childhoods. For bourgeois children, life experiences were highly gendered. For boys life started in the nursery, moved on to the preparatory school, then public school, university, army, church or business. For girls, the nursery was gradually replaced by education within the home and preparation for coming out as a debutante and marriage, where the restrictions of the parental home would be replaced by those of their husbands'.

Here we see elements of the 'new' childhood discovered by Ariès – the separation of the child and childhood from adults and the adult world; the notion that the child is engaged in a process of 'becoming' an adult; the distinctive clothes, pastimes and activities of children; the rigid separation of children from discussion and knowledge of sexual activity, and the extension of the life-stage childhood where children are infantilised and kept in their confined and restricted child-like state for a much longer period.

However, this childhood was far removed from the experiences of working-class children in the seventeenth, eighteenth and nineteenth centuries. Working-class children's lives were shaped by poverty and the struggle for survival, participation in a range of labouring activities, childcare responsibilities with younger siblings (especially for girls), play on the streets of the developing and expanding towns and cities and a much quicker integration in the 'adult world'. As Davin notes, working-class children:

> Were prepared for adult life through participation, and their early experiences equipped them for responsibility and independence at an age when their *betters* were still in the classroom. (1990: 39)

There is also little doubt that working-class children had far more freedom than their 'betters' – and indeed than future working-class children. Here we see a contradiction that is still discussed in NGO and academic circles today in the form of debate over child protection or liberation: should children be protected from the ravages of capitalism or liberated from the confines of childhood?

From the seventeenth to mid-nineteenth century, there was little in the way of child-specific state regulation, there was minimal state welfare and there were few voluntary and philanthropic agencies providing genuine 'relief' for the poor. What welfare there was, was punitive. The Poor Laws (Old and New) stigmatised the poor and – in the form of 'pauper apprentices' – split families and sent young children from their home towns to learn a trade and earn a living. The state attempted to control the poor (including poor children) by violence, punishment and containment. Ironically, given the Ariès thesis outlined above, when the state attempted to discipline working-class children it did so by treating them like 'miniature adults'. For example, at the Old Bailey, in 1814, on one day alone, five children under 14 were condemned to death after being found guilty of theft and burglary (Pinchbeck and Hewitt, 1973: 352) and in all, 103 children under 14 received capital sentences at the Old Bailey between 1801 and 1836 – though as Shore (1999) notes, none of these sentences were actually carried out. Nor were children spared other forms of 'adult' punishment. For instance, between 1812 and 1817, 780 males and 136 females under the age of 21 were transported to Australia (May, 1973: 9). While with the spread of market capitalism the poor had little option but to sell their labour power in order to survive – family poverty meant that men, women and children all engaged in whatever forms of labouring activity they could find, though often unemployment and under-employment made the struggle for survival more extreme. In these circumstances, the lives of the majority of children was exceptionally harsh, oppressive and exploitative.

In this context there were increasing calls from radicals and embryonic working-class organisations for state regulation of work, for improvements in the urban environment, for provision for poor families (including the establishment of a family wage), and for education (Lavalette, 1998, 1999a). Yet there was considerable resistance to these demands from *laissez-faire* economists and sections of the dominant class who argued that any such provisions would make British capital uncompetitive *vis-à-vis* its international competitors. For example, each attempt to regulate children's working hours in the early nineteenth century met with a furious response that limited the effectiveness of the legislation when it came into force (Lavalette, 1998). Entrenched interests resisted the spread of non-religious education (Simon, 1960). Any attempt to provide slightly more generous welfare was denounced by Poor Law Guardians and those involved with the Charity Organisation Society – desperate to stop any 'incentive' to loose living.

However, by the end of the nineteenth century things had changed quite dramatically. Now a more recognisably 'modern' childhood had been imposed on working-class children. Why and how did this change come about?

To come to terms with the changes that took place during this period it is important to look at the wider context. The end of the nineteenth century witnessed a major crisis within British society (Hobsbawm, 1994). The crisis reflected a number of interconnected elements: the relative decline of the British economy in the face of US and German competition; the threat to the British Empire, both from rival imperialist interests like Germany, Japan, France and the US and from internal rebellion; the revelations at the extent of poverty amongst the urban poor; and the rise of militant 'new unionism'. Faced with these threats sections of the dominant class within Britain focused on the need to pursue a 'remoralising' agenda that focused on the control of apparently unruly working-class youth and the promotion of a set of family values to curb drunkenness, violence, recalcitrance and family breakdown. State social policy was central to this agenda. It had the consequence of aiding the re-establishment of the working-class family, the promotion of a particular form of motherhood and the establishment of a set of legitimised activities for working-class children – separated by strict gender divisions – that carved out and promoted notions of childhood.

There were three linked developments that were of particular importance in establishing and legitimising working-class childhood. First, there were increasing state policy developments that focused on children. This took place, for example, within the fields of welfare, medicine, social work, education and the criminal justice system. These developments contained elements of both 'care' and 'control'. Thus concerns with child health, nutrition, abuse, poverty alleviation and the expansion of education brought elements of relief for the poor and disenfranchised, and a degree of protection for children. The expansion of welfare brought real advances and material benefits to the lives of the poor – including their children. But at the same time the legislation was framed in ways that promoted particular views of childhood and placed particular expectations on working-class children. The criminal justice system was brutal and treated poor children with incredible harshness. The development of social work brought the intervention of middle-class philanthropists into working-class homes, and saw them trying to constrict and regulate behaviour (Jones, 1984; Lavalette, 1999a; Pinchbeck and Hewitt, 1973).

The second element was changes to the employment structure and employment legislation that had the effect of restricting children's opportunities to work. Gradually, throughout the nineteenth century, the age at which children found employment increased. New industries were developing that afforded little opportunity for children to work. The consequence was that in the last quarter of the nineteenth century there were significant restrictions on children's ability to gain employment and increasing numbers were left unemployed or under-employed. Such children hung around the streets and were increasingly viewed as a problem of social order (Davin, 1996). Further, the expansion of compulsory education made it increasingly difficult to combine schooling and 'traditional' paid jobs. The consequence was the decline in child labour that was increasingly restructured into another form: 'out-of-school' employment, which was viewed as both healthy and beneficial (Cunningham, 1995; Cunningham and Viazzo, 1996; Davin, 1996; Lavalette, 1998).

The final element was the expansion of education. Education was promoted for a variety of reasons. For some sections of industry it was necessary to impart new skills to future workers; for others it was a way of socialising and disciplining children to maintain the existing social order at a time of increasing working-class rebellion; for others it was a means of training young girls in 'home-making' skills that would stand them in good stead as future 'mothers of the Empire'. For many working-class activists education was a right they demanded for their children. Thus there were conflicting demands behind the expansion of the education system, but the school created an activity and a location that was deemed essential for working-class children and in combination with the other elements mentioned above started to create a more recognisably 'modern' childhood amongst working-class children.

There is one final important element to note, however. While there were considerable efforts put into establishing and regularising an appropriate childhood, working-class children responded to these impositions in a variety of ways. Their responses established important cultural norms and symbols that, often subtly, undermined, re-directed and altered elements of the new imposed life-stage in class-specific ways. Thus while there was increasingly a recognisable degree of commonality between childhoods, there remained subtle and important class differences (Humphries, 1981).

The development of a working-class childhood is important for three main reasons. First, it emphasises that the state, state social policy and state institutions have been, and remain, vital structural elements imposing upon working-class children and restricting and reshaping their lives. Despite the fashion to assert the role of the child as an active agent shaping their lives and institutions we must not forget the powerful sources that limit and restrict our lives and *act upon us*. Second, the subjective element is important. Faced with such powerful impositions, working-class children have subverted, and continue to subvert, elements of the dominant culture of childhood. Third, this reminds us of the continuing significance of class in shaping the experiences of childhood in the modern world.

THE 'NEW SOCIOLOGY OF CHILDHOOD' (NSC)

Engagement with historical research has been important for sociologists of childhood. It has allowed them to establish the fact that childhood is not a static, merely biological, phenomenon, but is affected and shaped by wider social and cultural elements. According to the Danish sociologist Jens Qvortrup (1993) there are three important elements that can be discerned from historical and cross-cultural review. First, childhood is a structural element within society. From the conclusions to the review above we can attest to the fact that childhood is a permanent category within society. Children are recognised as distinct from adults, with particular needs. They are also expected to perform a range of tasks within society that are identified as particularly suitable and appropriate to children. But how children's needs are met, what roles and activities they are expected to perform varies across time and space. This means that it is possible to identify, compare and contrast different childhoods from different eras, epochs and cultures. Second, childhood is not isolated from society but integral to it and childhood is affected by societal developments, changes, crises and events. Third, 'children are themselves co-constructors of childhood and society' (Qvortrup, 1993: 14) – in other words, individually and collectively children have an impact on society and help shape it, and in particular have an impact on childhood and help shape it.

Qvortrup's neat summation paves the way for a discussion of the *new sociology of childhood* (NSC). Qvortrup's work represents an important starting point for sociological discussion of childhood and he has been very influential in the growing international interest in childhood studies. He combines an emphasis on both structure (recognition of the 'reality' of childhood as a stable social phenomenon) and agency (the roles, activities and practices of children), which shape their world. He attempts to marry elements of functionalist sociology – quite clear in his recent discussion of the work-like nature of education for children – with an emphasis on the rational, goal-directed action of children while they interpret their world. In this, Qvortrup's work reflects more general themes of continental sociology and brings these debates to the sphere of the sociology of childhood, a positive step which has helped bring theoretical rigour to the field.

However, the major theoretical approach dominant within Britain is the self-styled NSC. Unlike continental theorists of childhood, the NSC is far less concerned with childhood as a structural element within society but has instead developed an approach based on post-modern perspectives. Indeed they distance themselves from what they term, the 'absolutist pronouncements of the structural sociologies and Marxisms' (James et al., 1998: 26). There are four central claims made by the NSC. First, broadly following Ariès, childhood is a 'social construction': 'To describe childhood . . . as socially constructed is to suspend belief in or a willing reception of its taken-for-granted meanings' (1998: 27). However, in this version childhood is socially constructed – and constantly reconstructed – without reference to broader socio-economic context.

Second, children occupy and conduct themselves in worlds that are full of meaning for them, but about which adults are, at least partially, ignorant. These are 'children's childhoods'. Children are best placed to describe and analyse this world, better at any rate than adult outsiders.

> The children's world is . . . not unaffected by, but nevertheless artfully insulated from the world of adults; it is to be understood as an independent place with its own folklore, rituals, rules and normative constraints. (James et al., 1998: 29)

There have been some important research conclusions drawn from this claim. It has led to an important emphasis on listening to 'children's voices'. In the past, social scientific research on children and childhood often utilised secondary sources, where children were the object rather than the subject of research agendas. The move to listen to children, their views, interpretations and opinions is a welcome step forward. However, this has occasionally been interpreted as suggesting that research based on children's voices is more privileged, more insightful and more legitimate than other methodologies or approaches, a claim that we reject but which is addressed in more detail elsewhere (McKechnie, this volume).

Third, children are a 'minority group'. By using this phrase James et al. (1998: 31) are trying to assert that, politically, children – as a social group – are powerless and disadvantaged and that the new sociology is a theory of advocacy: it is dedicated 'to children's interests and purposes: a sociology for children rather than of children'. This approach has been closely tied into a 'children's rights' agenda where theorists have demanded the extension of various political, social and economic rights for children – asserting their equality with adults and rejecting any form of exclusion from social life.

Finally, children are an identifiable social group. Of course various social divisions dissect childhood but, they suggest, there is something common to all children and childhoods – it is a universal category – and as a result children have a common set of needs and rights (James et al., 1998: 32). Thus children – all children – are viewed as oppressed, and various social divisions are regarded as less important than what unites them as children.

These represent a very powerful set of claims. Without doubt the commitment to children's rights and perspectives has helped the NSC become hegemonic within childhood studies in Britain. But there are difficulties with the approach and here we focus on the most directly sociological of the NSC's commitments, their use of the concept of 'social construction'.

We have referred to the idea that childhood is a social construction throughout the chapter, yet now we are going to have to look at this expression more closely. Let us start by noting the appeal of social constructionism. This comes from the fact that it emphasises that human relations are not static and are not always the same. The great benefit of this is that when people say that 'women have always stayed at home and looked after children', or 'gay relationships are not natural', or 'white people and black people can't get on and are naturally antagonistic', or 'children have always been dependent on families for the first eighteen years of life and it is natural for parents to rear and look after their offspring for this period', or indeed that 'people are naturally selfish and greedy' – we can point to societies or earlier epochs when human relationships were significantly different, thus undermining the claim to 'naturalness' or some static human nature involved in the original claim.

Thus the social anthropologist Eleanor Leacock has noted that in 'primitively communist' societies life was exceptionally hard, but the relationships between men and women were much more equal – these were, she says 'egalitarian societies' (Leacock, 1981). In the ancient Greek world, homosexual relationships were valued as an expression of love, whereas heterosexual relationships were functional, concerned merely with procreation (Halifax, 1988). Racism has not always existed, but developed and expanded with the growth of the Atlantic slave trade (Callinicos, 1993). The notion that people are 'naturally' greedy and selfish is a peculiarly modern notion, reflecting a set of values that became more prevalent with the development of capitalist society (Callinicos, 1983). And as we noted earlier in the chapter, children have not always been raised or acted in the same way.

So the appeal of social constructionism is clear – it undermines a variety of commonsense claims about the world and key relationships within it. But the important question is really *'how are these various elements socially constructed?'* Answering this question leads the NSC to make two linked claims. First, social phenomena are constructed and reconstructed from within the realms of 'discourse' (James et al., 1998: 213). By 'discourse' they mean the hidden and overt assumptions of language usage (spoken, written and visual). Thus we can study children's different roles within society by looking at the changes to discourses about children (which children themselves often initiate): 'The child is brought into being through the dominant modes of speech that exist concerning age, dependency, development' (1998: 213).

Second, that social constructionism necessarily has an:

> intense relationship with cultural relativism . . . the 'socially constructed' child is a local rather than a global phenomenon and tends to be extremely particularistic. (James et al., 1998: 27, 214)

Cultural relativism is an approach that argues that we must study different cultures in their own terms, understand them in their own context and cannot judge them by reference to any supposed universal set of values or goals. James et al. give the following example of what this means in practice:

> [If] child 'abuse' was rife in earlier times and a fully anticipated feature of adult–child relations, then how are we to say that it was bad, exploitative and harmful? Our standards of judgement

are relative to our world-view and therefore we can not make universal statements of value. (1998: 27)

Reflecting the hold of post-modernism, the central message of the NSC is that we have to abandon any attempt to arrive at a full understanding of the world, or to assert that there is any broad directionality to human history. It is an assertion that many different accounts are possible of any piece of human behaviour or any event. There are, therefore, a number of discourses, each equally valid, and to assert that one has more importance or explanatory power or is 'truth' is part of an attempt to assert one's 'power' over others.

Superficially the approach seems very democratic and challenging – there are no truths, all opinions are equally valid, all interpretations equally significant. This seems to reinforce the notion that the world is polymorphous, non-unitary and non-consensual (Howe, 1994). But if we stop to consider the claims for a moment the conclusions are less appealing. The denial of any underlying reality, of any total structure of exploitation and oppression, necessarily prevents the consistent post-modernist from seeing one view of the world as any better than any other. There are simply different, equally valid, 'discourses'. But that precludes any possibility of affirming one account of history or one assertion of identity to be better than another. The Nazi and the anti-Nazi, the white racist and the black liberationist, the new lad and the old feminist, all should, logically, be regarded as having equally valid approaches to the world. Similarly, the account of the paedophile and that of their child victim would just be two – equally valid – discourses. While the cultural relativism of the NSC would make it 'inappropriate' for them to criticise the practice of female circumcision carried out on some young girls in parts of the globe because this is an activity with cultural meaning – and to criticise would be to hold a 'universal' ethic or set of values (and would just be another way of us trying to assert our power over these peoples).

Instead of seeing language or discourse as independent of social forces, it seems more appropriate to recognise that, though 'mediated', conscious-ness, language and ideas reflect material factors and relations within society. Thus while childhood and, in our example above, gay oppression, racism and gender relations are socially constructed, they are constructed within concrete contexts and structural relations which are located within particular historical processes. When we look at the social construction of childhood we cannot fully grasp this process without looking at changes to the totality of social relations within society – the creation of the modern family form, changes to productive relations, the role of the state – and how these affect the perceptions of and attitudes to children, and the children's responses to all this. Finally, while childhood is not static, it is not the case that there are an infinite range of 'reconstructions' of childhood – indeed, today's childhood in Britain is recognisable as the childhood established for working-class children at the turn of the twentieth century.

Finally, let us briefly address the notion that children are a minority group within society. For the NSC this means that all children have a common set of interests as children, and that they all find themselves excluded and disadvantaged. In the review above we emphasised class difference in children's experiences. Given this, while it is useful to note the ways in which legal strictures and regulations impact on all young people in the same ways (at least superficially), and while there is clearly an identifiable notion of childhood as a universal category applied to all children – we wish to stress the class-specific elements that divide children. In particular we do not accept that all children are oppressed in modern society: to put it at its most crude, we fail to see any oppression affecting the lives of the Royal children of Britain, and we fail to see what they have in common with those who live in inner-city slums (see Novak, this volume).

CONCLUSION

Sociological discussion of childhood has been concerned to show that childhood is not a natural, but a social, phenomenon. In different epochs and societies the lived experience of childhood has been different from that which we consider to be the 'norm' in twenty-first-century Britain. Nevertheless, various historical sociologies (particularly those which have tried to discover evidence originating from children themselves) attest to the fact that most societies see children as different from adults, with different expectations placed on their roles and activities. The human animal is one that takes a considerable time to develop fully, both biologically and psychologically, and most societies recognise this to some degree. 'Childhood' can fruitfully be considered the period thought suitable to young humans as they grow through this maturation process – and, linked to this, the activities thought appropriate for them at this stage of life. Both of these elements will vary across time and space and thus we can identify a number of childhood 'forms'. The precise form childhood takes is intimately connected with wider societal elements – and thus while childhood is socially constructed it is constructed within concrete, historical circumstances.

Such a general approach allows us to compare and contrast childhoods in different eras and societies. It allows us to recognise (and again compare and contrast) different childhoods within particular societies – childhoods are affected by an array of social divisions, but class divisions in particular have a clear impact on children's experiences and lives.

Finally, children themselves are active in shaping and responding to the imposed elements of childhood – confronting, accepting, rejecting and undermining imposed notions of children's roles and the form childhood should take.

KEY TEXTS

Ariès, P. (1962) *Centuries of Childhood*. Harmondsworth: Penguin.

Corsaro, W.A. (1997) *The Sociology of Childhood*. Thousand Oaks, CA: Pine Forge Press.

Cunningham, H. (1995) *Children and Childhood in Western Society since 1500*. London: Longman.

Davin, A. (1996) *Growing Up Poor*. London: Rivers Oram.

James, A., Jenks, C. and Prout, A. (1998) *Theorising Childhood*. Cambridge: Polity Press.

Lavalette, M. (ed.) (1999) *A Thing of the Past? Child Labour in Britain in the Nineteenth and Twentieth Centuries*. Liverpool: Liverpool University Press, esp. Chapter 1.

Qvortrup, J. (1994) 'Childhood matters: an introduction', in J. Qvortrup, M. Bardy, G. Sgritta and H. Wintersberger (eds), *Childhood Matters: Social Theory, Practice and Politics*. Aldershot: Avebury.

THREE

New Sociology and Old Psychology

SANDY HOBBS

INTRODUCTION

The object of this chapter is to examine the relationship between the work of psychologists, who have been studying many aspects of childhood for well over a century, and those writers who have adopted an approach which has been called the 'new sociology of childhood' (James and Prout, 1990, 1997; James et al., 1998). A reading of the new sociologists might lead to a conclusion that we may safely overlook research by psychologists because it is deeply flawed. In particular, psychologists are presented as having under-estimated the social aspects of the child and to have treated the child as passive rather than active. However, such implications fail to take account of the diversity of approaches to childhood that is to be found in modern psychology. Examples of valuable psychological research involving children will be examined. In addition, the value of stressing the 'active child' in all investigations will be questioned.

THE SCOPE OF PSYCHOLOGY

As a discipline psychology has been associated with the study of childhood for several decades. While the sub-category of developmental psychology has emerged it is only one facet of psychology. Anyone seeking to make claims about psychology in general needs to recognise that psychology for many years now has been both vast and varied. In Britain today there is an officially recognised body which seeks to control who may or may not call themselves 'psychologist'. There is an official title 'Chartered Psychologist' for those who wish to offer their services publicly. This might seem to imply the existence of a group of people with a shared body of knowledge and skills. However, such a picture is illusory. In 2001, the British Psychological Society held a conference celebrating its centenary. At that conference there was symposium in honour of Ullin Place who is mainly known for propounding a theory in which mind and brain are regarded as identical in his paper 'Is consciousness a brain process? (Place, 1956). Also present were a group of Chartered Psychologists who are registered spiritual healers. They were proclaiming the merits of what they call 'Soul Therapy'. These are only two contrasting examples from a wide variety of papers and discussions adopting a multiplicity of different approaches.

As we shall see, Sigmund Freud and Jean Piaget are singled out for particular criticism by the new sociologists of childhood. Are these writers representative of psychology generally? They certainly figure prominently when psychologists are polled on whom they consider the key psychologists of the twentieth century. A number of studies have been conducted in both the United States and Britain in which psychologists are asked to indicate which figures or books are the most significant or influential. For example, John C. Norcross and Thomas J. Tomcho (1994) found American psychologists rating Freud and Piaget amongst the leading authors, but also B.F. Skinner, William James, Carl Rogers, Charles Darwin, Alberta Bandura, Gordon Allport and Erik Erikson. These authors represent a wide variety of approaches to psychology. A similar variety has been found in other studies conducted in Britain and the United States; see, for example, Newstead (1983) and Heyduk and Fenigstein (1984). Piaget and Freud undoubtedly emerge from such studies as figures of significance, but then so do other psychologists with rather different approaches, such as Skinner, the radical behaviourist, and Rogers, the exponent of client-centred therapy.

Friman et al. (1993) have suggested that three main streams of psychology can justifiably claim to continue to thrive in modern psychology. Friman and his colleagues reviewed articles in leading psychology journals. The strongest may be termed 'cognitive', but the other two streams, psychodynamic and behaviourist, also have their strengths, if measured by output of scholarly articles. However, it must not be assumed that there is no psychology outside of those streams. Nor can it be claimed that those who belong to a particular stream necessarily share all that much in their approaches. One by-product of this situation in which rival approaches exist side by side is that there is a tendency for proponents of particular points of view to communicate primarily with others who share their position. This has been shown in the case of radical behaviourism through studies of which other articles the authors of articles in particular journals cite. It can be seen that with the establishment of journals for specialist work employing the techniques known as 'behaviour analysis' the levels of cross-citation between these journals and others specialising in other approaches is low (see Coleman and Mehlman, 1992).

It would be impossible for a single person to master all forms of psychology today. It would be foolhardy to defend all psychology since many approaches are incompatible with each other, Place and Soul Therapy being an obvious example. However, it is surely equally dangerous to imply that all of psychology can be dismissed.

THE NEW SOCIOLOGY, CRITICISING OTHERS

The use of the word 'new' might be taken to mean that the work of those sociologists now adopting this approach to studying children could be compared with some 'old' sociology of childhood. However, a reading of their work shows rather that what can be claimed as 'new' in their sociology is that they give central attention to children, whereas in the past sociologists on the whole tended to neglect childhood as a matter for investigation. The claim is substantially true, although if sociology were to be taken to include social anthropology, then the claim for originality is slightly weakened.

There is too another sense in which they claim to be 'new' and that is the contrast they claim to see between their approach and that of earlier non-sociological writers. Alison James et al. take this stance at the outset in their book *Theorizing Childhood* (1998) with two chapters called 'The pre-sociological child' and 'The sociological child'. In the first chapter they write critically of certain concepts they believe to underlie some discussions of childhood. They label these, for example, 'The Evil Child', 'The Innocent Child' and 'The Immanent Child'. Amongst the writers critically associated with these labels are Thomas Hobbes, Jean-Jacques Rousseau and John Locke. In dealing with two other concepts, 'The Naturally Developing Child' and 'The Unconscious Child', the main targets are psychology and psychoanalysis, particularly the former. Childhood, they assert, has been 'the sole theoretical property of developmental psychology' (p. 1). Psychology has 'firmly colonized children in a pact with medicine, education and government agencies' (p. 19). The tone of these phrases strongly implies a hostility to psychology as a discipline which might well be conveyed to the reader, despite the lack of substantial evidence to support this stance.

Jean Piaget is singled out for criticism as the most influential figure in developmental psychology propounding the notion of the naturally developing child; Sigmund Freud they associate with the concept of the unconscious child. Leaving aside the question of how fair their criticisms of these figures may be and how representative they are of their fields, one point which is striking is that the reader is expected to take their second-hand account of the views of Piaget and Freud largely on faith. There is a single quotation from Piaget whilst Freud, like Hobbes, Rousseau and Locke, is not directly cited at all in this chapter. A look at the reference section of their book shows that Freud's books go completely uncited and there is the single work by Piaget just mentioned, a book published in English in 1972, but which was a translation of a work appearing in French some years earlier. Piaget, a highly prolific writer who died in 1980 is thus hardly being quoted in a definitive formulation of his ideas.

It is worth exploring the work of Piaget in more detail than James, Jenks and Prout do. It is also worth bearing in mind the key failure they claim to see in the psychology of childhood: overlooking the child as agent. They also suggest that psychologists have underestimated the social facets of child development.

On this later point it is relevant to quote from Piaget's book *Sociological Studies* (1995). This book was first published in French in 1965 but the chapter from which this quotation is taken has appeared as an article in a French sociology journal in 1951. Piaget writes:

> . . . human intelligence is subject to the action of social life at all levels of development from the first to the last day of life. . . . We refuse only to accept that 'society' or 'social life' are sufficiently precise concepts to be employed in psychology. To hold that social life acts at every level of development is to say something as obvious, but also just as vague, as to attribute a contributing influence to the external physical environment. . . . (1995: 278)

Thus Piaget does not deny that the child (and the adult) interacts with a social environment. However, at least in the 1950s and 1960s when he published and republished this opinion, he argued that sociology had not developed sufficiently analytical concepts to help understand the development of human thinking. To justify condemning Piaget for underestimating the social aspects of the child one would have to demonstrate that his analysis of the sociology of that time was unfair. Yet it seems to be acknowledged by the New Sociologists that earlier sociologists had contributed little to the study of childhood.

Of course, like James et al., what I have offered here is a quotation taken out of context, However, to read it, side by side with their claims, must surely lead one to question whether their image of Piaget's approach is a fair one.

CLASSICS?

It might be thought that with major figures such as Piaget and Freud, their opinions are so well known as to make direct citations of their work unnecessary. However, there is good reason to doubt this. A number of studies have shown that supposedly 'classic' works in the social sciences are frequently misrepresented in secondary works. The conditioning of 'Little Albert' by John B. Watson and Solomon Asch's experiments on conformity are amongst the most cited research in experimental and social psychology respectively, yet studies of secondary citations of these works has shown that they are frequently distorted. Paul and Blumenthal (1989) point out that in the 1970s a number of papers had identified serious flaws in textbook accounts of Watson's research in which, by conditioning, he induced 'Little Albert' to react fearfully to a laboratory rat of which he had previously appeared quite unafraid. Yet, when they reviewed more recent textbooks they found that many of them contained similar misrepresentations to those which had already been pointed out. Such errors include getting the animal wrong (calling it a rabbit rather than a rat) and exaggerating the speed at which conditioning took place. Asch's research on American college students required them to make simple perceptual judgements on the relative length of lines. The student subjects believed they were being tested alongside other student subjects, but in reality these other students had been primed by Asch to give the same wrong judgement on certain specified trials. Asch thus set up a conflict between the apparent judgement of the rest of the group and the evidence of the student's own eyes. Sometimes, a student would 'conform', sometimes he would stand out against the group and rely on his own judgement. Frend et al. (1990) found that secondary sources tend to exaggerate the extent of conformity and imply that conforming was more common than not in Asch's set-up, whereas in fact the opposite was true. That the students conform *at all* was an interesting result but from that a distorted version of what actually happened has grown up. These are only two of a number of published examples, in which widely quoted works are misquoted or misrepresented. They provide us with a helpful warning: do not assume that, because a writer or a book or an article is familiar to you and is often cited, that the picture you (or anyone else) have of the writer, book or article is necessarily an accurate one. In this case, I suggest that James et al. may not be accurately portraying the work of Piaget and Freud. Later a little evidence will be presented which does not fit their stereotype of these writers.

CONTRIBUTIONS BY PSYCHOLOGISTS

Although psychology is a vast subject, it might be thought that the task of assessing psychologists' ability to understand children could be simplified by looking only at those who call themselves 'child psychologists' or 'developmental psychologists'. However, the boundaries between the fields of psychology are not firm. For example, one of the most prominent twentieth-century psychologists, B.F. Skinner, is not usually thought of as a 'developmentalist', yet his book *Verbal Behavior* (1957) is concerned with how language is acquired and his *Technology of Teaching* (1968) is concerned with the processes of education; both topics profoundly tied to the understanding of childhood.

I am not going to attempt a sweeping judgement of psychology's contributions to the understanding of children. Instead, I will take a couple of examples of psychological work which seem to me valuable and see whether the implicit criticisms of such work by the new sociologists is justified.

Betty Hart and Todd Risley, psychologists at the University of Kansas, for over thirty years have been concerned with intervention programmes aimed at helping pre-school children whose environments seemed to disadvantage them when they went to school. One of their most valuable works is *Meaningful Differences in the Everyday Experience of Young American Children* (1995). This reports a study in which they had the cooperation of forty-two families of contrasting socio-economic status. Some of the parents were professional, some were employed in the types of manual work, which are usually classified as 'working class', and other parents were unemployed, relying on welfare benefits. In this study Hart and Risley did not 'intervene' other than to regularly observe the young children in these families and their interactions with those around them. This was carried on from when the children were 13 months old until they were 36 months old.

They worked out a number of ways of describing variations in these interactions and found close relationships between these measures and the development of the children's vocabularies and the performance of the children on standardised intelligence tests. Since intelligence test scores have been shown to correlate positively with school performance, they can be said to have been examining differences in the experiences of young children which are likely to impact substantially on their later lives. They also found that, although there were some variations within each of the parental groups, on the whole, professional, working-class and welfare families tended to differ quite strikingly. Of course, it was not a new discovery to find children of professional parents doing better on intelligence tests than other groups. However, since they were in a position to compare not just IQs but also the ways in which these children interacted verbally too, they have given a plausible demonstration of at least part of the reason for such social class differences. Some of the ways in which parents differ in the ways in which they talk to their young children seem highly plausible as influences creating differences in the children's own verbal behaviour.

To give an indication of the importance of variations in the experiences provided to young children by their parents, Hart and Risley (1995: 183–7) discuss in detail a single observation that they made of a so-called 'welfare' mother and her daughter aged 23 months. They point out that the mother was 'concerned, nurturing, and affectionate'. The daughter has been toilet trained and is affectionately treated by her mother, who holds and kisses her. The mother does interact verbally, of course. She repeats the child's attempts at words and she describes things that are happening. However, she does little to develop conversation or encourage the little girl to practise words. Most of the feedback the child is given is critical or corrective. She does not encourage the child 's initiatives to the extent that many of the socially more advantaged parents do. One hour of observation is very limited as evidence. However, when the same pattern is found repeatedly and when similar patterns are found in other families, the potential cumulative power of differences in experience emerges as significant.

Note that the parents were not shown to differ in love, care or concern but in their behaviour towards their children, which they would not necessarily have believed significant nor adopted intentionally.

Having demonstrated such links, Hart and Risley were well placed to make suggestions as to how some of the disadvantages suffered by the children from poorer social backgrounds might be overcome. Calculating the cumulative differences between the experiences of welfare children and working-class children, they come to the conclusion that the welfare children would need to have over forty hours per week of intervention if that disadvantaging gap were to be overcome. That leaves out of the account any question of closing the gap between the children in working-class and professional families. Although it is possible that more effective methods of intervention might be eventually developed, in the short run Hart and Risley see guidance in childcare as the most practicable method of reducing such gaps. If the socially disadvantaged parents could be effectively taught the value of methods they currently do not use in their own verbal interactions with their children, that would be an economically more realistic way of reducing this particular source of social inequality.

Is it possible to criticise this research because of its failure to pay attention to the agency of the child? Clearly agency does not play a prominent part in Hart and Risley's analysis. It would be possible to treat those children who have been able to develop more substantial intellectual powers as having thereby enhanced their opportunities to influence their surroundings and their future lives. Here, as elsewhere, it can be argued that knowledge is power. However, it seems doubtful whether the explicit use of a concept of agency would have added significantly to Hart and Risley's understanding of what was going on.

We turn now from an example where psychological research appears to offer a basis of benefiting the child, to an example where benefits can already be shown: the treatment of children diagnosed as suffering from autism. A useful starting point of such a discussion is the book *Let Me Hear Your Voice* (1993) by 'Catherine Maurice', a parent adopting a pseudonym to protect the privacy of her children. Catherine Maurice gives a detailed account of the personal experience of realising something profoundly wrong with one's child, seeking help, and the initial failure of supposedly expert professionals to produce any effective results. She was introduced to ill-founded theories which were painful to her and other parents, in particular the claim that autism in the child was produced by the failure of 'refrigerator mothers' who failed to give the child sufficient signs of affection. Then she heard about Ivor Lovaas, a psychologist, who was said to have developed successful methods of helping some autistic children. She was initially suspicious of Lovaas and some people warned her against him. However, eventually she saw the merits of his methods with the result that dramatic changes came about in the lives of her children. Lovaas himself, in his afterword to Catherine Maurice's book, is modest about his own achievements thus far. Nevertheless he has been able to present telling evidence of the success of his methods. Bernard Rimmland, a fellow psychologist whose autistic child benefited from Lovaas's methods, writes persuasively in his Foreword in Catherine Maurice's book that Lovaas offers the 'treatment of choice' for autism. Although this is not yet a universally held view, there are now many other psychologists at work using and developing techniques derived from the initial work of Lovaas. These methods are now available in the British Isles as well as in the United States. The book entitled *Parents' Education as Autism Therapists: Applied Behaviour Analysis in Context,* edited by Mickey Keenan et al. (2000) is a useful guide to current developments.

An important feature of this book is that although all three of the editors are psychologists, adopting, as the book's title suggests, the 'behaviour analysis' approach, some of the contributors are the parents of children who have been diagnosed as suffering from autism. This arises from the fact that a number of parents have come to the conclusion that behaviour analysis techniques, which Lovaas developed, are as Rimmland says, the 'treatment of choice'. A group of these parents founded the charity known as PEAT (Parents' Education as Autism Therapists). Another British charity with similar aims is PEACH (Parents for the Early Intervention of Autism in Children).

What, then, are these methods developed by Lovaas and other behaviour analysts and which appeal to these parents? Central to them is the assumption that behaviour can best be understood if subjected to a functional analysis. This means interpreting the behaviour in terms of what goes before (antecedents) and what comes after (consequences). When a child is diagnosed as autistic it will be because that child is characteristically displaying behaviour which is variously anti-social, annoying, self-injurious and frightening. At the same time, he or she may fail to show 'normal' social interactions including, most notably, normal conversation.

Rimmland (1993) argues that physiological dysfunction underlies autism, but that does not mean that we must wait for the development of some physiological 'cure'. Autism can be dealt with at the level of behaviour. In other words, 'good', acceptable behaviour can be built up, and 'bad', unacceptable behaviour can be reduced or eliminated. This requires deliberate intervention, of course, and the principles governing successful intervention have been developed by behaviour analysts. Nevertheless, these principles are such that they can be learnt and applied by parents (and other non-professional helpers).

The key concept in behavioural intervention is that of 'reinforcement'. Reinforcement is a crucial aspect of the 'consequence' stage in the antecedent–behaviour–consequence analysis. When behaviour is reinforced, i.e. followed by a reinforcer, that behaviour becomes more likely to occur in the future. Thus, by the careful control of reinforcement, the intervening psychologist or parents can hope to build up the behaviour they wish the child to display (by providing reinforcement) and break down patterns of behaviour they wish to eliminate (by withholding reinforcement). Contrary to some misconceptions physical constraint plays little or no part in behaviour analytic treatment and can be justified only if it is undertaken in order to allow the processes based on reinforcement to be created.

To some observers, it might appear that such treatment is oppressive and carries with it a whiff of authoritarianism. However, there are one or two fairly straightforward responses which may be made to such a view. The most fundamental is that the shaping of behaviour by its consequences is not an invention of the behaviour analysts. It is a natural process which they can justly claim to have discovered. In other words, whether we are aware of it or not, all of our behaviour has been shaped by these A–B–C relationships. This applies to aspects of behaviour from the language we speak to the social and physical skills which we acquire to the preferred pastimes in which we engage.

Behavioural intervention with autistic children involves intentional shaping, of course, but intentional shaping is a normal part of our social relationships, particularly the relations between children and parents. Bringing up children involves a vast array of parental goals which they attempt to achieve for their children: toilet training, riding a bike, swimming, brushing one's teeth, for example. For reasons which we do not fully understand, the behaviour of autistic children does not develop within the range which we regard as normal. Behaviour analysts simply offer parents techniques which they can claim have a proven effectiveness in bringing the autistic child's behaviour closer to that of the 'normal' child.

If the carefully controlled shaping of the autistic child's behaviour seems oppressive, it is worth considering the life of the parents of the untreated child, living with an almost constant despair that one's child is just not developing like 'ordinary children'. If, on the other hand, one looks at the autistic child as somehow the 'victim' of behavioural treatment, then it might be worthwhile considering the child before and after treatment. Ask the question which child seems the happier.

One thing which is quite clear about the methods applied as a result of behaviour analysis, is that the idea of the child as active agent is not part of the central analytical framework. If it is to be claimed that behaviour analysts and the parents who take their advice are somehow misguided in not listening to the voice of the child, then alternatives need to be provided. Which ways of analysing autism can be effectively based on the concept of the active child? More importantly, which effective methods of dealing with autism can be derived from such an alternative analysis?

Autism in fact provides quite a considerable challenge to anyone wishing to analyse childhood primarily in terms of the active child and who relies heavily on discovering the child's point of view. It is characteristic of the autistic child that he or she cannot act and create in the ways that 'normal' children do and neither can they express themselves like 'ordinary children'. The outcome of the successful application of behaviour analysis is that the treated child acquires characteristics which we interpret as creative, sociable and expressive. As the title of Catherine Maurice's book implies, behaviour analysis allowed her to hear her children's voices.

Psychology as a whole is not monolithic. Accordingly, it is inappropriate to imagine anyone attempting to defend all psychological research as valuable. However, the varied nature of psychology also means that it is inappropriate to accept the sidelining of psychological research which seems implicit in the case made by James et al.

The cautious reader might now feel that I have made a case for taking seriously some psychological work on children but still wonder whether I have selected typical examples. Just as I asked how representative were Piaget and Freud the chosen subjects for critique by James et al., so the reader might question the representativeness of Hart, Risley and Lovaas. I frankly cannot answer that question, but then I am not claiming that all psychology is good, merely that some psychology has merits. Therefore, to assume that psychology can be quietly ignored is unjustified.

ORIGIN MYTH?

The cautious reader might also raise another question. If, as I claim, there is some good in psychological research, how have James et al. failed to notice this? I believe I understand why this error has occurred because this is not a unique situation. James et al. believe they are offering an exciting and valuable new paradigm. The history of scholarly endeavour is full of cases of new schools of thought and new fields of research being developed. One aim which pioneers may have is to place themselves historically, claiming worthy predecessors or damning the work of those whose errors were such that a revolution was necessary. Franz Samelson (1974) has argued that as Social Psychology was growing as a field there developed what he calls an Origin Myth, the essence of which was that the founder of Social Psychology was the nineteenth-century French writer Auguste Comte. Samelson argues persuasively that there is virtually no justification for this and that it involves a misreading of history. By calling it an 'Origin Myth' he is implicitly comparing these supposedly scholarly claims to the stories of particular peoples about how they came into existence. The story that the twins Romulus and Remus were suckled by wolves and later founded the city of Rome is but one of many examples.

A.D. Lovie (1983) has drawn attention to another origin myth in psychology. He notes that many texts of cognitive psychology claim that for a time in the early twentieth century the dominance of behaviourism was so great that psychologists gave up studying certain important subjects such as attention. Lovie was able to demonstrate that there was only ever a modest decline in research on attention, and that in any case, behaviourists were amongst those studying it.

Thomas H. Leahey (1992) suggests that the claims made by cognitive psychologists to have taken part in a revolution in which the

cognitive approach to psychology (implicitly correct) overthrew the behaviourist approach (implicitly incorrect) does not conform to reality.
Behaviourists were never a dominating, monolithic school and cognitive
psychologists do not themselves share a common scientific paradigm.
Here, then, we have another case of a group creating an origin myth for
themselves.

It would appear that like the cognitive psychologists, the new sociologists of childhood have felt the need to bolster the standing of their own
work by denigrating earlier work. Samelson (1974: 228) depicts social
psychologists as celebrating 'the heroes who slew the dragon of meta-
physics and rescued the fair maiden of empirical science'. It is tempting to
enhance one's own heroic stance by claiming to have slain a dragon.
However, it is unlikely that understanding will be increased by per-
petrating such myths. The new sociology of childhood will stand or fall
eventually on its own achievements rather than the imagined failings of
others.

THE ACTIVE CHILD?

In returning now to the concept of agency and its supposed neglect by
Piaget and Freud, it may be helpful to look at a couple of observations
these writers make. They concern rather young children, which may be
particularly appropriate since if we can establish an awareness of agency in
dealing with younger children it seems unlikely it would be overlooked
with older ones.

First consider Freud's account of his 18-month-old grandson Ernst:

> The child had a wooden reel with a piece of string tied round it. . . . What he did was to hold the
> reel by the string and very skillfully throw it over the edge of his curtained cot, so that it
> disappeared into it, at the same time uttering an expressive 'o-o-o-o'. He then pulled the reel
> out of the cot again by the string and hailed its reappearance with a joyful 'da' (there). (Freud,
> 1961: 9)

Ernst has invented this game, which Freud interprets as linked to the
child's reaction to the disappearance and return of his mother. Throwing
the reel is a re-enactment of his mother's departure, carried out as a
prelude to his mother's later return. We cannot tell whether Freud was
correct in this analysis. What is clear, however, is that Freud sees the child
as active in that he created this game. It is worth noting too that, if Freud is
right, Ernst was handling a situation in which his control was limited, the
presence or absence of his mother.

Turning to Piaget, consider this description of his daughter Jacqueline,
aged 13 months:

J. scratched the wall-paper in the bedroom where there was the design of a bird, then shut her hand as if it held the bird and went to her mother. 'Loo' (she opened her hand and pretended to be giving something). . . . What have you brought me? . . . A birdie. (Piaget, 1962: 119)

Here too we have imaginative play created by the child, though in Jacqueline Piaget's case, there seems no reason to look for an emotional problem to interpret it. The book by Piaget cited here is called in English *Play, Dreams and Imitation in Childhood*. These very words surely demonstrate that Piaget sees the young child as active. Playing, dreaming and imitating are not merely imposed on the child, though that does not preclude the possibility that what the child creates has been influenced by past events (see Cornwell and Hobbs, 1984, 1986, for fuller discussions of these examples).

What, then, of the general issue of agency which the new sociologists claim to be a fundamental error in psychological research on childhood? If by referring to 'agency' one is meaning that children 'take the initiative', 'create', and so on, this seems a fairly mundane point of which Freud and Piaget seem quite aware.

But is more meant? Does agency imply some sort of 'free choice' quite independent of outside influence? This idea is not a helpful one in scientific enquiry. While we must often admit that we do not know what circumstances led to a particular action, it is dangerous to suppose that any action is entirely 'spontaneous'. David Cornwell and I have argued that there are many relevant antecedents on record which seem to lay the groundwork for Jacqueline's imaginary bird (Cornwell and Hobbs, 1984).

A more plausible argument about 'agency' is that children's initiatives are not given sufficient prominence in accounts of childhood. This may well be true, but it demands a case-by-case argument rather than a blanket criticism of a whole discipline.

Finally, a concern with children's agency may involve the argument that children should be allowed more 'say', particularly with respect to research on childhood. Like a number of other writers, Jim McKechnie and I have argued that understanding of complex issues surrounding child labour has been hampered by a failure to take sufficient account of children's own point of view. Concerned adults have been so upset with the obvious evils of many forms of child labour that they have tended to react by seeking speedy ways to abolish it. For the child who is working, an urgent question is 'What else can I do if I don't have this job?' By taking account of the standpoint of working children, adult campaigners have come to realise that it is not enough to remove children from oppressive employment. Some acceptable alternative source of income and some meaningful education must be available (McKechnie and Hobbs, 1998). However, this argument for the merit of listening to children's voices refers to specific circumstances. As we have seen, it is questionable whether the same holds true for research on the early development of language or ways to treat autism.

CONCLUSION

The New Sociology of Childhood is indeed 'new' when one compares it with over a hundred years of study of children by psychologists. Ultimately it will be judged by the fruits of the research it engenders. One early clue to what the approach may achieve is to be found in the reports of the Economic and Social Research Council's Children 5–16 Research Programme, which was directed by Alan Prout, one of the 'new sociologists of childhood' discussed above, and was largely devoted to research compatible with the principles of the new sociology. Readers may judge that research for themselves, but it is worth pointing out how heavily dependent it is on strategies of enquiry centred on asking people questions. This is surely unnecessarily restrictive, particularly when one considers the achievements of psychologists such as those discussed in this chapter who employ a much wider range of techniques.

One of the arguments of this chapter has been that the critique of psychology by the new sociologists has been based in part on ignorance of the work of psychologists. That ignorance may have a variety of causes, one being the compartmentalisation of research and theorising in the human sciences, another perhaps being false preconceptions. It has been one of the aims of this chapter to give a fairer picture of the achievements of psychological research on childhood in the hope that the reader will give due attention to that research. Psychologists have much to give which is of value to those who wish to understand and help children.

KEY TEXTS

Hart, B. and Risley, T.R. (1995) *Meaningful Differences in the Everyday Experience of American Children*. Baltimore: Paul H. Brookes.

Keenan, M., Kerr, K.P. and Dillenburger, K. (eds) (2000) *Parents' Education as Autism Therapists: Applied Behaviour Analysis in Context*. London: Jessica Kingsley.

Leahey, T.H. (1992) 'The mythical revolutions of American psychology', *American Psychologist*, 47: 308–18.

FOUR

Children's Voices and Researching Childhood

JIM McKECHNIE

INTRODUCTION

In June 2001 the *Independent on Sunday* newspaper devoted a full page to a series of stories on film censorship. The reports were not as one might expect about the level of on-screen violence. Instead the journalists were reporting on the fact that the British Board of Film Classification (BBFC) were asking children about the classification of films. The aim of this initiative, from the perspective of the BBFC, is to gauge the extent to which it is getting the age classification right. To this end children will be asked for their judgement and opinions on whether the classifications of films used are appropriate. The main spokesperson for the BBFC indicated that such initiatives were being taken to 'give children direct say' in this area, which until now had been the preserve of adults (Morrison, 2001).

This is only one example of a growing interest in 'listening to children's voices'. Over the last decade there has been a move towards including the views of children on issues relating to their everyday life. In the area of social policy many organisations have as one of their founding principles the need to listen to children's views. One such non-governmental organisation (NGO) is Save the Children Fund (SCF). In one recent example SCF was involved in the production of a report based on children's views about a range of key policy areas. The report, *Our Lives*, presented the ideas of children (12–18 years of age) on a range of issues relating to the family, health, education, citizenship and protection from harm (Ritchie, 1999). The SCF has also put children's voices at the forefront of their research agenda. In considering child employment in Britain, the SCF has argued that policy needs to incorporate children's perspectives on the work they do (Pettitt, 1998).

In the examples cited above, the views of children are sought by adults. At the international level we can find examples where children *demand* that their voices should be listened to. The most dramatic example in recent years has been in the area of child labour. Groups of organised working children are to be found in Asia, Africa and Latin America. The organisations that have emerged from this include Bhima Singha and MANTHOC (Hobbs et al., 1999). These bodies argue that as child workers their views should be listened to when adults are deciding policy in this area. The most recent manifestation of this desire to be heard was the Global March Against Child Labour. The march culminated in Geneva in March 1998 to coincide with the International Labour Organisation meeting to discuss a new Convention on child labour. The Global Marchers argued that these meetings needed to include the views of working children in order to keep discussions grounded in the realities of young people's working lives.

These examples draw attention to a growing trend to incorporate the views of children into a range of areas from which they have commonly been excluded. How can we account for it? Part of the explanation is to be found in the effect of the United Nations' Convention on the Rights of the Child (CRC). This Convention has had an impact on policy-makers and wider society in part because a number of NGOs have highlighted the implications of the CRC for children's voices. Article 12 of the Convention commits signatories to take account of the views of children and young persons on matters or procedures that directly affect their lives. The UK government became a signatory of the CRC in 1991. In adopting the Convention the government is obliged to conform to it. A report is submitted two years after the adoption of the CRC, and then every five years after this, to detail progress in implementing the articles of the CRC.

Domestic UK legislation has also embodied this principle. The Children Act of 1989 and the Education Act of 1993 introduced the need to incorporate children's views in matters relating to their future interests. However, in 1994 the first UK report to the UN on the introduction of the CRC was criticised in part because it failed to fully address Article 12. It is debatable to what extent such concerns have been addressed by the British government. Nevertheless, the CRC has provided a framework for NGOs and advocates of child-related issues. By drawing attention to the failure to address international standards such bodies can ensure that the issue of 'children's voices' remains on the agenda.

While the idea of listening to the voices of children has been growing within the policy arena the concept is also reflected in the research field. The idea of allowing children to be heard resonates with ongoing debates about the nature of knowledge and the emergence of new paradigms within social science research. This is most apparent in sociology's rediscovery of childhood.

A 'NEW' SOCIOLOGY OF CHILDHOOD

Alan Prout and Allison James (1997) argue that a new paradigm for the sociology of childhood has emerged over the last decade. This 'new' sociology of childhood aims to bring the study of childhood to the centre stage of sociology and is viewed by its proponents as a counterweight to the dominance of psychology in the area of childhood studies. The re-emergence of sociological interest in childhood is to be welcomed though, as we have seen in Chapters 2 and 3, it is not unproblematic. It is not the intention of this chapter to cover this ground again. Instead, the focus is upon the research and methodological implications that are emphasised within the 'new' sociology of childhood.

One key element within this new childhood framework is the view that children and young people should be viewed as 'agents' or 'social actors' who are creating themselves in a range of different social contexts. This removes children from the role of 'objects' to be studied and emphasises that their views and experience could provide insight into the nature of childhood. In this context research is not carried out 'on' children but rather 'for' them. The implication of such an approach is that our methods of research need to place children as the central focus (Prout and James, 1997). At the heart of this perspective is the view that children must be accepted as accurate reporters of their own worlds. The emphasis is upon listening to their voices and using this material as the centre of any analysis of childhood (France et al., 2000).

Within the framework of the 'new' sociology of childhood it has been argued that the view of childhood held by researchers will be reflected in the study of childhood (James, 1999). The researchers' perceptions will be reflected in the methodology adopted, the groups that are studied and, ultimately, the interpretation of any data. Allison James (1999) identifies four discrete orientations towards 'the child' that have been reflected in research strategies. The different ways of 'seeing the child' are the developing child, the tribal child, the adult child and the social child. The link between these different views of the child and their research implications are clearly drawn out by Morrow and Richards (1996).

The perspective of 'the developing child' views children as posing different research problems compared to adults. Children are viewed as having different social competencies in comparison to adults. In this framework children's voices may be elicited but their views would be treated with some mistrust. The researcher interprets the data collected, which in turn is likely to be derived from cohort or longitudinal studies, experiments or observation. The 'tribal child' perspective views children as different research subjects from adults, but accepts that they have social competencies that are comparable to adults. The researchers aim is to attempt to get inside the autonomous world of children. Within this perspective participant observation and ethnography are common research methods.

The 'adult child' model views the child as comparable to adults in the research field. Researchers therefore employ the same research tools that they would use in any adult study. James (1999) suggests that an emphasis is placed on gaining the perspective of the child and listening to their observations on the adult world around them. However, James suggests that this tends to tell us about children's views of the adult world around them rather than that of childhood itself.

James's final model is that of the 'social child' where she argues that children are viewed as comparable to adults in terms of their status within research, but there is an acknowledgement that they have different social competencies. For James (1999: 244) this approach allows researchers to '. . . engage more effectively with the diversity of childhood . . .'. In adopting this view of 'the child' there is an implicit acceptance of children as social actors. To understand childhood, researchers need to employ methods that tap into the different skills, or competencies, that children have, for example, drawing, stories and written work. The use of qualitative research techniques, which draw on these competencies, offers the most effective research strategy in the study of childhood.

Given that the 'social child' reflects the underlying notions of the 'new' sociology of childhood it is not surprising to find that qualitative methods of research are viewed as having a key role to play in aiding our understanding of childhood. The rationale for this is that '. . . it allows children a more direct voice in the production of sociological data than is usually possible through experimental or survey style research' (Prout and James, 1997: 4).

However, listening to children's voices in the context of this new framework of childhood has other epistemological aspects as well. It is suggested that by attending to what children say, we gain access to the meaning they themselves attach to their experiences. Lloyd-Smith and Tarr highlight this in the area of educational research. These authors believe that by listening to children's views we gain insight to their reality: 'The reality experienced by children and young people in educational settings cannot be fully comprehended by inference and assumption' (Lloyd-Smith and Tarr, 1999: 61).

This emphasis on qualitative research methods has not only emerged in the 'new' sociology of childhood paradigm. Within psychology and developmental psychology, debates have continued about the value and role of qualitative approaches. In this context the primary driving force has not been that of 'listening to children's voices'. However, Jessor (1996) has suggested that the need to accommodate the subjective element into our inquiry of development, and understand the meaning of behaviour has been neglected.

For some researchers within developmental psychology the need to incorporate qualitative methods into their research is related to the role of culture in development. Textbooks of child development have acknowledged the role of cultural factors for a number of years. In the late 1970s Uri Bronfenbrenner's ecological model of development indicated the need to understand children's development within a number of contextual frameworks. The attention paid to Lev Vygotsky's theory in the 1980s and beyond has similarly drawn attention to the influence of social context on development. While there was an acknowledgement of the role of culture in development it was discussed at the theoretical level and researchers had difficulty in conceptualising this influence into their research. In the 1990s growing interest in integrating culture into development has emerged. Some have argued that this goal will only be achieved through a paradigm shift in developmental psychology (Coll and Magnusson, 1999). Within this shift there will need to be an awareness of the role of qualitative methods and non-experimental approaches to research. It is argued that employing such methods will create a greater understanding of the complexity of the relations between culture and children's development. This view is echoed in other discussions of developmental psychology (Jessor, 1996).

At a general level the discipline of psychology has had an ongoing debate about the merits of different methods of enquiry regarding human behaviour. For example, throughout the 1990s the main journal of the British Psychological Society, *The Psychologist*, devoted a number of special issues to the discussion of the role of qualitative approaches to research (*The Psychologist*, 1995, 1997, 1998).

What is apparent is that amongst researchers interested in understanding childhood there has been an emphasis upon qualitative methods of inquiry. In a recent text, which drew together examples of research studying children across a range of disciplines, the emphasis was clearly upon qualitative approaches with an emphasis on interviewing. The editors of the book suggest that the dominant research approach in childhood studies now emphasise interpretive and qualitative methods (Lewis and Lindsay, 2000). What are the perceived values of such an approach and what alternatives exist? We will consider these questions in the next section.

QUALITATIVE AND QUANTITATIVE APPROACHES

Approaches to collecting data within the social sciences have tended to be categorised as qualitative or quantitative. These methods of gathering information are viewed by many as contrasting approaches. For the moment we will accept this view and consider quantitative and qualitative approaches to developing our understanding of childhood. Within the new paradigm of childhood studies that has emerged within sociology qualitative research approaches are emphasised. The term qualitative research refers to a wide array of techniques. However, there is general agreement regarding the underlying aim of these different techniques. According to Denzin and Lincoln:

> Qualitative research is multimethod in focus, involving an interpretive, naturalistic approach to its subject matter. This means that qualitative researchers study things in their natural settings, attempting to make sense of or interpret phenomena in terms of the meanings people bring to them. (1994: 2)

A definition with a similar emphasis is provided by Bryman (1988: 46) who sees qualitative research as: '. . . an approach to the study of the social world which seeks to describe and analyse the culture and behaviour of humans and their groups from the point of view of those being studied'.

A number of different methods are available to achieve the goals outlined in the above definitions. They include participant observation, diary methods, case-studies, unstructured interviews, life history methods and group discussions. The key element is that in adopting such approaches the aim is to gather the views of the participants, to gain insight into the meaning they ascribe to events. Such approaches have been used extensively and have, for example, played an important role in educational research.

Qualitative approaches have certain characteristics. These include a strong emphasis on description and context. The former provides detailed information on the circumstances and setting being investigated. By doing this qualitative studies provide an awareness of the context within which data is being gathered. However, the issue of context goes beyond the immediate environment to include wider notions of context and culture. Perhaps the most important characteristic is that this approach aims to reflect the subject's perspective of the world around them. Qualitative approaches provide insight into the meanings participants ascribe to events, behaviours and value systems in their environments. It is the latter characteristic that strongly links qualitative research methods to the idea of 'listening to children's voices'. As Grieg and Taylor (1999: 46) comment: 'In an important sense, then, qualitative research enables the voice of the participant to be heard'.

There is a parallel between the emphasis placed on qualitative methods within the 'new' sociology of childhood and the role of these research techniques within feminist research. In feminist-standpoint research the focus is clearly upon gaining insight into women's experiences. Such experiences can most effectively be understood by employing qualitative approaches (Griffin, 1995). Within the 'new' sociology of childhood the aim is to gain insight into childhood through children's experiences.

Adopting this approach to research within the social sciences also reflects a specific orientation to investigation within the social sciences. A number of key philosophical assumptions underpin the qualitative paradigm. One of the most central assumptions relates to the nature of reality. Within this paradigm there is no 'objective' reality; rather we must accept multiple realities since reality is constructed by the individual involved in the research, participants and researchers (Cresswell, 1998). The very nature of qualitative methods is to unearth these differing realities. To achieve this, the researcher sets out to minimise the distance between themselves and the participants in the research project. Corsaro (1997) provides a good example of this in describing his study of children in Italian nursery schools and the lengths he went to in order to lessen the distance between himself and the children in the nursery.

Within the qualitative paradigm the research process emphasises inductive analysis. In this approach theory emerges from the data once it has been gathered, and may be constantly adjusted as more data emerges. For example, from some participatory observation in nursery settings you may gain information on the interactions between the children which may in turn lead you to the construction of a theory about children's friendships. The implication of this approach is that the research process is carried out within a theoretical vacuum; the researcher has no pre-conceived theory to test.

The philosophical underpinnings of qualitative research are best grasped when we contrast them with the other dominant research approach, the quantitative paradigm. In contrast to the inductive analysis that underpins qualitative research, quantitative research adopts a hypothetico-deductive analysis. Within such a framework hypotheses are generated based upon an existing theory. The role of research is to test the hypothesis. For example, an existing theory of children's friendship may lead us to predict some variation in the friendship patterns between male and female children. The researcher starts out with some notion of established theory and specific aims to investigate. In adopting this approach to investigating issues within the social sciences it is argued that the model adopted is one that is derived from the natural sciences. Researching children is therefore no different from the subject matter of chemists and physicists – they are knowable, objective and measurable.

The quantitative paradigm places an emphasis on controlled study, isolated from social contexts. This approach views reality as external to the actor and something that observers can agree upon. This is in contrast to the qualitative paradigm; there are no 'multiple realities'. The emphasis is upon objectivity, which places a distance between the objective researcher and 'the subject'. This approach, which is also referred to as positivism, places the emphasis on researching the observable. Phenomena that cannot be directly or indirectly observed through some assessment or measurement cannot be considered as the basis of knowledge. As such, 'subjective experience' is not within the interest of the social scientist unless it can be made observable and verifiable. The latter notion has meant that the emphasis is upon measurement and quantifiable data.

The dominant approaches for data gathering within this paradigm include experiments and surveys. The use of experimental methodology allows for the control of variables and the assessment of relationships between them, allowing researchers to make statements about causality. To produce reliable and valid information researchers must provide adequate definitions of concepts, operationalising them effectively and indicating how they are to be assessed. In the case of children's friendships there would need to be a clear understanding of what the term 'friendship' refers to and a means of assessing children's friendships devising in a way that met the criteria of reliability and validity. The expectation would be that any findings should be replicable.

QUANTITATIVE OR QUALITATIVE?

It is apparent that the quantitative and qualitative approaches can be contrasted on a number of points. If we focus on the notion of 'children's voices' the range of methods encompassed within the qualitative paradigm do appear to focus on gathering such information. However, the extent to which this observation can be supported may depend on how we conceptualise the idea of 'children's voices'. For example, survey methods, commonly used within the quantitative paradigm, could also be said to be collecting the views and opinions of children. The argument against this interpretation may be that the researcher, through constructing the survey, has already closed down the choices open to those who are participating in the research. The topics selected for study, the way in which children can respond in a sense restrict 'children's voices'. However, such an argument misses an important point. That is that all research, both within the qualitative and quantitative traditions, to some extent filters the voices of the research participants.

For some, such issues mean that the choice between quantitative and qualitative approaches is not a straightforward 'either–or' choice. We will return to consider this view later in the chapter. For the moment we will follow the tradition of considering these two approaches as alternatives to each other.

The choice between quantitative and qualitative approaches becomes more complicated when we start to consider wider criticisms of both paradigms. It is evident that both research traditions have problems. The quantitative approach, linked to its positivist roots, has been questioned on a number of grounds. The main concern is that following the natural science model, emphasising 'objectivity' and the control of variables in experimental settings, researchers are ignoring their influence in the research process. The desired 'objectivity' is not attainable. As a result, research in this paradigm has tended to produce limited insight or understanding of society. In particular it is argued that this approach has produced a limited understanding of societal problems (Jessor, 1996).

Jessor elaborates a number of other concerns. He suggests that the positivist tradition has resulted in a failure to address the role of context in research findings. The image created is that research findings exist in a vacuum or that they would be found across a range of contexts or cultures. A second source of concern is related to the participants in research. Adopting quantitative approaches loses sight of the individual. Results are discussed in terms of relations between variables and averages. In losing the individual we also lose their subjective experience. The research methods employed have difficulty in accommodating the meaning we ascribe to our behaviour. Failure to address these issues has meant that the data gathered is potentially superficial, the methods employed result in information that is 'narrow, rarefied and unrealistic' (Coolican, 1994: 172).

Concerns have also been raised about the qualitative approach and its constructivist base. For some the main problem with this approach is the very fact that it abandons many of the tenets of the natural science model. It has been argued that the emphasis on subjectivity within the qualitative approach is itself problematic (Morgan, 1996). In emphasising the subjective over the objective in data gathering such approaches face difficulties in meeting criteria of reliability, validity and replicability. Morgan believes that such concepts are at the heart of any science, natural or social. An additional criticism levelled at the qualitative approach is related to the fact that it accepts that there is a contextual nature to knowledge. The interpretation of what is happening around us will reflect context and culture. This leads to a conclusion that there is no objective reality, the result is relativity; all accounts of the world are equally as good (Stevenson and Cooper, 1997).

For Bryman (1988) three problems of qualitative research can be identified. First the nature of many qualitative studies raises questions about the generalisability of the findings. Second, the fact that research is not theory driven can result in a lack of theoretical depth. Emphasis on the participant's subjective views can constrain the development of theoretical models. Third, there is the problem of interpretation. Qualitative approaches emphasise the need to attend to the research participant's voice. The researcher is in effect trying to understand someone else's perspective. Questions arise about the validity of such exercises. Would two different researchers interpret a participant's voice in the same way? Within the qualitative tradition the issue of the researcher's interpretation has been viewed as problematic.

While criticisms such as the above have been levelled at qualitative research, some solutions have been proposed. For example, generalisability may be gained from multiple studies, replications or the use of multiple researchers investigating at the same time. Similarly concerns over the construction of theory and researchers' interpretation have resulted in some proposed solutions. For example, to tackle concerns about researchers' interpretations it has been proposed that they 'reflect' on their research process. This could entail keeping a journal in which researchers consider why they are pursuing different lines of inquiry and the approach they are adopting. This reflective document would then be open to external scrutiny.

It is apparent that both paradigms have their problems. How then are we to decide which to adopt in our goal to investigate childhood and listen to 'children's voices'? Henwood and Pidgeon (1995) draw attention to one approach. Following the suggestion of Bryman they propose two bases upon which to make this decision: technical or epistemological.

The technical perspective suggests that decisions regarding the use of quantitative or qualitative approaches should be resolved by considering the nature of the research question. Some questions will be better served using survey or experimental approaches. For example, questions relating to how many children work in the UK, what they do or how much they earn (see Stack and McKechnie, this volume) are couched in such terms that numerical information is needed to adequately respond to them. However, if we want to know what working children feel about their work or the importance of the earned income to them then qualitative approaches may provide a degree of insight that surveys cannot provide. Within this framework the descriptions of quantitative and qualitative approaches outlined earlier, and the problems that have been identified with both paradigms, could be viewed as examples of strengths and weaknesses. The conclusion that emerges from this perspective is that researchers should adopt the method that plays to the strengths inherent in both paradigms.

In contrast, the epistemological approach for deciding between quantitative and qualitative paradigms focuses on more fundamental differences. Within this approach the key questions relate to what is legitimate knowledge. The qualitative approach emphasises a constructivist notion of knowledge where understanding, or knowledge, is the result of the meanings that we arrive at as a result of social activities and our membership of social systems. Knowledge is therefore context bound and relative. There are no 'universal laws' to aid our understanding of human behaviour. Rather we need to employ qualitative approaches to understand the meanings, and potentially multiple meanings, people ascribe to behaviour and thought in the environment.

The epistemological basis of the quantitative approach is positivist, where knowledge is gained by applying the rigours of 'natural science' methods. The emphasis on quantitative, or numeric, data allows researchers to deal with concepts and theories by turning them into observable and manipulable data. In the epistemological option the researcher adopts the approach that is in harmony with their view of social science and the nature of knowledge. This contrasts with the technical in that combining quantitative and qualitative methodologies is more difficult to justify.

On what basis does the 'new' sociology of childhood emphasise qualitative approaches in childhood research? Given the key points emphasised in the new paradigm within childhood studies outlined by James and Prout (1990) it could be argued that the emphasis on qualitative methods reflects, what Bryman would call, the epistemological option. In addition, other factors may influence the researchers' emphasis on a particular methodology. Cresswell (1998) suggests that researchers are also influenced by ideological concerns. For example, qualitative approaches have been emphasised in feminist research because it was argued that other approaches maintain the exploitation of women's views in society. In this case feminist ideological considerations influence the choice of research method. If we apply this argument to the 'new' sociology of childhood post-modernism may provide the ideological influence that results in the dominant position of qualitative methods in this paradigm (see Lavalette and Cunningham, this volume).

The preference researchers may show for either quantitative or qualitative approaches may reflect decisions based on technical, epistemological or ideological grounds. However, the reality is that research is never so neat and tidy that one method is used to the exclusion of all others. Even where the preferred method has been chosen on epistemological grounds researchers still move between the two traditions (Bryman, 1988). This conclusion appears to hold true for the 'new' sociology of childhood as well. Prout and James (1990) acknowledge the potential value of quantitative approaches in the work of researchers such as Jens Qvortrup (1990). In the second edition of *Constructing and Reconstructing Childhood*, a key text in defining the 'new' childhood paradigm within sociology, the editors appear to step back from their earlier emphasis on qualitative methods: 'In retrospect, however, our claims for the primacy of ethnography seem somewhat one-sided . . .' (Prout and James, 1997: xv). The caveat is that survey methods and quantitative approaches need to ensure the inclusion of children in these approaches. This can, in some cases, mean the involvement of children in the design of the research process itself. While this appears to be a step towards the acceptance of quantitative techniques it is couched in the need to involve children in the design of such studies. Such a position appears to reflect the post-modern position emphasising the need to include the voices of marginalised groups, in this case children. While there is evidence of some movement from within the 'new' sociology of childhood the emphasis on qualitative methods is still apparent.

It could be argued that to fixate on qualitative approaches is to limit the scope of the researcher. A more productive approach would be to adopt a process that reflects the nature of the research question, what Henwood and Pidgeon term the technical option. Such a decision would result in an approach akin to methodological pluralism, where the research question dictates the appropriate method. There are a number of reasons why this may be more productive.

First, the dichotomy between quantitative and qualitative is a false dichotomy. In presenting the two approaches it is useful to draw attention to the points of contrast. When carrying out research, however, the reality is that the distinction between the two may be less obvious. Both approaches share similar problems. For example, both qualitative and quantitative approaches have to deal with issues of sampling. Similarly they have to deal with the problem of 'reactivity', or the way that research participants react to the researcher and the research process.

Second, by combining quantitative and qualitative techniques we may gain a fuller insight into the research question or our area of inquiry. Dockrell and Joffe (1992) demonstrate this point in their study of young people and HIV/AIDS. In their research they combine survey and unstructured interview techniques. They argue that the inconsistencies that emerged from these two sources resulted in a greater understanding of the issues. Such an approach has been used in other areas as well. Morrow (1994) has used a combination of techniques to look at children's out-of-schoolwork, while Prendergast (1994) looked at girls' menstruation experience through quantitative and qualitative techniques. Others have proposed the adoption of 'triangulation', where more than one method is used resulting in different forms of data. The results from these different sources are used to cross-check each other. It should be noted, however, that this can result in contradictory findings that are difficult to reconcile.

Third, the dominance of ideology may constrain the researchers' openness to other methods. We have already noted that ideological perspectives lead researchers to attend to the 'voices' of marginalised groups (post-modernism) or explore the issue of gender (feminism). Within both approaches there is an emphasis on qualitative methods. In some recent publications Ann Oakley has argued the feminist emphasis on qualitative approaches is based on a false choice between quantitative and qualitative approaches. Oakley suggests that the issue researchers should attend to is the 'appropriateness of the method to the research question' (Oakley, 1999: 156). By drawing on examples from health promotion she argues that the antipathy towards quantitative approaches could result in a failure to fully address the research question. For Oakley 'Understanding what acts mean to social actors is not the whole story; understanding society involves causal understanding, an understanding of how it is that what happens in society happens' (Oakley, 1998: 84). While Oakley is concerned with the qualitative bias of feminism the argument could be extended to the 'new' sociology of childhood. The influence of a specific ideology should not act as a barrier to the techniques that researchers use to develop their understanding of childhood.

Becker (1996) suggests that the similarities between the approaches are as important to recognise as the points of contrast. For Becker, 'The politics of social science can seduce us into magnifying our differences' (1996: 65). He goes on to suggest that this need not be the case and more importantly should not be the case.

CHILDREN AS RESEARCH PARTICIPANTS

While sociology has been discussing the emergence of a new paradigm within which to consider childhood this has to be viewed against the background of existing research interest in children. The strongest example of a discipline with an interest in understanding children is psychology, particularly developmental psychology. This background is acknowledged by those writing within the 'new' sociology paradigm. However, for some the tendency is to use developmental psychology as an example of what is wrong with existing approaches to researching childhood. In part, this perception of developmental psychology is linked to a view that considers research in this discipline as 'scientific' and seeking universal laws where children are viewed as lacking adult understanding. Piaget is often cited as an example of this position (see Hobbs, this volume). Such an approach emphasises the role of biological influence on the developing child and results in a deterministic view of development.

The potential problem with such a representation is that it fails to convey the extent to which a range of frameworks exist within developmental psychology to explain development. These frameworks range from those that emphasise the importance of in-built constraints, which influence knowledge and behaviour from childhood to adulthood. In contrast to that framework others view development as the result of social construction. In such a framework children's behaviour and knowledge are influenced by the environmental context. This includes the social and cultural influences on development (Cole and Cole, 2001).

All of the frameworks reflect what is generally referred to as the nature–nurture debate. The key point is that there are variations between the different explanations of development in terms of the emphasis they place on the role of environmental and biological factors. The reality is that all theories deal with the interaction between these two primary forces. In addition, theories such as Bronfenbrenner's ecological model have drawn attention to the influence of social systems upon children's development, while other researchers have highlighted the bidirectional influence of child and adult on each other's behaviour. Such influences have led developmental psychology to look critically at the context of research, including the influence of the researcher on participating children.

From the research perspective the main concern is that there is an acknowledgement that children have a wide range of competencies and skills which change over time. As such there are qualitative differences in the competencies of children and adults. That is not to imply that 'qualitative' is synonymous with 'inferior'. What it does suggest is that in research involving children we should be aware of these differences so that the methods of research employed reflect the ability of the participating children. If we fail to address this issue we may under-estimate the abilities of children or over-estimate their skills and abilities. From this perspective developmental psychology has provided a body of information relating to children's abilities, which have research implications. We will consider this by focusing on a number of examples.

First, the idea that 'listening to children's voices' places an emphasis on language. What is apparent is that children's production and use of language changes over time. As Garbarino et al. (1992: 90–1) comment: 'A child's verbal report is influenced by the child's age, the setting in which the conversation is taking place, by the person engaging the child in conversation and by the child's immediate situation that he finds himself in'. We should not assume that children's use of language maps directly onto that of adults. Some researchers have argued that the language used by the researcher may lead us to underestimate children's understanding (Donaldson, 1978).

Second, memory is an active process that involves the capacity to store, retain and retrieve information. Over our lifespan our ability to store, retain and retrieve information changes. In young children placing excessive demands on children's memory may impair their performance. Similarly as we develop a better knowledge of our own memory (metamemory), and form new strategies, our ability to recall improves. Related to memory is our third area of interest, cognition. The way in which we reason, solve problems and understand cause and effect has been shown to change over time. Our capacity for metacognition, or the ability to think about our own thought processes, shows change over time. Failure to attend to such variations when undertaking research may lead us to under-estimate children's ability or fail to hear their 'voices'.

While patterns of change have been identified in the areas outlined above within developmental psychology there are ongoing debates regarding how we explain such patterns. As indicated earlier there are a number of alternative frameworks within the discipline to account for such change. What is apparent is that research involving children needs to attend to such issues.

The picture is further complicated by the identification of the role of context in the research process. Margaret Donaldson's work has been seminal in drawing attention to the extent that the research context may influence the interpretation of children's skills and abilities. In a series of studies considering cognitive development Donaldson and her colleagues showed that children attend to the research context, interpreting its meaning and responding in a way that they feel makes sense in the context. These studies showed that the children's performance was improved by creating situations that made sense to them (Donaldson, 1978). This work, according to Donaldson, also demonstrated that the capacity to divorce ourselves from the context of any interaction may have a developmental underpinning. Older children were able to separate out the different elements, such as language and behaviour, within the research setting.

The examples cited above draw attention to the insight that developmental psychology can provide in the quest to understand childhood. In addition there are lessons to be learnt from the research methods used in developmental psychology. A large number of studies involving children employ interviews as the main source of data collection. While this has many benefits there are also some dangers. Young children have been shown to interpret questions very literally while other researchers have shown that young children will provide responses even to 'nonsense questions' (Hughes and Grieve, 1980). Subsequent research has shown that interpreting children's responses to 'nonsense questions' to be more complex than first thought (Waterman et al., 2000). However, the research reinforces the need for care in asking children questions since a response does not always signal comprehension of the question.

The context of the interview may also influence responses. Interviews involving an adult–child dyad need to be sensitive to the impact that this may have on the views expressed by children. An awareness of what is and is not acceptable to adults may influence what the child is willing to say. It is also evident that the child's experience of previous interactions with adults will influence the child's participation. Rose and Blank (1974) demonstrated that to children a repeated question from an adult may indicate that their previous answer was incorrect or not acceptable.

This should not be interpreted as indicating that the interview method cannot be valuable. It simply highlights the complexity of the research process. One reaction could be to consider other forms of response to questions which may be more amenable to children. Employing rating scales which have visual equivalents may be useful, for example, a range of simple faces with a range of emotional expressions from happy to sad could be used (Denham and Auerbach, 1995). Alternatively pictures may be used to explore children's understanding of a situation. While such approaches are useful the researcher needs to ensure that the stimuli used do not reflect the preconceived ideas of adults. In investigating children's notion of risk the type of picture stimuli would have to be relevant to risks within children's lives. The use of children's drawings have emerged as another technique to gain insight into the world of children. Drawings have been used to gain some understanding of children's cognitive skills and their interpretation of situations and emotional states. Such techniques create a range of interpretive problems, especially if the drawing is the sole source of information (Grieg and Taylor, 1999).

Such techniques are often used as devices to open a dialogue with children, to 'get them talking'. However, developmental psychology has also been interested in understanding children in the pre-verbal stage. To gain some understanding of children's worlds before they have a shared language system has resulted in psychologists developing a wide range of research techniques; for example, habituation studies and visual preference techniques. Such approaches rely upon the coding and interpretation of behaviour. A common example where children's behaviour is used is the caretaker–child relationship. The dominant technique used in this field is Ainsworth's Strange Situation method. In this type of investigation the caretaker and child experience a systematic manipulation of contact, separation and the introduction of a 'stranger' into the environment (Cole and Cole, 2001) The nature of the caretaker–child attachment is defined by the infant's behaviour in the different situations. The technique demonstrates that children's behaviour may provide insight into children's social relationships. In the case of the Strange Situation continuing research over a number of years has drawn attention to the cultural variations in the attachment patterns found as well as leading researchers to question the range of factors that influence the form and nature of attachments between children and their caretakers (Valsiner, 2000).

Up until this point the aim has been to demonstrate that developmental psychology has provided a range of insights that need to be considered when researching the voices of children. The last example drew attention to the use of observed behaviour and the way it can provide information on pre-verbal children's understanding and relationships. Some psychologists would argue that the use of observational techniques may be of value in all research, whether we are concerned with child or adult participants. In setting out to listen to the voices of children or any other research participants the assumption is that we should accept what the 'voice' tells us regarding the information that we seek. Two traditions within psychology, psychoanalysis and behaviourism, have been built upon doubts about whether we are able to gain insight into psychological processes by such methods. We could extend that argument to our current concern of understanding childhood. Is it the case that research participants have the relevant knowledge to be able to respond? Are they aware of all the circumstances? Are they withholding, or distorting, their views for some other reason?

This issue may be clearer if we consider a specific example: the issue of child employment in the UK (see also Stack and McKechnie, this volume). A body of information has grown up which, while limited, has provided some insight into this aspect of children's lives. However, one gap is related to our understanding of what actually goes on in children's workplaces, the activities they are involved in, the extent and form of social contacts they have or the skill opportunities they may have available to them. In America some researchers have attempted to address this issue. They collected information in two ways. First, they asked the young workers to provide this information. Second, they used observers to record what happened in the workplace. The outcome was a mismatch between what the employees thought happened in the workplace and what the observers showed that the workers did in the workplace (Steinberg et al., 1982).

While there are some methodological concerns related to this work (Hobbs and McKechnie, 1999) the general conclusion is that we should be cautious when 'listening to the voice' of the research participants and not automatically accept what is said. Nor should we abandon the critical analysis of what is said or the use of information from other sources. This latter point resonates with a number of the issues raised earlier in the discussion on qualitative and quantitative approaches. In seeking to understand childhood, methodological pluralism may be the most rewarding position to adopt.

CONCLUSION

While the growing interest in 'listening to children's voices' in the policy arena is to be welcomed, the issue of 'children's voices' raises a number of issues for researchers. The 'new' sociology of childhood has placed a specific emphasis on qualitative methods to achieve this. As we have discovered both qualitative and quantitative paradigms have a range of problems associated with them.

If our aim is to understand childhood then this goal may be best served by adopting a pluralist approach to research methods. Recognising the strengths and weaknesses in both paradigms requires researchers to choose the most appropriate research tool in the light of the research question.

We should also recognise that different academic disciplines may bring a range of perspectives to the study of childhood. By adopting a multi-disciplinary approach to research we may gain a greater insight into, and understanding of, childhood.

KEY TEXTS

Grieg, A. and Taylor, J. (1999) *Doing Research with Children*. London: Sage.
Lewis, A. and Lindsay, G. (eds) (2000) *Researching Children's Perspectives*. Buckingham: Open University Press.

FIVE

Rich Children, Poor Children

TONY NOVAK

INTRODUCTION

It is an obvious – although significantly neglected – fact that the living standards, opportunities and life chances of children differ enormously. In a society such as Britain's that is grossly unequal and deeply divided by social class it would be strange were it otherwise. Yet while inequalities between adults, for example in relation to 'race', gender or social class, are often recognised, when it comes to children relatively little attention is paid to the divisions which exist. It is almost as if the presumed 'innocence' of children has no place for the harsh realities of inequality and social division. Certainly there is a notable body of research and campaigning effort on the issue of child poverty, but like the study of poverty in general, this suffers from a tendency to view poor children in isolation. Only very rarely is the whole spectrum of childhood inequality considered, and the children of the poor placed alongside the children of the rich. Yet of all social groups and categories, inequality between children and the inequalities of childhood are probably the greatest.

THE INCOMES AND LIVING STANDARDS OF CHILDREN

Most children and young people do not have any significant income and wealth of their own. For the most part, what we know about the incomes available to children, and the living standards that this allows, is derived from that of their parent(s) and the households in which they live. Households below average income (HBAI) – a series of calculations produced by the Department of Social Security (now the Department of Work and Pensions) – ranks households and the individuals they contain against the average net income (including benefits, wages and salaries, and after taking account of taxation) of society as a whole. Adjusted for the differing sizes of households, these show that households with children are concentrated at the lower end of the income distribution: three-quarters of children live below average income, and only one-quarter above the average, a degree of inequality more marked than that amongst adults. More significantly, taking half of this average – the now commonly used measure of poverty – one in three children in 1999 was living at or below this level: an increase from one in ten in 1979.

This dramatic growth in childhood poverty, in both extent and severity, is of course but one reflection of the growth of poverty and inequality in Britain as a whole since the beginning of the 1980s. Britain has always been a greatly unequal society, and at any time in its history the gap between rich and poor – amongst children and adults alike – has marked its inequalities of class, whether in terms of wealth and income, health and educational opportunity, or any other feature of social life. During the course of the twentieth century, however, these inequalities, while by no means disappearing, began to narrow. The changes that brought this about were propelled on the one hand by a growing resistance and refusal on the part of working-class people to accept both their unequal lot in life and the naked operation of a market system that produced and reproduced this. On the other, there was a recognition on the part of the rich that some concessions were necessary if their systems of privilege were not to be entirely swept away. As a result, social reforms were gradually and cautiously introduced. Culminating in a so-called 'welfare state' between 1945 and the mid-1970s, these changes modified the most brutal consequences of a market economy: the recurrent threat of large-scale unemployment was largely removed; inequalities in income and wealth were reduced; and prospects for the futures of working-class children increased as fundamental needs for health, education and housing were removed, at least in part, from the operation of market forces and the ability to pay.

It did not, of course, last. The imperatives of a market system and the reassertion of the privileges of social class, of wealth and power, that was epitomised in the governments of Margaret Thatcher brought an abrupt end to the limited achievements of the welfare state. Between the early 1980s and the mid-1990s a series of economic recessions, spurred on by government policy, saw mass unemployment return and poverty increase dramatically. Working conditions worsened for millions as employers took advantage of the new insecurity to claw back what power they had lost.

At the same time, while the wealthy were rewarded with tax cuts to boost their already spiralling incomes, the welfare services on which the poorest most depended were reduced, abolished or stripped of their helping role (Jones and Novak, 1999). During the 1980s and 1990s government policy, rather than softening the effects of free market inequalities, added significantly to the growing divide between rich and poor. According to one study, while market forces, including both the dramatic rise in unemployment and its subsequent negative effect on wages, especially of the low paid, were primarily responsible for growing inequality in the first half of the 1980s, by the late 1980s changes in state benefits and taxation policies were having a greater effect (Atkinson, 1996). Children, and especially those children whose parent(s) depended on state benefits, invariably suffered as benefit levels were cut or made more difficult to claim and the household incomes of the poor reduced.

Other government changes specifically targeted benefits for children and young people, including the postponement of benefit paid to school leavers and the abolition of dependent child allowances to the sick and the unemployed. By 1987 there had been fourteen cuts in social security for children and young people that had deprived them of some £200 million of income (Andrews and Jacobs, 1990: 77). Then, in the 1988 Social Security Act, government removed altogether the right of 16- and 17-year-olds to claim benefit, and significantly reduced the level of benefit payable to all young people up to the age of 25.

The result was that over this period inequality of incomes in Britain grew to a greater extent and at a faster rate than in any other industrialised country, wiping out all the gains made in the post-war era, and increasing the gap between the highest paid and the lowest paid amongst those in work to levels not seen since the end of the nineteenth century. Trends towards a levelling of class differences in health or education were similarly halted, and in many cases reversed.

THE IMPACT ON CHILDREN

For a variety of reasons, children have been most affected by this growing divide: although children make up 22 per cent of the whole population, 29 per cent of children are in the lowest-income fifth of the population, and 11 per cent in the richest fifth. One reason for the growing polarisation in the fortunes of children is the way in which the dynamics of growing poverty have impacted most upon those families and households of child-rearing age. Thus between 1979 and 1993 the risk of living in poverty doubled for couples without children, but increased three-fold for those with children (Oppenheim and Harker, 1996: 55). The dramatic rise of unemployment in the early 1980s, and its persistence, has dramatically increased poverty amongst the children of the unemployed: in 1998/9 only 10 per cent of children in families with a full-time worker were found in the lowest income group, whereas the figure rose to 76 per cent of children in families with no working adult.

It is, however, not only unemployment that has impacted on the living standards of many children. The presence of children can limit the earnings potential of their parent(s), just as it increases household costs. Especially in the absence of affordable or adequate childcare facilities, parents may find themselves restricted to part-time work or required to take longer periods of time outside of the labour market while their children are dependent. This is particularly the case for mothers, who continue to bear the greater responsibility for childcare. Yet it is to women, and married women in particular, that employers have tended to look for their new sources of labour. Again the consequences of these changed patterns of work have a differential social class impact: whereas 65 per cent of professional and managerial women work full time and only 17 per cent part time, for women in unskilled and manual jobs the proportions are more than reversed, with only 8 per cent working full time and 55 per cent part time. Incomes followed the trend: in 1994 the earnings of full-time professional women averaged £400 a week, those of women in manual part-time jobs £70 a week (*Guardian*, 27 September 1995).

For single parents dependent on a sole income, achieving a job that pays sufficient to provide for themselves and their children in comfort and safety is a minority achievement. Some manage this quite nicely, but only 3 per cent of the children of single parents make it into the top fifth of income groups (compared with 12 per cent of all children), while 54 per cent remain in the poorest group (Department of Social Security, 2000: 75). As a result, the children of lone parents are more likely than children of two-parent families to find themselves in the poorest households: four-fifths of all lone-parent families are in the bottom two-fifths of the income distribution, a figure that rises to 90 per cent of lone parents without paid work. At the same time, and as a reminder that lone parenthood in itself is not necessarily a cause of poverty, 3 per cent of the children of lone parents enjoy the lifestyles of the highest income group (Department of Social Security, 2000: 75).

The children of ethnic minority families similarly share the poverty – and much less often the wealth – of their parent(s). All ethnic minority children are more likely to experience poverty than white children but for black and Pakistani or Bangladeshi children the risk is much, much higher: 74 per cent of Pakistani or Bangladeshi children live in households with incomes less than half the national average, as do 57 per cent of black children, compared with 34 per cent of children as a whole (Department of Social Security, 2000: 81).

What these statistics reveal then is a picture in which large numbers of children – and for those with single parents, parents of an ethnic minority or parents who are unemployed, a majority of children – are brought up in conditions below, and sometimes far below, prevailing measurements of poverty. Some children, conversely – and, like their parents, a minority – enjoy all the benefits and privileges that wealth and high incomes confer. For those who experience childhood as poverty and deprivation, the consequences, as we shall see, are enduring and far-reaching. Moreover it is, for many, more than just a temporary or short-lived experience. To experience the depths of poverty at any time during childhood may be seen as a potentially damaging experience; to spend a whole childhood in poverty can have the most devastating, and well-documented, long-term effects. Authoritative evidence produced for a joint study by the Centre for Analysis of Social Exclusion and HM Treasury shows that over a six-year period from 1991–6, while 37 per cent of all children were in poverty at the beginning of the period, 25 per cent stayed in poverty for four out of the six years, and 13 per cent remained in poverty for the whole six-year period. In other words, 35 per cent of poor children remain permanently poor: a figure that rises to 45 per cent for the children of single parents (Walker, 1999: 9).

HEALTH

Put a child from an unskilled or semi-skilled family background next to one from a professional or managerial background, and one will live nearly ten years longer than the other, be less likely to die at birth, in infancy and childhood, will suffer fewer diseases and live a healthier mental and physical life. It is no accident.

According to an editorial in the *British Medical Journal* in July 1999, 'poverty, as every doctor knows, is a major determinant of health, much more so than access to health services'. The latter remains important – the wealthier classes and their children still enjoy better access to state, not to mention private, health care (Ascheson, 1998). But it is in the causes of death and ill-health that class inequalities first have their impact.

Over twenty years ago the Report of the Working Party on Inequalities in Health chaired by Sir Douglas Black concluded that 'class differences in mortality are a constant feature of the entire human life-span. . . . At any age people in occupational class V have a higher rate of death than their better-off counterparts' (cited Benzeval, 1997: 154). Since then the situation has, if anything, got worse. Infant mortality – the number of children who die before the age of 1 – is one of the most widely-established measures of health and health inequality, used to measure economic and social development and health inequalities across the globe. In Britain overall levels of infant mortality have fallen over time, but inequalities between social classes remain largely untouched. Children born in social classes IV or V have a 50 per cent higher rate of infant mortality than those born in social classes I or II, while other studies using different criteria show even greater rates of difference: infant mortality in Salford, for example, being twice as high as that in south Suffolk (Yamey, 1999). Poor nutrition in pregnancy is one factor, leading to an average birth weight in social class V 115 g lighter than in social class I, while 25 per cent of mothers living in bed and breakfast accommodation in one London borough were found to have low birth-weight babies, compared to a national average of 7 per cent (Lee, 1999). Low birth weights account for 59 per cent of neo-natal deaths, contributing to a national infant mortality rate that now puts Britain on a par with Slovenia as a country with one of the worst records in Europe.

Once past the very unequal hazards of infancy, most children can expect to live to adulthood with very little chance of an early death. Those who do die early, however, are much more likely to be poor.

Death by accident is the biggest killer of children: about 500 die each year as a result. Poorer children are five times more likely to die in accidents than those from 'better-off' families, eight times more likely to be killed by a car (despite, it should be noted, fewer poor families owning one), and fifteen times more likely to die in a fire. 'The gap between rich and poor has widened since 1981, and is the steepest social gradient in childhood deaths' (*Guardian*, 22 December 1999).

Of course poorer children face more hazardous lives than richer children, and it is their poverty which is the cause of this. Overcrowded living conditions, lack of gardens and other safe play areas make poorer children more vulnerable. Poverty also brings added perils: families who have to cook on open fires, or light the house by candles, because the electricity supply has been cut, and the cheap, but less reliable, electrical appliances, child safety locks, smoke alarms and fire-proof furniture that are the lot of those who cannot afford more.

While childhood deaths mark an extreme of health inequalities, ill-health also has its own persistent and long-lasting impact. Children and young people are remarkably resilient, and this in itself has contributed to the neglect of their health problems and inequalities. According to one source:

> Perhaps the biggest obstacle of all to understanding the health needs of young people has been the assumption that adolescence and health go hand in hand, what Bennet referred to as 'a widespread belief that they are a fit and healthy group'. This assumption, which still pervades much medical thinking, is rapidly being shaken by evidence concerning the health of young people themselves and by a broader concern with the social and economic conditions they face as they enter adulthood. Economic recession, unemployment, low-paid jobs, and the sense of having no future are potentially all components of a social malaise that may affect the health of us all, but especially the young. (West and Sweeting, 1996: 50)

It is, however, not all of the young who will suffer such consequences, but rather those with lower incomes and from poorer social classes (Kumar, 1993). According to consultant paediatrician James Appleyard, one of the authors of the BMA report 'Growing Up In Britain', 'we are programming our children at an early age for lifetime problems. . . . The first five years are absolutely crucial to the development of children's bodies, minds and personalities. Deprivation in early life causes lifelong damage' (cited Lee, 1999: 1).

Moreover, it is not only the direct material impact of poverty which blights the lives of children in poorer families. As Richard Wilkinson has convincingly shown, the existence of inequality itself contributes to lower levels of health and well-being: Japan and Sweden, while not the richest countries in the developed world, have the narrowest income differences, and come first and second respectively in the world's ranking of life expectancy at birth (Wilkinson, 1994: 10). The psycho-social impact of class inequalities on health, rather than just the material effects of poverty, are as yet little understood, but the evidence of depression and suicide amongst young people shows a familiar class pattern. Those young people who leave school with no qualifications, for example, are three times more likely to be diagnosed as depressed by their mid-20s than graduates (*Guardian*, 12 July 2000), while a study of 1,000 young people from the west of Scotland, who were followed from the age of 15 to 21, found a significant deterioration in the mental health of those who faced unemployment: 'for almost all the mental health measures, unemployed males and females were in poorer health. Nine per cent of males and seven per cent of females who were unemployed reported attempting suicide, much higher rates than those found for those at work or in education' (West and Sweeting, 1996: 57).

EDUCATION

The cementing of class inequalities begins at an early age, and among the myriad of ways in which the privileges, or deprivations, of social class are passed down from one generation to the next, formal educational systems figure centrally. Schooling both reflects childhood inequalities and reinforces them, reproducing in each generation similar patterns that last into adult life.

In Britain the starkest example of the class inequalities in the schooling of children and young people is the deep-rooted divide between state and private schooling. As Nick Davies wrote in a special review of private schools in *The Guardian* (8 March 2000), 'there is no other country in Europe where private schools present a fully fledged alternative to the state system, open essentially only to the affluent'. In other countries, although private schools exist, and sometimes cater for a greater proportion of children than in Britain, their rationale tends to be based on religious affiliation rather than on wealth. In Britain private schools have for over a century (ever since they abandoned their founders' intention to provide free education for the poor, earning them the title of 'public' schools to which many still cling) sought to provide educational, social and interpersonal benefits to the small minority of children whose parents are able to pay.

With an annual income from fees alone of some £3.2 billion, Britain's 2,300 private schools currently cater for 7 per cent of the country's children, a proportion that has increased from 5.8 per cent in 1980. Yet the products of private schooling continue to dominate public life: almost half the students at Oxford and Cambridge have a private school background, from where they go on to fill 80 per cent of the judiciary and 83 per cent of High Court appointments. In other parts of the state apparatus, young people from private schools go on to take over half the places at the Royal Military Academy, Sandhurst, 80 per cent of the highest army ranks, and 40 per cent of the diplomatic service, while providing half of the permanent secretaries who run Whitehall (*Sunday Times*, 4 June 2000).

Their numbers equally dominate the major professions such as law and medicine: careers for which private school pupils are groomed from an early stage. According to one study:

> The future career plans of the private school pupils were generally made at a very early age. Indeed there was often evidence of extensive knowledge of job types within a particular career. Subjects wanted to go into criminal law instead of just law, and surgery instead of medicine. Many pupils reported a pressure from teachers and careers staff to decide on an occupational plan at the age of 14, in order to ensure they made 'the correct' choice of GCSE and then A level subjects. Additionally, an extensive programme of work experience was organised for pupils, often involving the parents of the pupils to provide access to hospitals, legal offices and accountancy practices. (Roker, 1991: 9)

In law, for example, half of the appointments to partners within the 'magic circle' of the five leading London law firms come from private schools, where they can expect to climb a ladder leading to current salaries of up to £1 million a year, and half of these were also educated at Oxford or Cambridge. According to a report published by the magazine *Commercial Lawyer*, 'You still have a better chance of being made a partner if you had a private education. The odds are stacked against you in the legal profession if you went to a state school. If you went to an ex-polytechnic, you can forget the magic circle' (cited in *The Independent*, 15 July 2000). Seventy-five per cent of private school pupils go on to take managerial and professional jobs, compared with only 40 per cent of those from the state sector (*Guardian*, 8 March 2000), and, along with the unknown numbers who fill the country's boardrooms, they form a small and largely self-perpetuating elite in whose hands the major economic and political institutions of the country substantially remain.

All this, of course, comes at a price. According to the Independent Schools Information Service, basic fees 'vary widely' depending on the particular school and the age of the child. For 'pre-prep' schooling, aged 2–7, fees are between £2,100 and £3,600 a year; for Junior or Prep schools, £3,600 to £7,500; and for Senior schools, aged 11 or 13–18, from £4,800 to £10,500, with additional charges for boarding schools. At the same time 'extras can add considerably to the bill'. In return, those with the ability to pay can receive a seamless web of private education from infancy to young adulthood. One such example is that of Mill Hill school in London; as the *Observer* reported:

> The pre-prep (£5,340 a year for 4 year olds) feeds into Mill Hill's prep school (fees £6,411 a year). At 13 they proceed to the main school on the same leafy 150-acre campus. This costs £8,250 a year, adding up to £100,000 per child for the full 15 years. The state sector spends barely a quarter as much. (*Observer*, 15 February 1998)

Fees alone, however, are not the only source of income for educating the children of the wealthy. Many private schools enjoy charitable status, with the result that they escape all tax on income from stocks, shares, trusts and property as well as escaping all VAT, corporation tax on their profits, capital gains tax and stamp duty on their property transactions, inheritance tax on new endowments and up to 100 per cent of their business rates. As Nick Davies reported:

> In 1996 the Independent Schools Council surveyed 838 of its members and concluded that they were saving £62.6 million a year. In 1992 the master of Haileybury, David Jewell, suggested that ending charitable status would add 30 per cent to fees – making charitable status the equivalent of a state subsidy of about £1,945 per pupil, some £200 more a year than the state now invests in the education of a child at primary school. (*Guardian*, 8 March 2000)

What this buys is a range of advantages over other children. According to the head teacher of Mill Hill's pre-prep school, for those aged 4–7, 'the difference is mostly a question of money and class size. We have an in-house music teacher, a full-time PE and dance specialist, and they start learning French at six' (cited in *The Observer*, 15 February 1998). Its prep school also has a rose garden, chapel, playing fields, six tennis courts and networked computer system, together with one teacher for every eleven pupils. Many other private schools similarly are able to afford such extensive facilities; with an average of eighteen acres of land each, 93 per cent of private pre-schools teach music, almost all teach French, two-thirds teach Latin, and a quarter teach German. In contrast, state schools have faced drastic cuts in music and sports facilities, school playing fields are sold off at the rate of twenty a year, state primary schools have on average one computer between eighteen pupils, and class sizes twice those found in the private sector (*Guardian*, 8 March 2000).

It should therefore be of little surprise that academic achievement of children in the private sector generally far exceeds that of children in state education. Ninety-two of the top 100 schools judged by A-level results are private. Nor can the superior results of private schooling be seen as a reflection of some innate superiority amongst the children of the wealthy: a University of London Institute of Education study tracked a group of 350 students who were equally able academically, half of whom went to private schools and half to state schools. Those who went to private schools did much better in their A-levels and were more than twice as likely to go to a top university (Lampl, n.d.: 2).

It is not, however, only the smaller class sizes and the vastly superior facilities of most private schools that mark the advantage of a fee-paying education. Just as schooling in general is one of the major institutions ensuring the reproduction of class inequalities, so those destined by birth and money to become the future ruling class of the country are trained in the culture and attitudes of their class. As Bryan Appleyard put it in the *Sunday Times* (4 June 2000):

> It is not just that private school pupils gain better qualifications – though they do – it is also that they are perceived to function better in society. . . . It is a sad truth that even the brightest state pupils tend to lack the wit, charm and confidence of their private school coevals.

'Wit', 'charm' and 'confidence', when interpreted as they invariably are in their class-specific contexts, go a long way. Along with the personal contacts and networks that ease privileged children into their future careers, they undoubtedly do much to make up for any lack of intelligence or ability. Research suggests that private schools lay great store by the development of such attributes; as an interviewee in one study saw it, 'the exam results are better . . . but it's more than that. Private schools give you confidence. You really feel you can do anything . . . you're made to believe it.' Another felt this had tangible results: 'I've had two interviews at University and you can see it makes a difference . . . they're just influenced by it' (cited Roker, 1991: 9). As the author of the study concluded:

> Pupil[s] believed that the high academic achievements of private school pupils was important; but it was this added confidence and forwardness that gave people from private schools 'the edge' over other young people in interviews for University and also, eventually, for jobs. 'It's a very subtle difference' [one] suggested, 'but it's very real'. (Roker, 1991: 10)

While private schooling marks the pinnacle of a class-divided education system, state schooling also mirrors this divide. Class inequalities within state education have been a persistent feature since its origins, and reforms over the years have done relatively little to change the situation. In the first place, a small but educationally significant part of the state system still reserves the right to select its own pupils. Grammar schools, although accounting for only 3 per cent of children at state schools, account for 22 per cent of top state performers at A-level, and 30 per cent of state school entries to Oxford and Cambridge, while the latter take only 20 per cent of their intake from the 85 per cent of children educated in unselective state comprehensive schools (Lampl, n.d.: 2). Even within the comprehensive system factors of wealth and social class bear heavily on achievements and future prospects. Although unselective in name, in practice those with sufficient income and wealth can play the housing market and pay the inflated house prices that are now commonly associated with the catchment areas of the best state schools.

Of perhaps greater significance, however, in perpetuating educational advantage and disadvantage even within the state system are the material benefits that favour the educational success of the more affluent, and the in-built and largely middle-class ethos and culture of the educational system itself.

The result is a state education system that systematically disadvantages those from poorer backgrounds. Whereas in 1998 more than two-thirds of children of the professional and managerial classes gained five GCSEs at grades A to C, only 20 per cent of children whose parents were in unskilled manual jobs achieved the same standard (*Guardian*, 11 May 2000). The consequences for future educational progression and, ultimately, for job prospects and careers are equally divided. Those who leave school with no qualifications are four times as likely to be unemployed than those who progress on to a university degree, while at every step of the educational ladder, future earnings are heavily determined by qualifications received. Thus males leaving school with O-levels or GCSEs will earn between 12 and 21 per cent more than those with no qualifications; those with A-levels 27–39 per cent more, and those with a degree 37–67 per cent more (Department of Social Security, 2000: 23). This link between education and future earnings, moreover, 'is getting stronger over time': between 1980 and 1994 earnings for men with A-levels increased twice as fast as for those with no qualifications (ibid.).

AN END IN SIGHT?

In March 1999 Tony Blair announced that his government was committed to the abolition of child poverty in Britain within twenty years. As a number of commentators have pointed out (see Fimister, 2001), it was both a bold and a limited commitment, whose ultimate success has yet to be judged. During its first term in office the New Labour government saw some significant inroads made into child poverty, with the numbers living below the poverty line reducing by an estimated one-third. Yet reducing the number by one-half will still leave Britain with one of the highest rates of childhood poverty in the industrialised world, and with a level still exceeding that when the last Labour government left office in 1979. Lifting all children above the poverty line will also, on current government policy, be a much more difficult task: New Labour's insistence on work as the route out of poverty leaves untouched those families with children unable to work and would call for a substantial redistribution of income, especially through the benefit system, that New Labour has shown itself reluctant to countenance. Even if it were to succeed, a target of twenty years will leave hundreds of thousands of children to endure its damaging effects in the interim.

What is more, lifting children above the poverty line will not put an end to childhood inequalities. The poverty line, set at half of average income, is itself an arbitrary and meagre definition of need, and to lift children from below to slightly above this line will still leave them facing substantial deprivation and hardship. As with adults, the continuum of childhood poverty stretches from the most wretched and miserable through a myriad of lesser deprivations. But poverty remains a matter of relative definition, and, like poverty in general, children's poverty is felt in comparison with others. In other words what it means to 'live normally' is judged by how other people live. It is entirely possible, and necessary, to eradicate the worst excesses of childhood poverty, but to give all children a normal life means addressing the huge gap that exists between those at the top and those at the bottom. Yet, despite the progress made by New Labour in raising the living standards of some of the poorest children, the gap between rich and poor continues to increase.

For children, compared to adults, the pressure to be like others is probably the most acute. As one mother said:

> You can accept it for yourself; it doesn't matter if you haven't got a pair of knickers without holes in or no stockings because you can cover up; you can accept it more for yourself, you can't accept it for your children, and that's the worst thing. (Cited in Beresford et al., 1999: 108)

Just because some children cannot afford what other children have does not mean they do not feel a need to be the same. Commercialisation of childhood has increased the pressure to compare and consume. Children are now a major target in the sales of everything from supermarket foods to financial services, to say nothing of music, clothes and fashion. Inequalities amongst children also open up new areas for commercial exploitation: most of the big financial institutions now operate special children's savings accounts, such as the Nationwide's Smart-2-Save (aged 1–11) or Bradford and Bingley's KidZone (aged 1–16). As the *Daily Telegraph* (9 February 2000) noted, reporting research commissioned by the Royal Bank of Scotland showing that while one-fifth of children get no pocket money at all, another fifth get an average in excess of £20 per week, with the earnings, gifts and other savings that some children enjoy, children are big business. Moreover, as the *Telegraph* helpfully reminded its readers, with children entitled, like adults, to an income of £4,335 per year before becoming liable to tax, those that can afford it have an added incentive to boost their children's wealth.

Poverty of course is not only a matter of money. In the final analysis, poverty is a social relationship, and the experience of poverty is framed not simply by a lack of resources but by the way people are treated and perceived by others around them. This, importantly, includes government policy, and the growing trend towards means-tested benefits – justified as a way of 'concentrating help' on those in the greatest need – reinforces the feeling of being separate and apart. The fear of being stigmatised, of being made to stand out, and in particular to be seen as inadequate or a failure is a constant pressure, and for many children a daily reality. According to James Roberts, aged 14:

> Kids whose parents don't have much money are forced to go to the cheap shops and if anyone sees them then they get picked on in the estate and at school. My friend and I have both had

these problems. You also get picked on in school if you get a free school dinner ticket; you get called things like 'poor boy', 'scavenger' and things that are a bit rude and I'm not allowed to repeat. This makes us feel sad, and sometimes angry with them, and then we get into trouble and get called troublemakers. (Cited in McMahon and Marsh, 1999: 14)

Learning the lessons of poverty is a painful experience, and it is one that most parents seek to avoid for their children. Parents go to huge lengths to shield their children from it, with mothers in particular sacrificing their own diet and health to ensure that children have enough to eat or can go on the school trip. Yet for millions it is a futile struggle against impossible odds and the cause of great conflict and tension that add to the pressures that poor children face.

For some children and young people, these pressures have proved catastrophic. For some it has meant family breakdown and the perils of life on the streets or 'in care' (see Jones, this volume). For others it has led to drug addiction, mental and behavioural problems, and a rising level of suicide. For many thousands it has created a position of economic and social marginalisation through which crime may offer the only viable route for survival. By 1997 there were approximately 150,000 16- or 17-year-olds not in education, training or paid work, a majority of whom received no income from the state. One survey conducted earlier in the 1990s found that 45 per cent of this group were or had been homeless, a quarter said they had had to beg, steal or sell drugs in order to survive, and a quarter of the girls were pregnant (cited in Wilkinson, 1994: 36). With girls from social class V backgrounds ten times more likely to become teenage mothers than girls from social class I, with 30,000 young people still leaving school with absolutely no qualifications and over 25 per cent of mostly poor young people leaving school with only the most basic qualifications to face an unemployment rate in excess of 16 per cent, state policy needs radically to rethink how it can deal constructively with a legacy that has pauperised so many children and young people for a generation and more. Getting 'tough' with young people left at the margins of society may win votes, but will do little to counter the damage that has been inflicted and the consequences this continues to have. Yet 4,000 young people aged between 10 and 16 are locked up in custody in secure units, young offenders institutions or prison, with their numbers predicted to rise. With a growing tide of incarceration answering the hopelessness, frustration and poverty of a great many young people, the gap between their lives and those of other children is enormous (see Goldson, this volume).

It would be possible, although in a short chapter such as this not practical, to detail the whole spectrum of childhood inequalities, with its privileges for a few and its disadvantages and deprivations for many. What can be said about children's health or education can also be said about every single aspect of their lives. This is of course merely to recognise that inequalities are pervasive and extensive. Combined together, as for many children they frequently are, they do immense and often long-lasting damage to a child's present and future prospects. That not all children suffer such a fate ought simply to remind us that we live in a deeply fractured and class-divided society. As such, the differences that mark children's lives – differences in education, physical and mental health, employment prospects, and general sense of confidence and well-being – are not merely the product of class divisions. They are also the starting-point for the reproduction of class divisions in the future. Britain's ruling class of tomorrow is already being formed in the private schools and other institutions through which privilege is passed from generation to generation; at the same time, and at the other end of the spectrum, today's 'failures' amongst the children of the poor are being prepared for the bleak future as adults that this society will offer them. Breaking this cycle calls for a much more radical assault on class privilege and the system that maintains it.

KEY TEXTS

The publications of the Child Poverty Action Group are an invaluable source of information, at least on the impact of poverty on children. One particular book that looks critically at current government proposals to abolish child poverty is *When Children Pay* by Rosemary Link and Anthony Bibus (London: CPAG, 2000).

The wider context of growing inequality in Britain is covered in Chris Jones and Tony Novak, *Poverty Welfare and the Disciplinary State* (London: Routledge, 1999).

Finally, as a reminder that inequality embraces the rich as well as the poor, John Rentoul's *The Rich Get Richer*, although not focused solely on children, gives some idea of how the other half (or, in this case, the other 20 per cent) live (Ratoul, 1997).

SIX

Children and Education: Inequalities in Our Schools

HENRY MAITLES

INTRODUCTION

Karl Marx claimed that when history repeats itself, the first time is tragedy, the second is farce and, although he was not specifically talking about education, the phrase does seem particularly pertinent to education. Most educational documentaries, articles, books, statements in parliament and debate generally seem to centre around a series of issues such as: falling standards compared to previous generations and our foreign 'competitors'; the failure of 'bog-standard' comprehensives to challenge pupils and improve educational levels; incompetent teachers; indiscipline and weak curricula. The 'solution' is increasingly portrayed as arising magically from marketisation and increased privatisation. Whatever the truth or otherwise of these criticisms of our education system, it is interesting that they are almost identical to those made by a number of Tory 'extremists', such as Rhodes Boyson, in the 1970s. Writing in 1975 Boyson listed his concerns in his chapter headings: 'Signs of Breakdown: Illiteracy, Violence and Indiscipline, Truancy, Collapse of Confidence' (Boyson, 1975: 1–2). In his reasons for this breakdown he highlights the use of the 'discovery method' and 'the comprehensive school' (ibid.: 2). His solutions included vouchers, greater authority and discipline, a national curriculum, payment by result and greater selection. Nearly all of these ideas have been taken on board enthusiastically by the Conservative governments from 1979 and, since 1997, by New Labour.

Prior to the 1960s (though still in operation in some parts of England and Wales) the 11-plus examination was a device that ensured that most working-class children were kept in their place within junior secondaries. By the 1960s, however, there were increasing criticisms of the 11-plus and the tripartite education system it supported. The criticisms arose from two linked concerns. On the one hand many Labour politicians were opposed to the system because it restricted 'equality of opportunity' (Crosland, 1956); on the other, there was increasing concern that education was not adequately providing pupils with the skills necessary for the modern labour market and this was hampering Britain's economic performance. Harold Wilson, leader of the Labour Party at the time, and soon to be Prime Minister, told the Labour Party Conference in 1963 that:

> To train the scientists we are going to need will mean a revolution in our attitudes to education . . . as a nation we cannot afford to force segregation on our children at the 11+ stage . . . we cannot afford to cut off three-quarters of our children from virtually any chance of higher education.

The rhetoric was clear and so was the strategy – 'modernisation' of the economy required a more technologically skilled workforce and this required both a greater number of graduates and an increase in the general level of education. This goal was backed by increases in the financing of education, not only in real-term expenditure but also in terms of the proportion of GDP spent on the service. For example, between 1953 and 1972, total public expenditure increased by almost 83 per cent, but in education, expenditure went up by nearly 243 per cent; spending on education as a percentage of GDP grew from just over 3 per cent in 1955 to 6 per cent in 1969.

The increased spending was matched by moves towards comprehensive schooling, and, even in narrow attainment terms, there were great successes in a relatively short number of years. For example, illiteracy fell from over 3 million per year to 2 million in the mid-1970s; pre-war, 90 per cent of children left school with no qualifications; in 1990 it was less than 7 per cent; a study in Scotland involving 40,000 pupils showed a levelling up of attainment, as opposed to the general view of a levelling down (McPherson and Raab, 1988). All evidence suggests, indeed, that the greater the egalitarianism in the system, the greater the levelling-up process and the better for society as a whole. There is thus little doubt that comprehensives are, in their own way, a success story. One head teacher concludes:

> In spite of media hostility, bad legislation and lack of support from the government, poor quality leadership from many LEAs, the retention of selection in some areas, a period of difficult social development in the country, an inappropriate curriculum and a level of accountability which constantly exposes any perceived failings in the system, comprehensive schools have succeeded magnificently. (Dunford, 1999: 30)

Comprehensive education, even if only partly introduced, has led to more children leaving school with more qualifications. Further, there is no evidence to back up claims that A-levels and GCSEs in England and Wales and Higher Grades in Scotland are getting easier and that this explains the better results; in reality good teachers and comprehensive schools have led to great improvements in standards.

But despite these improvements in educational attainment and a corresponding jump in positive outlook by students, there was clearly a section of the community – those most affected by poverty and deprivation – who were not sharing in this general rise in standards, attainment and outlook. Sociologists worked to outline the links between poverty and education. Most attempted to examine the field at two levels of explanation. For example:

> Education is related to poverty at both the micro and the macro level. At the micro level is the underachievement of an individual coming from a home which might be insecure, lacking in material resources and possessing a wealth of society's disadvantages. At the other end there is the persistent underachievement of particular social groups concentrated in social class five. (Robinson, 1976: 24–5)

In the late 1960s and 1970s education policy attempted to deal with disadvantage at both the macro and the micro level. However, while policy at the micro level – focusing on the school and related matters – can be effective, the outcomes are limited because of the preponderance of the macro factors – structural inequality and poverty – which require redistributive action at societal level. None the less, in the late 1960s and 1970s, even though the long post-war economic boom was coming to an end, there was still a feeling that the massive social inequalities could be tackled and the consequent educational (and other social) inequalities would be lessened in their wake. Analysing policy at both the micro and macro levels, this chapter is going to look at educational reform in the light of the underlying relationship between social deprivation and educational inequality.

MICRO-LEVEL POLICIES: SIZE MATTERS

The New Labour government in 2000 chose to stimulate debate about elitism and socio-economic deprivation and its effect on education by highlighting the case of a young student called Laura Spence, a Tyneside comprehensive school student who was denied a place at Oxford University despite having excellent A-level grades. The message from government was clear – old elitist barriers in education must be abolished and there should be equality of opportunity for all. Clearly, in terms of higher education (HE) it is true that our universities continue to be populated by the children of the better off: the latest figures suggest that a mere 17 per cent of the lower socio-economic groups go on to university, while 45 per cent of the higher socio-economic groups do so. Indeed, at the 'top' universities, nearly 40 per cent of students come from independent schools, where spending per student and smaller class sizes ensures that their privileged background is reinforced. And here is the conundrum. The elitism of the HE sector is built upon the inequalities of education – both between the public and the state sector, and within the state sector itself – at primary, junior and secondary levels.

One of the key elements of 'micro-level' inequalities relates to pupil : teacher ratios and class size. The latest figures suggest that the average pupil: teacher ratio is 10.6 : 1 in independent schools compared to 18.6 : 1 in state schools. The independent schools thus have much smaller classes and consequently better interaction – outlined in all Scottish HMI and OFSTED reports as essential to good learning because it facilitates discussion and dialogue and promotes confidence building.

Research from the United States, and in particular New York and California, suggests that reducing class sizes in secondary schools can have a major impact in terms of the quality of learning and teaching, heightened classroom participation and communication skills, enthusiasm for increased reading, a noticeable decline in the number of disciplinary referrals, a rise in teacher morale, improvements in both student absenteeism rates and teacher health absence rates and much improved parental involvement. In these projects in the USA, the major improvements were where classes were reduced from over 30 to under 20 (American Federation of Teachers, 2000; California Department of Education, 2000; Educational Priorities Panel, 2000; HEROS, 2000).

The governments in Westminster and Edinburgh, in contrast to most of those involved in education, continue to argue that smaller classes in upper primary and secondary schools are not important to academic success and that 'scarce' resources must be pumped into nursery and primary 1 and 2. However, even within this priority area, the government's own figures between 1995 and 2000 make grim reading. In England as a whole, the average class size, as opposed to overall school pupil : teacher ratio, moved from 26.8 to 26.5 (0.3 of a pupil!) and in some areas (East, London, South East, South West) class sizes actually rose. In Scotland, the average class size rose in primary 1–3 from 24.9 to 25.9 and the percentage in classes over thirty went from 13 per cent to 16 per cent (Social Trends, 2000: 51). Indeed, in terms of other countries in Europe, the most recent figures indicate Britain compares unfavourably in terms of pupil : teacher ratios.

Reducing class size does not even seem to be part of the long-term plan. Glasgow City Council, for example, has embarked on a new Private-Public Partnership building/refurbishment programme for all of its twenty-nine secondaries, yet at no stage has it been suggested that extra space should be created to accommodate the classrooms that a significant reduction in class sizes would entail.

Teachers' opinions on this are generally ignored. Research currently being undertaken by the author, involving half of all secondary social subject departments in Scotland, suggests that about nine times as many principal teachers conclude that smaller class sizes would improve the learning experience for students as believe removing disruptive pupils was the key. Government effort, though, goes into searching for temporary exclusion schemes to deal with disruption: smaller class sizes are not usually thought worthy of consideration.

It is worth noting that a major reason why parents want to send their children to private schooling is the smaller class sizes that the greater resources per student can lead to. David Blunkett claims that his strategy *vis-à-vis* private schools is to make state schools so good that parents will not want to use the private schools, but it must be noted that spending per pupil will need to almost double before the fees, charitable status and endowments of the private school funding can be effectively equalled.

Although the British government and the Scottish Executive boast about current education funding levels (Labour Party, 2001: 18), surveys of European government expenditure (UNESCO, 2000: 11.336–58) show that in terms of education spending as a percentage of GDP, Britain is nineteenth out of thirty-eight, spending less than, for example, Belarus, Estonia, Finland, Ireland, Latvia, Lithuania and Moldova, and far behind 'rich' European states such as Sweden, Norway, Denmark and France. Indeed, a recent report (*Guardian*, 2001: 1) argues that government spending on education in 2000, as a percentage of GNP, was at its lowest since 1962.

Reducing class sizes does have cost implications. As an example of the costs involved, a small secondary school in Aberdeen has been given £250,000 per year to reduce class sizes in S1/S2 (Key Stage 3 equivalent) to fewer than twenty pupils. Unfortunately, the school has also decided to 'set' the classes (that is, divide the school year groups into classes on the basis of ability) and thus overall improvements will be muddied – it will be possible to claim that it is the ending of mixed-ability teaching (rather than smaller class sizes) that is the key to any performance improvements. Funding-wise, £250,000 per annum for every secondary to reduce class sizes (some £100 million per annum for Scotland alone and perhaps £1 billion per annum for England) is, according to the government, too expensive, involving tens of thousands of extra teachers and more rooms, whereas 'setting' the classes costs effectively nothing. Although it is generally believed that 'setting' leads to higher attainment, the current evidence shows no such thing. For teachers struggling with large mixed-ability classes, the idea of set classes can appear attractive and there is evidence that the more able can do better. Yet a recent study (Hallan and Ireson, 2001) suggests that progress in English and Science was not related to setting and pupils with low attainment in Maths at Key Stage 2 made more progress in Key Stages 3 and 4 if mixed-ability teaching was used. Further, some primary teachers have found teaching a low-ability-only group demoralising and claimed that it made their teaching poorer.

Clearly internal school issues affect pupils and their educational outcomes. Class size, teacher : pupil ratios and the style of teaching adopted all matter. Yet to focus narrowly on these issues ignores the impact of structural inequality within education. It is to this issue we now turn.

MACRO FACTORS: POVERTY AND EDUCATIONAL UNDER-ACHIEVEMENT

Over the last twenty years, since the publication of the Black Report, it has become accepted that there is a direct and causal link between poverty and ill-health. People with the poorest health in Britain (indeed in all major developed countries) live in the areas of highest deprivation and that deprivation seriously, and indeed fatally, affects life chances. Yet, while this link is accepted in many areas of welfare, in education policy and research today there are few attempts to look at structural inequalities and their impact on education. For example, in a recent work, *Scottish Education* (Bryce and Humes, 1999), there is an overview of everything affecting Scottish education *except social class*. Although there are welcome separate chapters on race, gender and disability, there is no chapter on class or poverty or deprivation – indeed these topics are reduced to discussion in two pages in one section (out of a book of over 1,000 pages). A thorough search of educational journals does not show any systematic evidence of work outlining the educational effects of poverty. Indeed, journals outlining research in education are full of research ideas and practice, all valuable, but in densely packed sections on new research projects and research reports from, for example, the Scottish Council for Research in Education, there is not one piece of ongoing work defining the links between deprivation and low educational achievement. It may be true, as Brian Boyd (1999: 731) claims, that 'the link between poverty and attainment is well established in the educational literature', but there is no evidence that this has any reflection in government circles and/or policy. A brief, though not systematic, review of the academic journals demonstrates this point. For example, in the long-standing National Foundation for Educational Research in England and Wales (NFER) journal, *Educational Research*, there were a number of articles on social class and its effects on educational achievement published between 1971 and 1973 (Ferguson et al., 1971; Finlayson, 1972; Harker, 1971; Krausen, 1973; Squibb, 1973; Wein, 1971), but the index for Volumes 40–2 (covering the period 1998-2000) reveals there is not a single article relating to the importance of social class or poverty or disadvantage to education.

In part, this reflects the post-modernist trend in sociological thinking, which has challenged universalistic views of the world and, in particular, Marxism. Marxists attempted to develop a comprehensive theory of the relationship between social class and structures in society, including of course education. Whilst not ignoring the work of the school or the educational worker, the Marxist approach contends that the macro factors – poverty and deprivation in society – are the keys to an understanding of under-achievement. Whilst other factors – 'race', gender, sexuality, disability, individual school structures and overall policy – are important, they are important within the context of class society and examining any of these other aspects in isolation can be misleading (for a fuller discussion, see Callinicos, 1989; Cole et al., 1997; Hill et al., 1999). Post-modernism has, at its core, perhaps two main points: first, it challenges the idea of social class as being the determining factor in society; and, second, it concentrates on the local – the micro level, rather than the macro level. There is little doubt that these themes have become the orthodoxy, not just of New Labour but of many, if not most, educational researchers. Today in Britain virtually all educational research is on specific areas of schooling rather than on the effects of poverty – and this I suggest is a reflection of post-modernist themes in education. This is not to argue that all those involved in research are themselves post-modernists (most would deny it) but, rather, that the influence of post-modernism has been to ensure that educational research has gone down the route suggested above at the expense of a holistic approach. Apple and Whittey (1999: 10), argue that this post-modernist trend is no less than a 'conservative restoration' in which the competitiveness of the economy and the educational necessities for this become paramount over the education of the whole person.

Despite its paucity, when one examines what research there is on poverty and education, the links between disadvantage and educational inequality can be clearly established. As early as 1973 the National Children's Bureau was warning of the links between disadvantage and behaviour, attainment, school experience and parental interest (Wedge and Prosser, 1973: 54). This found that 'among children generally, the single factor most strongly associated with high attainment is social class'. Another report in the same year found that schooling can actually exacerbate the inequalities between the social classes: '. . . we find that the inequality existing before children reach school is increased by their early schooling . . . the inequalities between children grow while they are at school' (Field, 1974: 17–18). Interestingly, Gillborn and Mirza (2000: 14-17) found a similar widening of inequality between white and black children in present-day schools.

We should not really be surprised at this, because the educational system itself contains a bias against the disadvantaged: it is quite startling to visit schools where students can articulate orally complex answers but find it very difficult to express the same in written form and are consequently heavily penalised by the exam system. The Halsey Report (Halsey, 1972) called for schools to 'understand the families and environments in which the children live' and for teachers 'to be sensitive to the social and moral climate in which their children are growing up' but the obsessions of governments with exam results and league tables (more below) makes this virtually impossible.

What is interesting, of course, is whether there has been any change, over the almost thirty years since these works entitled *Born to Fail* and *Unequal Britain* came out. One might have hoped so, but unfortunately the educational gap has grown larger between poor and wealthy rather than narrowed. The most recent report on educational attainment in England,

Educational Inequality – Mapping Race, Class and Gender (Gillborn and Mirza, 2000), commissioned by OFSTED, came out at the same time as Chris Woodhead's resignation. Whilst not exactly buried, neither is this piece of research well publicised. Analysing the results, Lavalette et al. show that:

> . . . children from managerial/professional backgrounds are 3 times more likely to gain 5 A–C grade GCSEs than those from unskilled/manual backgrounds. In 1988 some 52% of children from managerial/professional backgrounds gained 5 or more higher grade GCSEs 12% of children from unskilled/manual background reached this benchmark. In 1997 some 69% of children from managerial/professional backgrounds achieved 5 or more higher grade GCSEs, with 20% of children from less privileged backgrounds achieving this level. (2001: 98)

What this emphasises is that from 1972–97 things did not get better in terms of educational inequality, rather they got worse. Interestingly, Gillborn and Mirza (2000: 19) have the evidence to show that 'the familiar association between class and attainment can be seen to operate within each of the main ethnic groups'. The 1999 report from Gordon Brown's Treasury department made similar links between class and achievement. The report stated:

> . . . children from disadvantaged backgrounds are much less likely to succeed in education. On difficult to let estates one in 4 children gain no GCSEs and rates of truancy are 4 times the average. . . . There is a strong relationship between children's performance in maths and reading tests between the ages of 6 and 8 and their parents' earnings. If one father's earnings are twice the level of another, his son's maths test score is on average 5 percentile points higher than the other's, and 2.7 percentile points higher up the reading test distribution.

The education gap has widened and this reflects the widening wealth gap. In other spheres (such as health) some of the most damning evidence on the relationship between inequality and poor health has compared areas in the same city. There has been much less of the kinds of detailed analysis of the 'education gap'. None the less, where it has been undertaken the evidence is powerful. Looking at educational disadvantage in Glasgow, Michael Pacione (1997) compared all the secondary schools in the city in terms of educational attainment and social disadvantage. In a complex and thought-provoking piece of empirical research, Pacione showed how attainment and disadvantage are linked. He was able to divide the schools in the city into seven clusters: Clusters I and II, for example, have below average clothing grants and free school meals, above average pupils in households with heads in social classes 1 and 2 and low absenteeism and truancy and above average educational attainment. Schools in clusters VI and VII all are far below average in terms of attainment and attendance and have a high proportion of pupils in receipt of clothing grants and free school meals.

More recently a report by Rosemary Long in the Glasgow Evening Times (Long, 2001: 12–13), 'Grim facts of life shame Glasgow', showed the appalling effects of poverty on education. In the poorest parts of the city, the proportion of people leaving school with no qualifications was significantly above the national average (in Baillieston +145 per cent, Cathcart +168 per cent, Govan +86 per cent, Pollok +75 per cent, Shettleston +71 per cent, Maryhill +360 per cent, Springburn +306 per cent) whilst in better-off areas just outside the city limits the figures were below the national average (for example, Eastwood −50 per cent, Strathkelvin and Bearsden −42 per cent). Similar trends were shown in terms of comparison to the national average of those going on to higher education (Maryhill −55 per cent, Springburn −74 per cent, Cathcart −72 per cent, Baillieston −62 per cent; whereas Eastwood and Strathkelvin and Bearsden were +50 per cent and +31 per cent respectively). Poverty is clearly the key factor here; for example, household income in Springburn averages £13,360 per annum, while in Eastwood it is £22,960. Examining the 2001 Scottish league table exam results and a relatively weak factor of deprivation, the take up of free school meals in Glasgow (weak because the take up is less than the entitlement, so that the contrasts are less marked), the effects of poverty and educational attainment are clear. The 'top' seven schools in the league tables are the seven schools that have the lowest take up of free school meals, and the 'bottom' schools academically have the highest take up. Similar analyses, producing similar results, have been done in Sheffield and England as a whole (Davies, 2000: 8–10, 18) and could be done in any city.

TESTING TIMES

If the general thrust of this chapter is correct and educational disadvantage is intrinsically linked to socio-economic disadvantage, educational reform should be viewed in terms of impact on this. That does not mean that activity at the micro level is wasted or irrelevant. The kinds of things that schools try to do to help social inclusion, such as homework clubs, breakfast sessions and positive attendance rewards, are useful and beneficial but they cannot fundamentally alter the imbalance caused by social deprivation.

The Conservatives from the early 1980s onwards were determined to ensure that as much of the market as possible was introduced into education, in line with their general philosophy. Taylor (1993: 46) summarised the thinking behind the reforms of the various Conservative governments:

> The thrust of educational reform has been towards making schooling more relevant to the needs of a market economy, controlling the demands of education on the public purse, improving the efficiency and effectiveness of teaching, and satisfying public and political demand for tangible educational outcomes. . . . [This is] Neither the language nor the agenda . . . of the 1970s.

Commenting on this, Nisbet and Watt (1995: 96) claimed that, 'Among all these changes, the interests of the educationally disadvantaged seem to have been overlooked, or have had to take second place'.

Testing was one aspect of this. The 1988 Education Reform Act introduced compulsory testing at 7, 11, 14 and 16 years. Teachers, cognisant of the stress levels on very young children, opposed this in both Scotland and England and Wales but nevertheless the introduction of testing was achieved. Linked to testing were league tables, introduced in 1993 as an 'aid' to parental choice. For most families, of course, it is no such thing; the higher ranked schools are usually private, specialist, grammar or comprehensives (usually over-subscribed) in middle-class areas. Besides, the league tables are themselves so flawed that even the government use them with some trepidation. The nature of raw data tables can hide much more than they show, particularly if the evidence of the link between social inequality and educational attainment outlined above is valid. Quite simply, the effort by government to measure a person's ability by exam performance is quite meaningless. Getting good A levels, GCSEs or 'Highers' is generally less a sign of outstanding excellence and achievement and more the good luck of being born to parents who are relatively well off. The paradox is that money follows the 'successful' schools in the league tables as parents are keen to get their children, where feasible, into these schools. This leads to the development of over-subscribed schools close to 'sink' schools. This situation can only further deteriorate if New Labour succeeds in its plans to introduce performance-related pay, which has the potential to pitch teacher against teacher, as well as school against school.

SCHOOL EFFECTIVENESS

This is not to say that there are no differences between schools in similar areas; often schools in similar areas can have moderately different results. I well remember as a principal teacher of social subjects having to justify why 'my' subject results were worse than some schools and praised if better than others. Often the differences between schools in similar areas are minute yet pondered over – the result being that the eye is taken off the underlying differences in a city, as outlined in the research in Glasgow above; the real difference is not between schools in similar areas but between schools in affluent areas and those in areas of poverty. None the less, research in the 1980s (Mortimore et al., 1988) outlined a number of reasons why some schools did better than others in similar areas. Mortimore assumed that social class accounted for more than 90 per cent of achievement and outlined a number of factors that explained the other 10 per cent: first, a collaborative way of working between staff (including senior staff) and pupils; second, a commitment to equality of opportunity; and, third, first-class teachers who turned down the chance of an 'easier' life in an 'easier' school because they were politically committed to improving the chances of working-class children. In other words, the principles of collaborating, commitment and comprehensive teaching improve the educational performance of the disadvantaged – the opposite of what right-wing educationalists would have us believe in their attacks on 1960s educational methods. Research like that carried out by Mortimore has been sidelined and ignored by policy-makers, primarily for ideological reasons. 'Effective' schools, as defined by the Conservatives in their terms of government and now echoed by New Labour, are said to be those that had a hierarchy amongst staff, greater discipline, streaming and selection. In a damning critique of the 'school effectiveness research and school improvement industries', Slee and Weiner (1998: 5) maintain that:

> . . . while purporting to be inclusive and comprehensive, school effectiveness research is riddled with errors: it is excluding (of children with special needs, black boys, so-called clever girls), it is normative and regulatory . . . it is bureaucratic and disempowering. It focuses exclusively on the processes and internal constraints of schooling, apparently disconnected from education's social end – adulthood.

Unfortunately, it is on this school effectiveness anvil that our educational policy is now being forged. And there are further unfortunate effects of this culture of league tables, target setting and school effectiveness. Recent research from Nick Davies (2000) shows the unfortunate side effects of this school effectiveness dogma, and Gillborn and Youdell (2000) suggest that, although unconsciously in many cases, educational rationing is in use in schools. The agenda set out by the league tables leads to Gillborn and Youdell describing a 'triage' system operating in schools. Triage is a system used in hospital casualty departments to prioritise those patients who need urgent or immediate attention, as opposed to those whose case is not urgent or, indeed, those who are beyond meaningful help. In schools, it can lead to a situation of concentrating on those under-achievers at the margin of the 'good' grades, with whom some effort can lead to improved grades. The other groups, the 'safe' and those 'without hope', can be left with little attention – effectively their education is being rationed as schools become desperate to get pupils into the 'good' grades. Gillborn and Youdell (2000: 198–9) conclude that throughout the study of their schools:

> the importance of GCSE grades A–C has continually surfaced. They are the key performance indicators for schools, subject departments, individual teachers and pupils . . . the proportion of final year pupils attaining five or more higher grade passes remains largely unchallenged as the central criterion of success or failure . . . an A–C economy has developed, such that higher grade passes have become the supreme driving force for policy and practice at the school level . . . secondary schools are increasingly geared to maximising their performance in relation to the 'bottom line', whatever the cost elsewhere. In the A–C economy, the needs of the school, so far as the league tables are concerned, have come to define the needs of the pupils.

The concentration on exam targets also affects virtually any attempt to develop better-rounded people. Thus, initiatives (however limited) such as education for citizenship are always couched in terms of their impact on school targets and, indeed, often arguments are heard that these initiatives are a waste of time as they do not help the school, or the teachers, make their targets. Gillborn and Youdell (2000: 199) comment that '. . . our case study schools have responded by interrogating virtually every aspect of school life for the possible contribution to the all consuming need to improve the proportion of pupils reaching the benchmark level of five or more higher grade passes'.

PRIVATE GOOD, PUBLIC BAD?

The introduction of the market into education was an attempt by the Conservatives to challenge some of the efforts of comprehensive education and liberal teaching of the previous decades. Paradoxically, as Ball (1996: 2) points out, the Major government (1992–7) characterised the increasing pass rates in exams as both a testimony to their commitment to raising standards and a reflection of declining standards! The outcome of 'failing' schools was to be closure, followed by re-opening, often under a super-head who would turn the school round. The reality was very different. Spooner (1998) and Tomlinson (1998) analysed the effect of this policy in Leeds and Hackney Downs respectively. Commenting on the Hackney Downs experience, Tomlinson (1998: 167–8) comments that '. . . the case of Hackney Downs offers an example of how not to develop a relationship . . . the 'blame and shame' policy characterises the treatment of schools in this country in the 1990s, which results in school closure accompanied by public humiliation'. As a final irony, pupils were transferred to Hamerton House school, which had no better exam results than Hackney Downs, and the total cost of closing Hackney Downs was estimated to be the same as keeping it open and in reasonable repair.

Yet New Labour, despite a rhetoric which talks of 'economic success . . . social cohesion . . . skills and abilities of our people . . . world class system of education and training' (Labour Party, 1997) and 'education remains Labour's top priority. Excellence for the many, not just the few is our driving passion' (Labour Party, 2001: 18), persists with the 'name and shame' policy, albeit under the name 'Fresh Start'. Whilst successes are trumpeted (*TES*, 2001a), there were obvious major problems (Davies, 2000: 163–70) with extremely limited benefits from large financial outlay. Further, Davies claims that the results have been massaged to make things appear better than the reality. In January 2001, it was reported that the policy of dealing with the (in Alistair Campbell's words) 'bog standard comprehensives' had been a failure (*TES*, 2001b).

However, it could be argued that in at least one area, the Education Action Zones (EAZs) policy, there was an acknowledgement of the effects of poverty. Indeed, the EAZs were to be the 'standard bearers in a new crusade inviting business, schools, LEAs and parents to modernise education in areas of social deprivation' (Department for Education and Employment, 1998). Centrally involved in EAZs are companies such as Shell in Lambeth, British Aerospace in Hull, Plymouth and Teesside, and Tesco, ICI, Cadbury Schweppes, Kellogg's and McDonald's in various locations. Whilst economic incentives are a central part of the policy, Power and Gewirtz (2001: 47), in an analysis of the bids submitted and remedies proposed, comment that:

> There would seem to be some mismatch between the injustices identified and the remedies proposed. . . . These injustices clearly call for a policy of redistribution . . . but these additional finances are relatively small. . . . In addition resources do not seem in general to be directed towards the elimination or reduction in economic hardship.

With this perception, it is little surprise that in the *TES* (2001c) it was announced that the government was considering rethinking and relaunching the EAZ scheme with some major changes. These changes, announced as policy proposals in late August 2001, involved ever-increasing private involvement in schools, including whole local authority education provision being run by profit-making local companies. Paradoxically, squeezing school finances has encouraged local authorities, whatever their political hue, to adopt these schemes (*TES*, 2001d).

CONCLUSION

Ultimately, New Labour is so wedded to its neo-liberal agenda that no matter what it does in educational terms it fails to challenge the poverty that is the underlying cause of most of the problem. Without this, there is the plethora of policies informed by micro-level concerns that pitch schools against each other in competition for scarce resources. New Labour's policies have led to further marketisation, the continuation of selection at age 11, the introduction of 'Fresh Start' initiatives for 'failing' schools, the continuing of league tables, under-funding (especially in comparison to the private sector), large class sizes (especially from the third year of primary school onwards), the development of specialist schools and, announced in August 2001, greater encouragement for religious schools throughout England. Will these reforms help or worsen educational inequalities caused by disadvantages and poverty? The evidence suggests these micro-level reforms will not improve educational inequalities. Indeed, they will almost certainly make things worse. The experience of the first term of the New Labour government and the first phase of their second term suggests that, unfortunately, we will see the education gap grow as the wealth gap continues to widen.

KEY TEXTS

Gillborn, D. and Youdell, D. (2000) *Rationing Education*. London: Oxford University Press.

Hill, D. and Cole, M. (eds) (1999) *Promoting Equality in Secondary Schools*. London: Cassell.

Pacione, M. (1997) 'The geography of educational disadvantage in Glasgow', *Applied Geography*, 17: 169–92.

Slee, R., Weiner, G. and Tomlinson, S. (eds) (1998) *School Effectiveness for Whom?* London: Falmer.

SEVEN

Working Children

NIAMH STACK AND JIM McKECHNIE

INTRODUCTION

Opposition to children working, when it first emerged in Britain in the late nineteenth century, challenged deep-rooted traditions that work for the majority of children was natural and necessary. The significant shift from the position where children had a duty to contribute to the family income to one where children's work was viewed as undesirable, represented a radical change in the perception of children and childhood. By the early twentieth century, for a variety of reasons, there were few instances of children working full time. However, children's work was never eliminated, it was merely transformed. Children continued to work but in a part-time capacity before and after school and at the weekends. This pattern of working has been viewed as a harmless activity undertaken for 'pocket money'. This interpretation of children's work has been reinforced by the construction of the notion of 'children's jobs'. These assumptions will be examined in this chapter.

In the UK today the legislation regulating the employment of children dates back to the 1930s. Current research indicates that this legislation is outdated and ineffective. Child employees have become a marginalised workforce that is all but invisible in society. The net effect is that the majority of children working today have no protection in relation to employment rights or health and safety. In spite of international treaties and an EU directive encouraging changes in policy in relation to child employment, successive British governments have shown themselves to be resistant to policy changes in this area. The reasons for, and consequences of, this lack of political will, will be explored in this chapter.

CHILD EMPLOYMENT AND INDUSTRIALISATION

It is a commonly held belief that industrialisation was responsible for removing children from their domestic environment and bringing them into the workplace. In reality, even in pre-industrial times children worked from the earliest age possible in order to contribute to the family income. Children, depending upon their age, ability and gender, were assigned jobs as part of the family workforce. The proto-industrial period, which preceded the Industrial Revolution, saw small-scale industry emerge in the agricultural sector in the form of cottage industries. During this time market activities and the production process were brought more forcibly into the home and the expectation that children should contribute to the family economy was formalised. Traditions during this period saw lace-makers' children taught to handle bobbins at the age of 4 years, and children of farmers working sixteen-hour days at harvest time. The belief that children should work was so dominant at this time that Poor Relief was withheld from families who had children over 5 who were not working (Horrell and Humphries, 1999). It is apparent that in the pre-industrialised period work was already considered a natural part of life for children. As such, parents, governments and charitable organisations saw it as their responsibility to ensure children had work. Against this background industrialisation was not responsible for children's entry into the workforce, but rather it extended children's employment opportunities out of domestic industries and provided additional jobs in the factories, mills and mines.

As such, opposition to child labour was considered somewhat radical when it first emerged, as it challenged the embedded traditions that work for the majority of children was natural and necessary. Opposition came from reformers such as Robert Owen, Lord Shaftesbury and Richard Oastler. Their emphasis was not on the fact that children worked but rather the conditions that some were now working under were unacceptable. While such campaigners drew attention to this issue they cannot be viewed as responsible for changing child employment in the UK. To understand the transition from a position where children were expected to work to one where they are excluded from work we must look for other factors. These include legislative policy, technological advance, and societal and economic changes.

For many, changing attitudes to child employment during the Industrial Revolution were mirrored in the legislation, particularly the Factory Acts. The 1802 Factory Health and Morals Act was the first legislative reaction to the conditions under which children were employed. This Act was aimed at apprentices in the cotton and wool mills and introduced restrictions to the maximum working day of twelve hours. Subsequent Acts, such as the 1833 Factory Act, focused on children in the textile industry and included similar maximum daily hours and age restrictions for beginning work. There are three important points to note in relation to the initial Factory Acts. First, their aim was to regulate children's work, not eliminate it. Second, the Factory Acts are a decisive point historically because they are the first instance in which the government removed sole autonomy for children's upbringing from parents and made it subject to regulation.

Third, they introduced the idea of compulsory schooling with the Half-time system.

While legislation played a role in changing the pattern of child labour it would be misleading to suggest that it was universally accepted or adopted. In particular the Half-time system, where children combined work with a basic education, proved ineffective. The costs for employers and parents meant that the system was bypassed. While ineffective, the Half-time system did establish the link between education and childhood. The Education Acts of 1870, 1880 and 1918 reinforced this link. From a practical viewpoint comprehensive education legislation was easier to enforce than child labour laws and had the additional advantage of dealing with children's unemployment and under-employment as well (Cunningham, 1990).

While legislation played a part in changing child labour in the UK, changes in the production process and technology have also been identified as factors influencing child employment. At the beginning of industrialisation the machinery lent itself to the employment of young children with small frames and 'nimble fingers' but as technology advanced the machinery became more sophisticated. With the introduction of developments such as the self-acting mule in the textile industry, and the transition from water-driven to steam-powered factories, the specific need for child labourers was reduced. It has been argued that employers' perceptions of their workforce also underwent a transition. Initially employers during the Industrial Revolution believed that the machinery would run itself and could be tended by the cheapest source of labour, which invariably comprised children. As industrialisation progressed employers became aware that older operatives could be more efficient. Technology was never solely responsible for either drawing children into the workforce, or for excluding them from it, but was one element within a complex process.

The third force that has been linked to explanations of changes in child employment in the UK stems from social and cultural factors. Industrialisation had an impact on the family structure and the internal dynamic of the family members. The majority of children were no longer employed by parents and extended family but by strangers. Parents no longer controlled children's training or welfare, while work and home became increasingly separated. Davin (1982) argues that parents' anger at the exploitation of their children may be partly responsible for the turning tide of opinion regarding children's work. Alternatively, Pinchbeck and Hewitt (1973) suggest that outrage towards children's work happened not because working conditions were worse than in pre-industrial society, but because they were more visible. As children's work moved out of the home and into the public arena it became subject to public scrutiny and comment.

In addition, the family structure underwent dramatic changes during this time. In the mid-nineteenth century we see the emergence of the demands for a 'family wage'. Where before all members of the household were expected to contribute to the family income, the demand for a 'family wage' saw the emergence of the 'male breadwinner' earning a wage, which was sufficient to support the family. While such demands were unsuccessful they did have an impact on the working-class families' perception of child employment. Thorne (1987) talks about how children at this time became 'sentimentally defined', their 'proper place' narrowed to family and school. Children's work could no longer be equated with adult work; it was only acceptable as a form of education or a harmless pastime.

While demands for a 'family wage' were largely unsuccessful, economic change has been linked to changes in child employment. Family incomes during the latter part of the nineteenth century did start to rise. For Nardinelli (1990) this allowed family strategies to change. According to this argument rising male earnings allowed families to 'invest' in their children. By educating their children they could gain better long-term returns in contrast to the short-term rewards from a child's earnings. Rising family income did allow families to control the supply of labour; however, it is not clear that the underlying motives for this are the ones identified by Nardinelli.

In the latter half of the nineteenth century the number of child workers declined from the high peaks of the 1830s and 1840s (Horrell and Humphries, 1999). It would be naïve to attribute this decline to any one of the causes outlined above. Some have argued that the decline in children's full-time work should be viewed as an interaction between changing technology, changing family dynamics and state legislation (Bolin-Hort, 1989). Similarly, it would be wrong to conclude that these changes ultimately removed children from the labour force in the UK. For example, the introduction of compulsory education did not stop children from working per se but only from working full time. Legislation was targeted at the factories and mines of the Industrial Revolution, yet many children worked outside of these environments. Instead of witnessing the decline of child labour in the UK what occurred was the transformation of children's work.

This transformation can only be fully understood if we attend to the wider cultural backdrop. It has been argued that what emerged in the latter part of the nineteenth century was a process by which children's labour became marginalised. This resulted from changing political and ideological views. Social policy formation started to impact directly on children's lives. The realisation that changing economic circumstances meant that an educated labour force was needed resulted in education becoming the defining activity for children. In adopting this definition of childhood, society at large implicitly accepted one ideology of childhood. That view emerged from bourgeois society, whose children never worked, but was accepted by the working-class since it served their needs in defining roles within the working class family at a time when it was under pressure (Lavalette, 1999b).

The net effect of the dynamic interaction between all of these factors was to marginalise children's work. This took two forms. First, children were marginalised in that they were restricted in the types of jobs they could do.

Out-of-school jobs and, by definition, part-time work was now the accepted form of work. Second, the forms of work they undertook were labelled as 'children's jobs' to emphasise their distinction, and separation, from adult work. An additional consequence of this change was that attention to child employment diminished. By the early twentieth century the 'problem' of child labour had been 'solved' and the spotlight was removed from this part of children's lives.

ESTABLISHING MYTHS OF CHILD EMPLOYMENT

By the early part of the twentieth century children's work had been consigned to the past. The 1918 Education Act, which introduced compulsory education and a school leaving age of 14 years, effectively ended full-time employment for children. This Act also introduced controls over the work that children could do. This in part was in reaction to the exploitation of child labour that had taken place during the 1914–18 period in the UK. The reluctance to go as far as completely prohibiting children's work was influenced by a number of factors. First, governments were unwilling to enforce any legislation that would interfere with particular industries; for example, agriculture and delivery work. Second, there was still a belief that work was an important practical experience. This was particularly relevant for working-class children where work was viewed as a means of instilling moral character and discipline. Third, part-time work was believed to combat juvenile delinquency; if children's spare time was taken up by work then they could not be running wild and disrupting public order.

In 1924, the Home Office, which had responsibility for child employment issues, carried out a survey to assess the effectiveness of the 1918 Act. The survey found that the numbers of children working and the hours that they worked had both decreased; in addition, the survey claimed to find no negative consequences to children's part-time work. This report was used to convince the general public that child employment legislation was effective. However, the findings have been criticised because of methodological weaknesses and bias in the interpretation of the results (Cunningham, 1999). In effect, the Home Office emphasised the positive aspects of work and questioned the significance of contradictory findings.

With the 'evidence' indicating that children's employment was not problematic, further study and discussion were not needed. The next official attempt to address the topic of child labour emerged in 1931 and was in reaction to the plans of the International Labour Organisation (ILO) to formulate a convention on child labour. It was feared that the ILO's recommendations under the convention would be too stringent and would interfere with children's employment. In reaction to the ILO's plan new surveys were carried out. This time there were more reports of weaknesses in the legislation. It was apparent from the returns that the regulations were not being enforced. In addition, a number of voices were raised questioning the received wisdom regarding the 'educational benefit' of work. Some educationalists argued that children's part-time work, particularly early morning work, was having a negative effect on their education.

In spite of these concerns the Home Office view prevailed. The ILO proposals were to be obstructed if they were found to be inconsistent with Britain's interests. However, the 1931 Home Office report had another consequence: it acted as the main evidence source for the 1933 Children and Young Person's Act. This Act constitutes the basis of child labour law in Britain to the present day. It provides guidance on the number of hours children can work, when they can work and the types of jobs that they can do. Implicit within this Act is a specific view of children's work; a view that perceives work as a positive socialising experience with the added benefit of constraining children's asocial behaviour.

Since the introduction of this Act concern over child employment has ebbed and flowed. During the Second World War children were once again drawn into the labour force. The legislation that regulated children's work was relaxed to allow children to help in the war effort. Such moves were legitimised by the need to help the war effort and as such were unavoidable. However, by the end of the war period there was a growing concern over the exploitation of child workers and the impact this had on education. This became linked to debates about the 1944 Education Act. Once again the government established a review process.

The evidence gathered in this review pointed to two conclusions. First, working was not a marginal activity engaged in by the minority of children. Second, employment was not a positive learning experience but rather was one that had a negative effect on education (Cunningham, 1999). Even with a growing body of evidence raising concerns over child employment the final outcome was that the conservative forces of the Home Office dominated. By the late 1950s, despite concerns being raised on a number of occasions, the legislation on child employment was largely unchanged from the 1933 Act. Beyond the boundaries of Whitehall social opinion about child employment was also changing.

In the post-war period the dominant link between child employment and poverty was broken. Up until this time child labour had been an experience associated with the working class. As social provision improved after the war the link between children's work and low family income was broken, the stigma linking poverty and child employment was removed. The net effect was to give respectability to this activity and enabled middle-class families to allow their children to work. This transition was reinforced by the production of reports highlighting the positive aspects of such employment experience. The Crowther Report of 1959 and the Newsom Report of 1963 highlighted the beneficial effect of such work. Society at large began to accept the view that child employment was not only a 'safe' experience for children to have but also a positive one. Such views were based upon a set of assumptions. These include the belief that legislation was effective and that such work was 'safe' with no negative effects for children.

CONTINUING MYTHS AND MISCONCEPTIONS

In the early 1970s the dominant assumptions about the 'harmless' effect of child employment were severely challenged by a government report produced by Emrys Davies (1972). The results of Davies's national study drew attention to the fact that large numbers of children worked, that the legislation was ineffective and that employment was not harmless. Rather, Davies argued that child employment had a deleterious effect on education. Working children were less able, had poorer commitment to school and were more likely to truant. The issue of child employment was once again on the political agenda.

During the time that the study was being conducted responsibility for the child employment issue moved from the Home Office to the Department of Health and Social Security (DHSS). In response to the report, the DHSS acknowledged that the existing legislation may not be sufficient and the Employment of Children Act was passed through Parliament in 1973. The central thrust of the Act was to replace the multiplicity of local authority regulations with one set of regulations. Compliance with the regulations was to be improved by increasing the level of fines. This Act also introduced the idea of assessing a job's suitability before the child began work. Although the Act became law it was never implemented, owing to 'financial constraints'. The only related action that was taken by the DHSS in 1976 was when they issued a set of model by-laws in an attempt to standardise local authority regulations.

Research addressing the nature and extent of full-time school children's part-time employment since Davies's work has been sporadic. Studies which have taken place have originated from diverse sources including work by campaigning organisations, academic research, media interest and some government-funded work. The Low Pay Unit published the findings from a series of studies across the UK between 1980 and 1998, which aimed to dispel the myths about children's employment and establish that it was not a marginal activity. MacLennan's (1980) findings indicated that 35 per cent of children were involved in part-time employment. Later research conducted by MacLennan et al. (1985) and Pond and Searle (1991) indicated that, at any given time, approximately 40 per cent of school children in London (MacLennan et al., 1985) and 43 per cent of school children in Birmingham (Pond and Searle, 1991) were working. Both these studies, although quite large in scale, were criticised for being restricted to local job markets and for not being representative of the UK as a whole. However, support for their findings was found in two studies, which were conducted in Scotland. Lavalette et al. (1991) in urban and McKechnie et al. (1994) in rural Scotland, found approximately one-third of children were involved in part-time employment at any one time. In addition, the Scottish researchers assessed not only the part-time jobs that children had at the time of the study but also any jobs that they may have had in the past. When this perspective is taken there is evidence that as many as two-thirds of children have experience of part-time work by the age of 16.

The findings of a nationwide survey by Hibbett and Beatson (1995), based on a representative sample, supports the findings of the regional studies. Comparisons between studies can be problematic because of variations in definitions and methodology (Hobbs et al., 1996). However, a consistent picture does emerge. It is the norm for children to have experience of paid employment outside of the family before they reach the end of compulsory education.

In the first half of the twentieth century the types of jobs that children were employed in were perceived as 'children's jobs'. This implied a narrow range of jobs that were considered to be 'light' and 'harmless'. Research in the 1990s questioned the myth of 'children's jobs', for two reasons. First, as Hobbs and McKechnie (1997) showed, children work in a wide range of jobs including delivery work, door-to-door sales, shop work, babysitting, the hotel and catering industry, gardening, cleaning, model-ling, and working in garages and on building sites. Such findings are supported by other studies: for example, Jolliffe et al. (1995) recorded children working in over twenty different job categories. This diversity of employment questions the idea of children working in a narrow range of 'children's jobs'. Second, research findings show that many children are employed in the service sector. This includes employment in shops and the hotel and catering sector. Many of these jobs parallel adult activities and as such contradict the concept of 'children's jobs'.

While children may be employed in a wide range of jobs, many of which are associated with adult work, the level of reward is low. It should be noted that there is no legislation on minimum wage levels for children under the age of 16. Pond and Searle (1991) reported an average hourly rate of pay of £1.80 but cautioned that this average did not indicate the variation that they found in the sample. Seven per cent of adolescents in Pond and Searle's study were earning fifty pence or less an hour. More recently, Middleton et al. (1998) found that working adolescents are paid on average £2.22 an hour, but that almost 33 per cent were earning £1.25 an hour or less. Without any regulations to provide minimum levels of pay for this group, children remain a source of cheap labour.

As we noted earlier, on a number of occasions throughout the twentieth century the efficacy of the legislation has been questioned. The research findings from the studies undertaken in the 1990s suggest that there continues to be serious doubt about the usefulness of the existing policies. The legislation provides information on when children can work, how long they can work for, the types of jobs they can do, and requires local authorities to monitor levels of employment. Research findings show that in every one of these areas the legislation is broken (Pond and Searle, 1991; Hobbs and McKechnie, 1997). There is little evidence that there is any political will to implement existing legislation.

One could argue that this may be of little concern if the type of work that children do is 'harmless'. In the last twenty years a number of studies have considered the impact of such work on the lives of the employees. Some researchers have focused on health and safety issues. Studies have shown that between 18 and 36 per cent of children have reported some form of accidental injury related to their work (Hobbs and McKechnie, 1997; O'Donnell and White, 1999). Other researchers have looked at the impact of work on education. This research has supported concerns expressed since the early part of the twentieth century that work can have a negative effect on education. In the last few years a more balanced debate has emerged highlighting that work may have positive and negative outcomes for children. However, it must be recognised that research has consistently shown that working a high number of hours per week is associated with poorer educational attainment (McKechnie and Hobbs, 2001). We will return to the work–education relationship in the next section. For the moment it should be noted that employment is not a neutral experience and we should be cautious in assuming that it is 'harmless'.

At the beginning of the twenty-first century a rather depressing but consistent picture emerges regarding child employment. It is apparent that the same concerns about such employment have been raised on a number of occasions. These concerns relate to the effectiveness of legislation and the 'harmless' nature of work. The response is usually the same: an inquiry and debate, but no action.

This scenario has been replayed most recently in 1998. As a result of the growing research evidence throughout the 1990s, a Private Members Bill was introduced in Parliament. The government's response was to set up a committee to review the issue. This feeling of history repeating itself is reinforced when we look at the outcome. At the time of writing no report has been published and no significant changes in legislation have been introduced. While this may give the impression that little has changed, there has been some progress. First, the research evidence based on child employment in the UK has grown dramatically in the last twenty years. This has allowed researchers to question long-standing commonsense assumptions about child employment. Second, UK policy on this issue must now take cognisance of international conventions. In the next section we will pursue this latter idea and identify key policy issues that are emerging.

POLICY ISSUES

In the last three decades child employment has been the focus of policy debates on two occasions. The most recent, as we have just noted, was

1998. Prior to that we have to turn to the 1970s and the discussions which followed the 1972 Davies report. In the latter case the debates resulted in the 1973 Employment of Children Act, which has never been brought into force. To date, the 1998 review of child employment has produced no significant outcomes.

In contrast to the failure of successive British governments to fully engage with this issue, international debates relating to child employment have moved forward. The United Nations' Convention on the Rights of the Child, the EU directive on the Protection of Young People at Work and the International Labour Organisation's Convention 182, have turned the policy focus in the direction of children and work.

Against this background what are the policy issues relating to child employment that Britain faces? Given the limited space available we will highlight some key issues that demonstrate the need for an effective policy response.

Child employment legislation

In June 1994 the European directive on the Protection of Young People at Work was ratified. All European member states were given two years to implement the necessary changes into their own legislation. The then Conservative government sought and received an opt out from this directive to allow more time to review the adequacy of its own national legislation and to ensure that any legislative changes addressed national needs; for example, the need to protect the cultural practice of early-morning paper delivery. This position was inherited by the New Labour government in 1997. In 1998 a review committee was established to consider the legislation on this issue. It was assumed that this review would have reported its findings by June 2000, the end of the opt-out period from the EU directive. No formal statement has been forthcoming from the government on this issue. However, movement has been noted on two issues. First, the government issued a model by-law to all local authorities. The aim of this appears to have been to harmonise local child employment legislation. Second, the total number of hours that children under the age of 16 years can work during the school week was reduced from seventeen hours to twelve hours, as prescribed in the EU directive.

The above gives the impression that some action has taken place. However, tinkering with the legislation becomes a questionable activity when all of the research testifies to the fact that national and local regulations on child employment are ineffective. Jolliffe et al. (1995) found that 85 per cent of adolescents in their study were breaking one or more of the regulations and as such were illegally employed.

The ineffectiveness of the legislation is in part due to the lack of enforcement. Rikowski and Neary (1997) found that only fifteen out of 128 local authorities in England and Wales had a specifically designated Child

Employment Officer, or even an Education Welfare Officer, whose main brief related to child employment issues. In a separate study, one Education Welfare Officer stated that, 'The system has become farcical. When it comes to children working in the city we are absolutely unable to operate. From our point of view all controls over youth employment have collapsed' (Moorehead, 1987).

The explanation that is usually proffered to explain this is a resource-based one. Local Authorities argue that they do not have the resources to deal with this issue and central government argues that the resources are included in existing budget allocations. However, we would argue that resources are not the main explanation to account for the ineffectiveness of the legislation. Rather, we would suggest that even with adequate resources the legislation would be ineffective because it is out of date, perceived as irrelevant by those children who work and is overly bureaucratic. In addition, society at large views this activity as at worst 'harmless' and more commonly 'beneficial' to children. These views are based upon the myths that have grown up regarding child employment in Britain (Lavalette et al., 1995). Given this state of affairs legislation needs to be reviewed at both the micro and macro levels.

At the macro level there needs to be some debate about the aim and role of legislation in this area. Do we need legislation? If so, what form should it take? What should be the goal of legislation? Whitney (1999) has argued that the present legislation is inconsistent and illogical. More importantly, it fails to reflect contemporary society or the lives of teenagers within it. Reflecting on this, Whitney reviews four possible ways forward:

- Carry on with the status quo.
- Make virtually all child employment illegal.
- Deregulate and make virtually all child employment legal.
- Develop a modern, national, integrated approach to legislation.

For Whitney the first option is not acceptable given what we know about child employment in Britain. The second and third options are also rejected. In the former case this is because it would be impractical and impossible to police a system that seeks to stop children working. In the latter case, having little or no control over child employment would, according to Whitney, lead to greater potential exploitation of this labour force. The final option is Whitney's preferred solution. Developing a modern, national, integrated approach would provide greater flexibility to those who wish to work but offer protection from exploitation. To make this system effective, legislation should focus on the responsibility of the employer, rather than the employee, having to conform to a set regulatory framework.

This latter focus on the employer is echoed in the work of other writers in this area. Some have focused on the micro aspect of policy and argued that any legislation needs to be constructed on an evidence base rather than commonsense assumptions and historical precedence. McKechnie and Hobbs (2000) propose a number of ways that this might be achieved but argue that all alternatives need to be properly evaluated.

Causes of employment

In attempting to explain why children work, the traditional emphasis has been on economic factors. This is in part due to the influence of theories derived from the child employment literature in the so-called developing economies of the world. In this context the primary explanation that emerges emphasises the role of poverty. While this is undoubtedly a key factor in influencing such employment in developing economies it has limited use within the context of the UK.

It can be argued that poverty was a key factor when explaining child employment in the UK from an historical perspective. It is questionable that poverty is the main causal factor in contemporary society. However, this issue has generated alternative views. Mizen et al. (1999) argue that poverty has been neglected as an important factor in child employment. In contrast, others have argued that while poverty plays a role in some cases of child employment it cannot be viewed as the single, or even main, cause (McKechnie et al., 2000). Research evidence has tended to support the latter position. It could be argued that if children are driven to work by poverty then we would expect to find higher percentages of children working in more deprived areas. Research findings do not support this position (Lavalette, 1994). Where differences are found it indicates that children in more affluent areas are more likely to work. In poorer areas fewer job opportunities may exist.

At the same time studies have shown that some child employment is linked to family poverty. Researchers have found cases where children hand over their income to their parents or use their earnings to buy food for the household. Where this does happen the child's income can make a significant contribution to the family's overall income (Middleton et al., 1998).

If poverty is not the central reason for working, then what motivates children to work? A number of qualitative studies have identified a range of factors. These include working to gain financial independence from parents, combating boredom, gaining work experience and earning money to buy a range of consumer goods. There is clearly a need to gain fuller insight into the reasons why children decide to work. For example, such decisions may be related to attitudes towards education.

Gaining some understanding of why children work will provide insight into the supply side of this labour force. However, there is little known about the demand side. Why do employers employ children? As we have demonstrated, children are employed in a wide range of jobs. Many are associated with adult forms of work, and the majority of jobs fall under the general 'service sector' banner. It could be argued that many of the businesses that employ children are small. Economies of scale are limited and employment costs can be a significant part of the overheads. In these circumstances employing cheap labour that is not covered by minimum wage legislation or statutory employment rights must be appealing. In addition, child employees are a relatively pliable workforce, reflecting the youthfulness of the labour force, their weak power position and the lack of organised labour structures. Within the market system the employment of children may simply reflect the logic of the market.

From a policy perspective understanding why children work will provide only part of the picture. There is a need to investigate the demand side of the equation. If children are going to work should we continue to view them as a secondary workforce, or should they be viewed in the same way that society views adult part-time workers? Such a change would require an approach that recognises the rights of all employees, irrespective of age.

Work and education

The emphasis on the role of work and education in children's lives has swung to and fro over the years. Before and during the Industrial Revolution work was the focus of many children's lives. By the beginning of the early twentieth century education was increasingly seen as the most appropriate activity for children. This did not mean that children no longer worked but rather that they combined their employment with education. The legislation reflects the view that combining part-time work and school is beneficial in that it allows children to gain experience of the 'real world' of work.

The 1970s research by Davies was motivated by concerns over the negative effect employment was having on children's education. Davies's conclusions reinforced this view highlighting the fact that working children had poorer attendance, poorer academic ability and were less engaged with school. Since then researchers have argued that employment may have positive and negative consequences for school students. Studies have shown that the negative effects that Davies identified are more likely to emerge if students work in excess of ten hours per week. Working fewer hours per week has, in some studies, been linked to better attendance and academic performance measures.

Such findings have been explained within the context of a 'balance model'. In this framework employment is perceived to have the potential to be 'good' or 'bad'. What influences the outcome is the interaction between the quantity and quality of the employment experience (Hobbs and McKechnie, 1997). In highlighting the quality aspect of employment it becomes apparent that in addition to the number of hours committed to work, the nature of the job, the individual's experience of work and when they work, will all play a role in influencing the outcome within the 'balance model'.

However, these findings are limited to examining relationships rather than looking at issues of causality. In other words, although these findings tell us that long hours at work can be related to lower academic performance they do not tell us if long hours at work cause the lower academic achievement. That working long hours has a negative effect on education is one interpretation. It could be the case that children who perceive themselves as less academically inclined prefer to weight their commitments more heavily to alternative activities such as work.

From the policy perspective the work–education relationship is of particular interest. If legislation is to continue to allow children to combine part-time work with education what are the optimal circumstances for this? Being able to address this question would enable legislation to maximise any potential benefits of this experience while minimising any costs. A second related policy issue is that research investigating this issue may provide some insight into children and young adolescent's views on the education system. To what extent do children's choices within the work–education arena inform us of their views on the education system? As we have indicated it is possible that students opt out of the school system by investing more of their time in part-time employment. Such decisions may be a reflection of disaffection with the prevailing system. Within the education sector debates about the balance between vocational and academic content are ongoing. School students who commit more time to part-time work may be reflecting in their behaviour questions about the relevancy of the curriculum and its failure to deal with the 'real world'.

Engaging with school students' views on this matter may provide some insight, which could aid in the construction of effective employment and education policy. The issue of listening to the views of children in this area takes us into the final area we wish to consider.

Children's voices

As we noted in the introduction to this policy section, debates about legislation and policy are now played out against an international backdrop. One of the most significant instruments is the UN Conventions on the Rights of the Child. Within the Convention it is clearly stated that children should be given a 'voice' in policy matters that directly affect them. In debates about child labour at the international level the idea that child workers' voices should be attended to has gradually been accepted. In the developing countries working children have sought to organise themselves and claim the right to be heard on this issue. They want to be recognised as legitimate workers, receive recognition for their contribution and have practical, relevant responses to their problems (Boyden et al., 1998).

Within the UK there is little evidence that this aspect of the Convention has had any impact on policy-makers. The recent 1998 review committee on child employment legislation failed to take any cognisance of children's views on employment policy. By failing to do this there is a failure to understand that child employees, like any other worker, evaluate the employment experience. In attending to their views on work, policy-makers could avoid placing their adult interpretations on children's work experience.

While 'listening to the voices of children' has become a recognised issue for policy-makers it is not unproblematic. Many questions need to be addressed, such as: Whose voices are to be heard? Are they representative of all children's views? How are we to prioritise their views amongst all the others? While problems exist in applying this principle from the policy perspective, it should be viewed as a challenge that we should rise to rather than a problem to be avoided.

CONCLUSIONS

Within this chapter we have shown that child employment is not a thing of the past. We would argue that there is a degree of continuity in children's economic contribution through work from an historical perspective. Over time the forms of work have changed and children have emerged as a marginalised workforce, virtually invisible within present-day society. Such changes reflect the economic, political and ideological changes within society.

Within the UK a number of myths have dominated societal views on child employment. Research evidence from the last three decades undermines the commonsense assumptions upon which these myths were based. In turn this calls into question the validity of policy and legislation debates within the UK. The evidence indicates that the majority of children in the UK will have experience of paid employment before they reach the end of compulsory schooling. Against this background policy-makers need to reconsider the role of work and education in children's lives.

KEY TEXTS

Cunningham, H. and Viazzo, P.P. (eds) (1996) *Child Labour in Historical Perspective 1800–1985.* Florence: UNICEF.

Hobbs, S. and McKechnie, J. (1997) *Child Employment in Britain: A Social and Psychological Analysis.* Edinburgh: The Stationery Office.

Lavalette, M. (ed.) (1999) *A Thing of the Past? Child Labour in Britain in the Nineteenth and Twentieth Centuries.* Liverpool: Liverpool University Press.

EIGHT

Children, Class and the Threatening State

CHRIS JONES

Once considered vulnerable citizens whose welfare and rights deserve to be promoted, [children] are now viewed as a problem, a drain on the public purse. They should knuckle down and do as they are told. (Rickford 1995: 24)

INTRODUCTION

This chapter focuses on some of the poorest and most vulnerable children in British society. It attempts to give some insight into how and why British governments have, since the beginning of the twentieth century, become involved in the lives of those children, either whilst still living with their families or by removing them into the so-called 'care' of the state. In the process, an historically informed policy analysis is presented, at least in outline, which attempts to explain the fluctuating interest of the state in the lives of such children. As the argument unfolds, it becomes ever more difficult to discover any sincere humanitarian concern with the plight of society's poorest children as a key force behind the child welfare policies and practices which have emerged over the past century. Instead a multiplicity of other propelling influences are identified which point up the dominance of a peculiarly hard-hearted capitalist 'mind-set' which sets humanity aside in its pursuit of wealth and power.

State social work provides an interesting vantage point from which to explore this changing relationship of the British state with children and young people. In so doing it offers insights into how a society views and values some of its children and younger people. Social work is especially useful in that it highlights the manner in which the state's relationship with children is closely bound up with, and influenced by, their class position. This is possible owing to the simple, but often neglected, fact that state social work has always been class specific. Social work's gaze of concern and action has been, and remains to this day, on the children and young people amidst the most distressed and impoverished sections of society. Overwhelmingly the children 'of social work' are drawn from the poorest sections of the working class, which inevitably embraces children of minority ethnic groups who are over-represented within the disadvantaged.

There might be times when state social workers intervene in more prosperous families, but these are the exceptions and not the rule. The research evidence for this class specificity is overwhelming (Schorr, 1992). But this has not prevented social work agencies and practitioners from presenting themselves as universal providers with an interest in all children. These claims have tended to confuse analysis and understanding, and have compounded the difficulties that many have in recognising that childhood is not a homogeneous experience shared by all children. As with every other aspect of life, gender, 'race' and not least class are key influences in determining life chances and experiences. They are also important features in determining the manner in which the state relates to its population. Examples are not difficult to find which illuminate this, whether it is schooling, the criminal justice system, healthcare or social security. In all these areas if you are working class and poor, and worst still, working class, poor, black, young and male, one can expect a quite different (and worse) experience to others from more prosperous and privileged backgrounds.

WELFARISM AND PROBLEM FAMILIES

We start our analysis by looking at some of the key welfare legislation which has impacted on the lives of poorer children and young people to determine the motives and reasons which prompt societal concern and interest in these areas. The years immediately after the Second World War are understandably highlighted in all histories of British social policy as one of those epochal moments in the development of British social welfare. Amidst the reforms which included the abolition of the much-despised Poor Law (an historically vilified institution by the mass of the British working class), and the introduction of the National Health Service, was the 1948 Children Act which created the childcare service. This Act was a landmark in the development of British state social work and like much subsequent childcare legislation carried a vision and plan for children which was far wider in scope than just those children who were to be the direct target of the state's intervention.

The 1948 Act and the 1946 Report of the Curtis Committee – which informed its content – captured and reflected many of the key principles of what came to be called the social democratic welfare state. It broke, albeit in a qualified and tentative manner, with the more punitive traditions of the Poor Law and Workhouse, which, until 1948, had been the key institution for the care and warehousing of some of the poorest children in society. This children's legislation, as with many of the other welfare reforms at the time, was full of optimism and hope about the potential of even the most damaged and impoverished children to develop into useful and productive citizens. Informed by psychodynamic psychology and influential followers of Freud such as John Bowlby, the newly formed childcare service epitomised a positive welfarism which was common across the emerging social democratic welfare state.

This more optimistic view about some of the poorest in society did signify a shift in state policy and thinking. The 1948 Children Act departed from the highly punitive perspectives which had dominated policy and practice for over a hundred years towards these sections of society, which had been variously condemned as 'undeserving' or a 'residuum'. In virtually every aspect of state policy this most deprived, impoverished and damaged section of the population had been subjected to purposeful neglect, guided by the anxiety and policy imperative that nothing should be done to encourage their reproduction. In the years immediately after the Second World War this negative policy response was to change with new welfare legislation which was different in both style and content.

The softer welfare approach exemplified by the 1948 Act, whilst seemingly an improvement on previous practice, was not without qualification. For example, when one looks at some of the discussions which took place at the time it is clear that there was no wholesale repudiation of the biological determinism which had asserted that the behaviour of the poorest was somehow fixed by their genes and therefore was incapable of being amended. The sub-committee of the Women's Group on Public Welfare which published the influential report *The Neglected Child and His Family* (1948), noted for example:

> In the light of the strong evidence by many witnesses that parents in problem families are little influenced in their conduct by what is beneficial to themselves, let alone what is socially desirable (as is shown for example in their failure to get needed medical or dental treatment or to persevere with contraceptives) the Committee felt that reliance on their co-operation was a somewhat slender hope. It is not difficult to decide that the unfit should be prevented from propagating. (Women's Group on Public Welfare, 1948: 120)

The dilemma, they noted, was where to draw the line to mark out those whose 'unfitness' was 'sufficient to justify sterilisation' (ibid.: 120). The acknowledgement that there was a dilemma was important and gave rise to limited reliance on the scalpel, but the option of sterilisation has never been removed from state practices and continues to be used although with little attention or concern. It is sobering to recognise that genetic and biological approaches to acute poverty have never been rooted out of the British welfare repertoire and, as we shall see, it returns with a vengeance later in the century with the redesignation of problem families as an 'underclass' and a return to policies of studied neglect and containment (Jones and Novak, 1999).

BLAMING MOTHERS

The shift towards 'welfarism' did not, however, signify a radical new understanding of the problems confronting some of the poorest families and children in the country. Their poverty and associated hardship was still seen primarily as being rooted in their behaviour and values. In contrast with the past, the main difference was the sense that something could be done about it now through various interventions of the state welfare system, since the causes of poor morality and values were attributed to family upbringing, which could be changed and not to biology, which could not. But even with this important change the poor were still to blame for their condition, and little or no attention was given to the wider socio-economic and political structures and systems which offer more compelling explanations for the causes of poverty and damaging social inequalities.

Within this paradigm the working-class family became a crucial site for state intervention and attention (see Donzelot, 1979). It was within the family and its dynamics that the answers were to be sought to explain why British society was burdened by up to a tenth of its population locked in acute poverty and deprivation, despite the advances in welfare provision and successive governments' commitment to ensuring relatively full employment through the pursuit of Keynesian economic policies. This focus on the family as a site of welfare activity was reflected in the redesignation of the 'residuum' as 'problem families'.

The assumption that these families were responsible for their own difficulties has informed all subsequent state social work practice. It led to a distinctively more personal and intrusive intervention by the state into the lives of the children and families so designated. This was not only a direct consequence of a conservative analysis of poverty but was also informed by a set of theories and perspectives which maintained that the solution to these problems rested also within these families. It was argued that a highly personalised intervention by a social worker could re-educate and re-moralise the problem family. The target of the re-moralisation strategy was the mother. The working-class mother comes to take centre stage as the main 'carrier' of poverty (see Henriques, 1955; Wilson, 1977). The following passage taken from a report cited by the Women's Group on Public Welfare characterises much of the official discourse on mothers as being the prime culprit responsible for child neglect and poverty: 'in all 36 cases there are obvious defects such as irresponsibility, apathy, laziness, or lack of intelligence on the part of the mother' (Women's Group on Public Welfare: 33). Or later in the same report:

> In a memorandum on Problem Families submitted to the Committee, Dr Soothill, Medical Officer of Health for Norwich, says 'they have no idea of a proper paying out of money – one failing is that they do not bother to start repairing a thing until it is worn or damaged beyond repair, for example, shoes. Some of them are great or even forceful 'borrowers', and others are

quite incapable of refusing a loan even though they are fully aware that it will not be repaid. (Ibid.: 55)

The creation of a childcare service in 1948 marks the beginning of a period whereby the state reaches down into homes and households that had previously been regarded as hopeless. Now there was talk of rehabilitation and treatment with social workers explicitly expected to be caring and sympathetic and therefore capable of forming therapeutic relationships with the mothers. It made for an interesting social welfare experiment which was not only class specific but also highly gendered. This latter quality was reflected both in the belief that women made the best social work practitioners (if not managers) because of the 'qualities of sensitivity and sympathy that are required' (Forder, 1966: 207), and in the central position assigned to working-class poor mothers in the reproduction of poverty. Henriques, an influential writer on working-class family life at the time, wrote of mothers in problem families:

Nearly all these mothers are bad, negligent and stupid mothers because their own mothers were bad, negligent and stupid. They had never learnt anything different when they were young. But the ghastly tragedy of it all is the probability that the children of these mothers will also grow up to be bad, negligent and stupid mothers, for that is what they have been taught to be. And so the horrible circle is perpetuated. (Henriques, 1955: 84)

CHILDREN AS HUMAN CAPITAL

There are many factors which contributed to this reorientation of state policy towards the most impoverished children and their families. Needless to say, governments would like us to believe that it was moved primarily by compassion and concern for the plight of children. Compassion there may have been, but as is typical with much British welfare policy there were also compelling economic arguments which informed this new attention on some of the most deprived households in society. The parallels with the Children Act 1908, another landmark Act with respect to the state's interest in working-class children, is compelling. As John Stewart noted:

Considerable concern was expressed in the 1900s about Britain's child population amidst fears of 'racial decline' and imperial and economic competition. In particular, it was the children of the poor who appeared to present the greatest danger to Britain's world position. (Stewart, 1995: 93)

In 1948 we find similar concerns being expressed. This time the context was shaped by the demographic trends revealed by the PEP Report on Population (1948) followed quickly by the Royal Commission on Population's Report (1949). Both pointed to declining birth rates and an ageing population and expressed considerable anxieties about the implications for the supply of labour in an expanding economy (see Wilson, 1977). The problems both in the 1900s and then forty years later which prompted state childcare legislation were largely issues about the capacity of working-class families to produce children who would be physically and mentally fit for either the market or the armed forces. The context of both Children Acts was about seeing all children as potential national assets, none of whom could or should be wasted. As one commentator noted at the later period:

> It should not require the cold statistics of the sociologist to awaken the official conscience. Nevertheless, the declining birth rate and the ageing population make it imperative that, quite apart from humanitarian considerations, every child should be given the maximum chance of survival, and more important still, should reach adult life in as perfect state of physical and mental health as is possible. (Martin, 1944: 106)

At the turn of the twentieth century, the evidence revealed by the Boer War appalled elite opinion. Recruitment during the war adversely affected by the discovery that over 70 per cent of the men had to be rejected because of poor health. This led to the creation of the Interdepartmental Committee on Physical Deterioration whose report in 1904 provided further detailed evidence of the state of the country's working population and their children (Thane, 1982). It made for disturbing reading. Influential opinion came to the view that the imperial race was at risk and more specifically that Britain was losing its competitive edge to Germany and the USA because British workers could not match the physical prowess and fitness of their foreign counterparts. The response was a flurry of state social welfare activity which also embraced children. There was, for example, the introduction of compulsory physical education in schools in 1902, subsidised school meals for children in need in 1906, the creation of a school medical service in 1907, followed by the more wide-ranging Children Act of 1908 which amongst other things addressed juvenile smoking and drinking and led to the formation of juvenile courts. What is of particular interest is that legislators begin to refer to children 'as the capital of the country' and assets in need of 'investment' and protection (Stewart, 1995: 91). Of course there were those who advocated for these reforms on the basis of child welfare and protection and these voices should not be neglected, yet the impulse for state intervention and expenditure is much better explained and understood in terms of anxieties over labour where children of the working-class poor now become seen worthy of attention in terms of their value as future workers and soldiers. Without these 'economic' concerns it becomes difficult to explain both the timing of the state's activities and why a shift from neglect to intervention should occur.

Positive developments in state welfare policy, however, rarely outlast the context which gives rise to them. The 1908 Children Act may have pushed the state into new directions in the face of fears about physical efficiency and imperial decline in the context of increasing international competition. But the return of economic slump in the 1920s and 1930s saw the fate of poor children slip from the national agenda. The changed economic and political context of 1948, however, was to bring forth a new burst of activity.

Very similar concerns framed the context of the 1948 Act. We see the same arguments used to justify the state's renewed interest, especially with respect to the children of the problem families. According to such influential studies as *Our Towns* (1943) – another best-seller from the Women's Group on Public Welfare – not only were problem families characterised by their above-average family size such that they were estimated to constitute 10 per cent of the population, but their children rarely made it to the labour market in any fit state to be usefully employed. Tom Stephens, who was a leading social work figure after the Second World War and helped create the Family Service Units, gave the following account of what supposedly befell children in problem families:

> The dirt diseases such as scabies and impetigo will never be stamped out as long as there are neglected children. All kinds of vermin are transmitted from dirty homes to cleaner ones. . . . The alarming spread of V.D. is taking place to a large extent among girls of low morale who come from wretched, undisciplined homes. Not only prostitutes, but also the homeless, unemployable youths and hardened tramps who form a considerable part of the chronic prison population are largely a product of the same kind of family. The case for the total eradication of this evil is overwhelming. (Stephens, 1945: 5–6)

By the time the population reports were published in 1948 and 1949 working-class children, and especially those of problem families, were recast in terms of their value to the labour market. It became imperative that no children should be wasted or lost to productive capacity. In the debate on the Children Bill, one MP made this explicit when he said that 'from the national point of view we cannot afford to lose 120,000 children or to have their lives wasted' (Lindsay, *Hansard*, Volume 452, 28.6.1948). This was echoed by the PEP Report's comment 'that to cut down the wastage of human assets is to reduce the difficulties which confront a population policy' (PEP, 1948: 137).

These two Children Acts, forty years apart, reveal the manner in which labour market considerations significantly influence and shape the capitalist state's relationship to the most disadvantaged children in society. It is by no means the only consideration, but it is notable that the state becomes interested in working-class poor children – many of whom are damaged by their experience of poverty and suffer because of their parents' inability to cope with the pressures – only at those times when there are clear concerns over the supply and reproduction of usable labour. Conversely, in periods of high unemployment, as in the latter decades of the twentieth century when there is no longer any sustained demand for unskilled male manual labour either in the short or long term, it is evident that the state rapidly withdraws from this policy approach to one which is much more openly regulatory, disciplinary and restrictive.

BACK TO CLASS

The importance of labour market considerations is evident across the range of the state's children's policies. In schooling, for example, there was a wave of reforms which transformed the organisation of schools from the late 1940s through to the 1960s. For some this was a matter of breaking free of the class-ridden structure of schools which privileged only a tiny proportion of Britain's young people. But for the state, one senses that there were other pressing imperatives that had relatively little to do with pro-gressive social ideals but much more to do with securing the vitality of capitalism in Britain, which demanded that the state should reach down increasingly into the working class for the skilled and professional labour required by the growing economy. This is how Robert Ensor put it:

> The nation's egalitarian policies do not merely provide 'ladders' of opportunity, but we toothcomb the whole school population in our endeavour to find able children to climb them. (Ensor 1950: 133)

This sentiment was echoed in a whole raft of educational reforms and reports that were produced through the 1950s and 1960s including the 1963 Newsom Report (Wynn, 1970: 22) and the Robins Report (1963), which paved the way for the expansion of higher education. These reports, in their search for working-class talent, contrast sharply with the educational reforms of the neo-liberal period from the late 1970s onwards, which as Nick Davies (2000) notes has resulted in a school system which is now more deeply fragmented and socially differentiated than at any time since the Second World War. According to Davies, the school system in Britain today is:

> a very long way from the thirty-year-old dream of a network of comprehensive schools. In their place, we have developed a two-tiered system in which the children most in need of education are tipped into second-class schools with sparse resources and no sixth forms, while those who are naturally most able are given more resources and their own A-level classes. The second-tier schools are stigmatised, together with their pupils. The fact that middle-class children tend to prosper in this system while the poor fail, rubs political salt in the social wound. 'It is not standing still. It is getting worse and worse. It is becoming more and more polarised. There is a horrendous backlash going to happen, and yet there is almost a wilful blindness to it.' Jan Woodhead, head teacher at Abbeydale Grange, said that. (Davies, 2000: 35)

For the poorest and most disadvantaged children this polarisation has entailed abandonment by the state as it locks them in (sometimes literally) under-resourced, unpopular and unhappy schools. As a consequence, governments have been compelled to introduce increasingly draconian control measures to manage the tensions, including considerable use of school exclusions and the creation of specialised sin-bins. Who are these children who, in Davies's terms, are 'cleansed – pushed out of schools' (2000: 132)? According to Davies the politicians argue that they are children who are basically ill-disciplined, often as a consequence of poor parenting. Yet as Davies contends this emphasis on ill-discipline conceals and distorts a more telling set of explanations:

> First, that the children who spill out of schools have bubbled over the edge of a boiling cauldron of trouble, and that this has far less to do with discipline than it has to do with an epidemic of emotional damage, particularly among the 30% of children who live in poverty; second, that these children are the most visible part of the central problem of our schools – how to teach the new mass of disaffected children who see no point in learning, how to give any reality at all to the once vibrant idea that education is the natural escape route from poverty. (Davies, 2000: 133)

It is rarely the case that the developments in any one discrete area of the state, whether education, health, social security or social work, are unique to themselves. Rather, it is common to find that state social policies, whatever their location, tend to share common trajectories. So it is hardly a surprise to discover that state social work in its interventions in the lives of working-class poor children follows a similar pattern to that of state schooling. Moreover, as with schools, what makes the analysis so disturbing is that we can discern a turn towards neglect and constraint precisely at a time when, on the one hand, levels of poverty and social polarisation are deepening and widening and, on the other, the consequences of such poverty and inequality are beginning to be increasingly felt. In cities such as Liverpool, there is no longer any debate amongst health workers that poverty and its effects account for why the city figures so highly on all the negative health indicators and that the people of the city live four years less than the average for Britain (Liverpool Health Authority, 2001). But as need increases and evidence mounts which demonstrates that enduring poverty corrodes the physical and emotional well-being of children and their carers, we find the state in retreat instead of being more prepared to assist and support the most vulnerable.

Some people might take exception to this analysis not least those who believe, since New Labour's 1997 election victory, that there has been a significant turn for the better, and feel that the worst of neo-liberalism's worship of capitalism and the market have been tempered by a more compassionate government. Such opinion is not entirely fanciful. New Labour, unlike its Conservative predecessors, has not been averse to acknowledging poverty as a social evil, and has developed an extraordinary repertoire of rhetoric and initiatives which suggest a commitment to greater equality and social justice. But in practice the gap between the rich and poor is widening under New Labour and its policies have been seriously deficient to meet the extent of need. Moreover, it is a government so anxious not to disturb the more prosperous that its agenda to tackle the gross abuse of poverty is feeble and lacks any vision of the social and economic reconstruction that is required. This is revealed in some starkness when we begin to examine the lives of those children and households who experience the most enduring long-term poverty and all that comes with it.

REDUNDANT CHILDREN

For the very poorest in Britain, the past thirty years has been a torrid time (Jones and Novak, 1999). Their historic value to society has been as unskilled labour power. They have no other intrinsic value within a capitalist society. For this segment of the working class, the demand for their labour power has almost evaporated. As Davies argued:

> They are in the deepest sense redundant. Looking at them from a strictly economic point of view, these former workers and their families are worthless. More than that they are an expensive burden – at least they will be if they are to be properly housed, clothed and fed, if they are to be given decent schools and hospitals. So, why bother? . . . From an economic point of view they are worth nothing, they will be given the bare minimum. For these redundant humans, the creation of poverty is the final solution. (Davies 1997: 299–300)

By the last decade of the twentieth century the imperative for active state policies to rescue as many children as possible for the labour market had long disappeared. Whereas the 1950s and 1960s were times when it was possible to believe that education could be a route out of poverty for some working-class children, the latter decades of the twentieth century saw the introduction of state policies intent upon playing down the expectations of such children and young people and encouraging them to view any job, however menial and mind destroying, as a reasonable aspiration. As Mizen (1995) noted, the plethora of training schemes developed during the 1980s and 1990s were not about helping young working-class people develop a range of transferable skills that would equip them for successful and rewarding employment in the new 'flexible' labour market. Rather:

> Across the majority of schemes, the emphasis on giving young people generic skills gave rise to training dominated by on-the-job training with employers, exercising little of a trainee's existing capabilities and giving them scant opportunity to develop new work-related strengths and abilities. On the whole, training on a scheme involves repetitive and unrewarding tasks directed by the existing demands of each employer's organisational structure and immediate labour process, without any real commitment to provide quality skills training. . . . Youth training has [also] largely served to reproduce young women's marginalisation from access to skills training, through further segregating them into narrow areas of training characterised by even lower-skilled work. (Mizen, 1995: 138, 139)

For those children and their families who came to the attention of state social work the experience has tended to be even worse. What few analyses have been done reveal that many of these children are drawn from households which are dependent on benefits rather than wages, and that their family carers are often long-term unemployed, even unemployable (Becker et al., 1987). But it is not simply material hardship which has blighted their lives but also the emotional stress which comes from living in hardship and the tensions over managing on limited budgets which are then added to by the daily grind of living in a society which equates material well-being with moral worthiness and respectability. Is it any surprise to discover then that working-class children are experiencing mental health problems of epidemic proportions (Davies, 2000)?

The ideas of rehabilitation and positive intervention which flourished so briefly within social work in the immediate aftermath of the Second World War have long gone. With historical hindsight it now seems that the need to reach down to the most vulnerable and marginalised children in ways which would genuinely assist them to reach adulthood in good physical and mental health was in fact very short-lived. For the social work profession the rhetoric of treatment and its claims to restore the children of problem families and save them from lives in prisons or psychiatric care were aspects of its campaign to gain legitimacy and acceptance. But one suspects that it never figured very centrally in its practice – case-work is not the most straightforward method to apply – and that state sponsorship of social work had much more to do with its capacity to supervise and regulate the most difficult, intractable and expensive of its welfare-dependent populations. As the 1959 Younghusband Report noted, the familialism of social work had much to commend itself as an economic form of welfare:

> There is also clearer understanding of maintaining the elderly and the mentally and physically handicapped in the community wherever practicable. . . . The services are now more consciously planned and administered so as to help the family care for its own members. It has been put to us that the new emphasis on preventive and domiciliary care is sound economy as well as sound social policy, and that it is certain to prove less costly than the alternatives of admission to residential care. (Younghusband Report, 1959: paragraph 551)

And the cheapness of social work featured in every governmental report and policy which underpinned social work's evolution into the local authority social services departments of England and Wales which were created in 1974. The 1968 Seebohm Report, for example, argued that by creating generic social services departments it would be possible to:

> [P]revent children having to be taken into residential care and could save heavy expenditure in other directions. The cost of keeping a child in a remand home is now £20 per week or £1,000 per annum; the cost of keeping a child in an approved school is nearly as much. . . . A qualified social worker earns £1,060–£1,435 a year to which must be added the cost of supporting

services. If an additional social worker can remove the need for two children coming into residential care, the benefit to the community in terms of money is obvious. (Seebohm Report, 1968: 16)

As with most areas of life in contemporary Britain, it is all too often this 'bottom-line logic' that determines what is done. This capitalist logic has increasingly seeped deeper into welfare areas which were once influenced by factors other than economy, efficiency and effectiveness. The fact that issues of cheapness and economy now have such a bearing when discussing the lives and welfare of some of the most distressed children in the population says much about our society and leaders: leaders who have no qualms about committing huge expenditure on their own children's development and education to ensure that they secure privilege and power but resist any suggestion to commit public resources to those in far greater need. For the children and families of state social work this focus on ensuring that they do not burden the state with additional expenditure informs their relationship with the state, which over time has become characterised by restriction, regulation, surveillance and control.

THE ABUSIVE STATE

The contact which children and young people have with state social work services is variable, but generally falls along two principal axes. The first is as members of a household or family and the second is in their own right when the social work agency takes over the parental function and they come into 'care' which is now called being 'looked after'. In both cases, we can find evidence of both good and bad practice. In the former, children and young people talk of their social workers who removed them from deeply abusive and neglectful environments and provided them with positive support and new caring and loving foster homes (Morris, 2000). Many social workers and their agencies regret deeply that the positive experiences of child-saving rarely make the headlines.

Despite the complaints of social work agencies and various professional social work organisations about the manner in which the press highlight their failings with children and young people, it is virtually impossible to arrive at any overall assessment now which is not negative and critical of state social work. To be blunt, the failings far outweigh the gains; the experience of children and young people within the state, either as members of a household in need or whilst being 'looked after' either in residential or foster care is one in which the negative features far outweigh the positives. Indeed, in far too many cases, the relationship of children and young people with state social services can be characterised as disrespectful and abusive, with the abuse being on a continuum from low-level neglect at one end to extreme physical and sexual torture at the other.

In recent years the British media have given a high profile to cases which fall at the extreme end of this continuum and provided graphic and disturbing accounts especially of residential institutions where torture and abuse of children and young people has been endemic. In much of this coverage, especially where it concerns the criminal prosecution of the perpetrators, a somewhat distorted view has been promoted which suggests that the primary problem of residential childcare has been the ease with which those minded to abuse children have been able to find employment, sometimes at senior levels, and have thereby contaminated the institutions and damaged children with impunity. There may be some truth to this, but when analysis and enquiry stops at this point some significant questions remain unanswered. A simple example: throughout the Waterhouse enquiry into the particularly outrageous abuse of children in residential institutions in North Wales, it became evident that many of the children and young people had told people in authority about their plight: people such as the police, senior managers in social work agencies, clergy and others who were not directly responsible for their care. Yet nothing was done. This appeared in the *Guardian*'s coverage of the North Wales Inquiry:

> One boy, who described a particularly long and vivid catalogue of abuse said he grabbed hold of the jacket of an executive from social services . . . who was visiting the home. He pleaded with him to do something. 'He just wouldn't listen. He wasn't having any of it' . . . one witness after another describes how they grew up in a world of threats, 'We were treated like animals, creatures, rubbish . . .'. (*Guardian*, 24 September 1997)

This is no isolated example. It is now clear from the testimony of many children and young people who have experienced the state through social work services, that their voices are not heard: they are not taken seriously and their concerns are continually ignored (Barter, 1996; Morris, 2000). This in turn gives rise to an overwhelming sense of powerlessness with the realisation that people can do things to you with almost total impunity. The voices of the children and young people in the care of the state are not heard.

If we move down the continuum of abuse from this extreme end, we find children and young people complaining relentlessly that they are subject to arbitrary decisions without any consultation. This young man's account of coming into care is typical:

> The day after my twelfth birthday my social worker came to pick me up as usual. I fell asleep in the car and woke up looking at a house which turned out to be a kids' home. I hadn't been told that I was going into care or that I couldn't go home at the weekends anymore. (Cited in Chapman, 2001: 56)

The plight of black children in care graphically illustrates the manner in which class and race prejudice intertwine to compound injustice. Despite pressure over recent years from a variety of black organisations who have bitterly complained about the processes whereby disproportionate numbers of black children come into care and their subsequent experiences in care (Bryan et al., 1985; Barn, 1993) there appears to be little improvement. Black children continue to complain that they are negatively stereotyped from the outset:

> One thing I want to say is that as soon as you are in care and you're black they think, oh, troublemaker, let's bung 'em up somewhere – criminal. I've been pulled up often for no obvious reason. (Cited in Merrick, 1996: 209)

A young person from the Manchester Black and In Care Group echoed this sentiment: 'The image of myself was reflected back as an image associated with drugs, violence, simpleness, exotic, problematic, bad and mad' (cited in Jones, 1993: 84).

Similar accounts of indifference, prejudice and ignorance flow from gay and lesbian youngsters in care. Differences are important to note but the commonality of experience and outcome is overwhelmingly negative. Young people who have been in the care of the state are hugely over-represented in the prison population, amongst the homeless, the long-term unemployed, addicts of alcohol and other drugs, those with severe mental health problems, and those with chaotic and unhappy adult lives with profound difficulties in generating supportive and nourishing human relationships (Schorr, 1992). This litany of disaster and ruined lives demands explanations which take us far beyond identifying and prosecuting perpetrators of abuse in children's homes, indifferent social workers or introducing new forms of criminal checks on those seeking to work with vulnerable and often damaged young people. These are the sorts of responses which are encouraged by the media's coverage and which are often readily endorsed by government but wholly inadequate to the problem.

ISSUES OF RESPECT

The development of a more appropriate understanding and policy framework which has some possibility of achieving radically better outcomes demands as a first step that we pay attention to the views of the children and young people who have experienced these systemically abusive and disrespectful interventions in their lives. Similarly we must pay attention to the views of parents and carers who find themselves losing their children to the state. These perspectives demand primacy. However, in the British context, such a demand is both radical and controversial as it contradicts a profound and deeply rooted social welfare assumption that those who live and struggle in poverty and hardship are, by their social and economic position, inferior to the mainstream of the population and do not have views worthy of serious consideration (Phillips, 1999: 131). Such an assumption embraces a great number of the working-class poor but falls with particular rigour on those who have difficulties in supporting and raising their children and keeping them out of trouble with the police and other agents of state authority such as schools. As numerous social scientists have indicated for over sixty years now, these difficulties are determined to be 'private' or 'family' problems and not 'social problems' in that explanations and solutions are sought in personal and family relationships/dynamics and disconnected from broader socio-economic and political arrangements which remain so powerful in the determination of life chances.

It is the argument of this chapter that state policy aimed at the most disadvantaged children in British society is constructed around a set of historically rooted and continually reproduced assumptions that hold these children and their families as not worthy of respect: people who count for nothing. It is from this premise that policy is variously constructed and implemented. The form and content may have changed over time depending on historical sensibilities and contingencies but there remains a striking continuity of disrespect and disdain. To arrive at such a conclusion it is essential to strip away the rhetoric of liberal and humanitarian sentiments which saturate the debates and policy pronouncements. When the rhetoric is peeled away and we look at state practice and funding, and when we listen to those on the receiving end, a stark picture emerges which is characterised by preoccupations with social control, surveillance and limiting expenditure. On the few occasions when significant resources are committed and action is taken, it is more often than not prompted by the demands of the labour market or, in earlier times, the demands of the empire, rather than by a genuine concern with the care and protection of the most impoverished families and their children.

The consequences are both significant and far-reaching. For the children and their households it means enduring encounters with a disrespectful state whose services are inadequate or non-existent in times of need, and threaten and undermine when eventually deployed at crisis points. As Richard Wilkinson has argued, lasting damage to health and well-being follows when one feels:

> devalued, useless, helpless, uncared for, hopeless, isolated, anxious and a failure; these feelings can dominate people's whole experience of life, colouring their experience of everything else. It is the chronic stress arising from feelings like these which does the damage. (Wilkinson, 1996: 214–15)

Yet, as poverty frames and shapes the entire lives of so many children in Britain today, their plight is worsening, as these social workers make clear:

Many of the clients are more stressed than ever and certainly more stressed than when I started as a social worker 20 years ago. They have such grotty lives with no hope. Most of the kids we work with have no hope and I see the situation getting worse and worse. It seems that society has no need for them anymore. No one seems to care and the Government just wants them shoved aside. So some of the families are in terrible downward spirals where I agree that their kids need to be taken off them but if you go back you can see if something had been done earlier then this could have been avoided. (Cited in Jones, 2001: 557)

And as this child protection worker noted:

Most of our time is spent on a massive sprawling council estate on the outskirts of the city. It's got a crappy shopping centre and there is nothing there for the kids. There are lots of families there who are totally entrenched in poverty and all that brings with it. They are really struggling and in a mess. They really need some help. What they need is some money but of course nowadays nobody's actually offering what they need. Nobody is offering them jobs, any type of support or access into social networks that might get them out of the place. All they might get is a social worker who will go round to their house and ask a lot of questions – a bloody cheek many of them think – and because there are no immediate child protection needs they will get nothing. (Cited in Jones, 2001: 557)

We now have a rather bizarre situation emerging where the voices of some front-line state social workers are sounding increasingly like those of their clients with both complaining that they are not listened to, and from different sides of the fence, both bitter at what they see as inadequate services and inadequate recognition of the severe and multiple problems arising from twenty-five years of widening social inequalities and deepening poverty. New Labour has not broken with neo-liberalism and this has dire consequences for those in any way dependent on state welfare to survive. Moreover, New Labour has re-energised historical class relations based on contempt for those who are unable to survive the brutalisms of capitalism without support. Of all capitalist societies, Britain is the one most noted for its rigid and stark class fissures – where how you speak and look and where you are born remain so significant in determining life chances. At the core of those class relations there is a simmering class hatred which informs and shapes the perspectives of the dominant classes with respect to those at the 'bottom'.

The leadership of New Labour has energised this animosity by making it clear that they want no association with this segment of the population by demonising welfare dependency. For all its talk of social exclusion and poverty it has failed to indict the Conservatives for the brutalities and indignities they inflicted on the weakest in society for nearly twenty years. New Labour has refused to engage in any radical analysis of poverty and perpetuates neo-liberalism's project by diverting attention to so-called 'failing' schools, local education authorities, social service departments, teachers, doctors and so forth as if these were the problem.

Other capitalist societies do much better than Britain for their weak and vulnerable. How can it be that one of the great economies of the world can be so parsimonious in the quantity of its welfare provision and so brutalising in its administration of those few resources? According to David Piachaud (*Guardian Society*, 29 March 2000: 7) the 'UK is emerging as a serious contender for the title of the worst place in Europe to be a child' with the worst child poverty rates in the European Union. The fact is British society with its historical legacy of class contempt, provided a rich and fertile ground for a particularly harsh version of neo-liberalism with its politicians, business elite and opinion-makers in the media, all too ready to ridicule and strip away what were already relatively modest and qualified gains which had been secured through the welfare state reforms following the Second World War. Class hatred and neo-liberalism make for a potent mix which has life-threatening consequences, especially for those children and their families at the bottom of the social order. It is a threat that cannot be disposed of through piecemeal social reform. What is required is change of a quite different and fundamental kind.

CONCLUSION

As with so many areas of British social policy, child welfare reveals a history of development which is devoid of meaningful compassion and concern. Perhaps we should not be too surprised given that British elites had created charities to campaign against cruelty to animals long before creating comparable charities for combating child cruelty. The absence of compassion has not been fully explored here, but at least the elements of an alternative explanatory framework have been presented which ought to be helpful for policy analysis in Britain. At the core of this framework is the notion of 'useful labour' and the manner in which this concept underpins and shapes so much of the state's policy interventions. Of course, as this book as a whole reveals, this concept has a class specificity which reveals the state's concern with those who must work to survive as against those whose wealth and privilege exempt them from that necessity, and for whom the concept of useful labour is completely alien as they travel the globe's playgrounds of the rich. For the poorest, a quite different world is inhabited. One in which they endure some of the most profound of human indignities – poverty and disrespect – which is only modified when episodic and special social and economic conditions make their potential for useful labour of interest to the state. Whilst it would lead to lazy policy analysis to reduce everything to labour power and labour market conditions, the history of child welfare in Britain does offer a sobering example of the kind of social policy arrangements which emerge in societies which tend to view its citizens (or in the British case, subjects of the crown) of being of different value and worth, and then determines its policy interventions on the basis of narrow class informed economic demands rather than human need.

KEY TEXTS

Davies, N. (1997) *Dark Heart*. London: Chatto and Windus.
Davies, N. (2000) *The School Report*. London: Vintage.
Jones, C. and Novak, T. (1999) *Poverty, Welfare and the Disciplinary State*. London: Routledge.

NINE

Children, Crime and the State

BARRY GOLDSON

INTRODUCTION

[It is] easy to blame these poor children and to ascribe their misconduct to an innate propensity to vice; but I much question whether any human being, circumstanced as many of them are, can be reasonably expected to act otherwise. (Evidence to a House of Commons Select Committee in 1817, cited in Tobias, 1972: 11)

. . . from the outset juvenile justice has existed principally as a function of a broad nexus of State control . . . a means of the steady expansion of State control . . . the system is riddled with paradox, irony, even contradiction . . . [it] exists as a function of the child care and criminal justice systems on either side of it, a meeting place of two otherwise separate worlds. (Harris and Webb, 1987: 7–9)

The problem of children breaking the law is one of the great preoccupations of modern times. In recent years juvenile crime has attracted sustained high-profile attention from politicians, child welfare services, criminal justice agencies, the media and the public. Indeed, it would seem that crime, and the fear of crime (within which the behaviour of children and young people has been prominent), is never very far from contemporary public consciousness.

However, little of this concern is new. Juvenile crime, the anxieties that it induces and the formal and informal responses that it incurs, has a long history. Such history is complex. It is complex not least because it is derived in a dualistic conception of childhood itself. In this way children, from the beginning of the nineteenth century onwards, have been perceived both as *vulnerable victims* in need of care and protection, and as *precocious threats* who require control and correction (Hendrick, 1994). Such conceptual dualism has particularly applied to working-class children and the children of the poor, those who have been, and are, exposed to structural disadvantage. Moreover, it follows that state policy responses to such children, and the practical interventions of state agencies, have been driven both by care/welfare and control/justice priorities. In tracing the emergence and consolidation of state policy with regard to children who break the law, therefore, it is important to appreciate that such responses do not conform to a tidy linear development of progressive and benign reform. Indeed, good intentions, driven by enlightened benevolence, may take their place in any explanatory account, but analyses of juvenile crime policy must also be set within a context of its social origins, the economic and political interests behind it, its internal paradoxes and the nature of its appeal in respect of social control.

This chapter will aim to unravel the development of policy in relation to children and crime, and to trace the evolution of the juvenile justice system in England and Wales, from the beginning of the nineteenth century to the present. Any such overview is inevitably schematic and incomplete but it will be argued that the competing imperatives of care/welfare/protection and control/regulation/punishment have been, and are, delicately balanced and permanently negotiated and re-negotiated in the determination of state responses to juvenile crime.

DELINQUENCY DISCOVERED

As childhood as a social construction changes, so also does the nature and patterns of control over it. (Qvortrup, 1994: 14)

At the beginning of the nineteenth century the construction of childhood as a separate and independent social category from adulthood had yet to be institutionalised. Children played a full and active role within the economy (see Stack and McKechnie, this volume). Similarly, the practices of the criminal justice and penal systems did not discern between children and adults: there was no distinct legal category of 'juvenile delinquent' or 'child offender'. The age of criminal responsibility was set at 7 years. As such once a child reached their seventh birthday they were held to be equally accountable before the law, and exposed to precisely the same penalties – many of them extraordinarily severe – as an adult. Indeed, such severity included capital punishment and children who were spared the ultimate penalty were either transported overseas or detained in prisons with adults. In 1817 the Prison Discipline Society reported that there were 315 boys under the age of 17 held in Newgate adult prison. Moreover, children were often treated more harshly than adults in such institutions on the basis that such treatment would serve the purposes of early deterrence.

Bourgeois philanthropy, social reform and 'child saving' began to emerge around this time and dovetailed into prevailing moral anxieties and reactionary political concerns. This was a time of industrial revolution and society was in the grip of major social and economic transition, flux and uncertainty. The philanthropists were moved by their revulsion at the appalling conditions endured by the children of the poor, and the Establishment was concerned with the prospect of serious social disorder should the 'criminal classes' join forces with the burgeoning presence of organised workers and militants. Intervention was legitimised on both counts (Goldson, 1997a). In short, the prevailing view was that society needed to protect children (especially the ever-increasing numbers of street children), but it also needed to be protected from them: an expression of the victim–threat dualism to which we referred above.

It was largely such concern that inspired the first systematic inquiry into juvenile crime which was undertaken by the Society for Investigating the Alarming Increase of Juvenile Delinquency in the Metropolis in 1815. The Society's report was published in 1816 and it concluded that the main causes of delinquency included the improper conduct of parents; children's educational deficits; the lack of suitable employment opportunities for children and the over-severity of the criminal code:

> Dreadful is the situation of the young offender: he becomes the victim of circumstances over which he has no control. The laws of his country operate not to restrain, but to punish, him. (1816 Report, cited in Muncie, 1999: 55)

The Society proposed that distinctive responses should be established for child 'offenders', underpinned by reformist and rehabilitative objectives (not infrequently conceptualised in terms of moral rejuvenation), as opposed to simple retributive and punitive reactions. Similarly, in 1817 the Society for the Improvement of Prison Discipline and the Reformation of Juvenile Offenders argued that it was increasingly necessary to separate the child offender from his/her more hardened adult counterpart in order to avoid the moral contamination of the child. Accordingly in 1823 a specialist convict hulk (prison ship) was introduced for children, and in 1838 the first penal institution exclusively for children was opened at Parkhurst. Perhaps more significant, however, were the efforts of voluntary organisations which were mobilising support for the creation of separate institutions for 'delinquents' outside of the formal prison system.

Perhaps the most prominent champion of specialist institutions for children was Mary Carpenter whose prescriptions for the treatment of both 'destitute' (deprived) and 'delinquent' (depraved) children were recorded in her extensive writings (Carpenter, 1851, 1853). Carpenter and her supporters preferred the concepts of reform and moral reclamation to those of deterrence and punishment as the basis for intervention, and she was a formidable advocate for Reformatories and Industrial Schools. In 1854 the Youthful Offenders Act allowed courts to send children convicted of an offence to a *Reformatory* for between two and five years (*controlling* the 'threats'). In 1857 the Industrial Schools Act provided that children who were found begging, suffering from parental neglect and/or seemingly beyond parental control could be sent indefinitely to an *Industrial School* (*protecting* the 'victims'). Moreover, the new institutions not only promised to control and protect, but also to insulate each constituency of children from the 'contagious' spread of 'moral contamination'. By 1860 approximately 4,000 child 'offenders' were being held in forty-eight certified Reformatories in England and Wales. The development of the Industrial Schools was slower but, notwithstanding this, by the end of the century more than 30,000 children were contained in one or other form of institution. Whilst the practices of incarcerating children in Parkhurst Prison ceased in 1864, and the new institutions can be conceptualised (at least in part) in terms of humanitarian reform, taken together the Reformatories and the Industrial Schools also comprised a major extension of social control over working-class children.

By the end of the nineteenth century, therefore, delinquency had not only been 'discovered' but a recognisably 'modern' construct of the juvenile 'offender' had been institutionalised through emerging and consolidating strands of policy. In turn, such a construction invited specialised forms of response and the control apparatus developed and expanded accordingly. At this point in time the role of the state was essentially limited to providing legislative approval and financial support for voluntary effort and the initiatives of the reformers. However, as policy responses to juvenile crime entered their next stage of development the role of the state evolved from a position of burgeoning influence to one of direct control.

ENTER THE STATE: RECONCILING 'WELFARE' AND 'JUSTICE'?

... it is by making the system appear less harsh, that people are encouraged to use it more often. (Cohen, 1985: 98)

The need for special jurisdiction for children had been periodically raised throughout the nineteenth century and by its end some towns had implemented separate juvenile courts. However, it was not until the election of a reformist Liberal government in 1906 that state action was taken to place such courts on a statutory footing and, in so doing, to complete the administrative separation of the child and adult jurisdictions. In introducing the Children Bill, Home Secretary Herbert Samuel proposed that the 'courts should be agencies for the rescue as well as the *punishment* of juveniles' (cited in Gelsthorpe and Morris, 1994: 950), and the subsequent Children Act 1908 can be seen as an attempt to reconcile *welfare* and *justice* imperatives. The Act provided the new Juvenile Courts with both civil jurisdiction (welfare) over the 'needy' child (victim), and criminal jurisdiction (justice) over the child 'offender' (threat). This served to raise further questions of the relationship between deprivation and depravation and, as Harris and Webb (1987: 9) have observed, 'it made the juvenile court itself a locus for conflict and confusion, a vehicle for the simultaneous welfarization of delinquency and the juridicization of need'.

The Children Act 1908 has been described by Pinchbeck and Hewitt (1973: 144) as a 'Children's Charter' which 'provided a more comprehensive and child oriented legal system and more generous and liberal provisions for children in all walks of life'. However, the ideologies of welfare that informed the Act also legitimised the incremental extension of state intervention and supervision of (almost exclusively working-class) children. Classical conceptions of punishment and deterrence were certainly challenged by welfarist notions of individualised 'treatment' but neither completely supplanted the other. Instead, an awkward co-existence of welfare and justice imperatives consolidated a 'penal-welfare complex' (Garland, 1985: 262), within which policies and practices could no longer simply be seen as either singularly humanitarian or exclusively repressive.

The 1920s witnessed a resurgence of interest in children and crime, not least among academic psychologists. Although the crime rate had decreased during the war years (1914–18) it had started to rise in the 1920s during the period of 'Great Depression'. However, despite the likely relation binding widespread poverty, unemployment, hardship and crime, the conceptual emphasis was placed at the level of family relationships and individual personality. Medico-psychological perspectives became very influential within which the work of Cyril Burt exercised particular purchase. Burt (1925: viii) conflated notions of neglect and delinquency and argued that addressing juvenile crime was 'but one inseparable portion of the larger enterprise for child welfare'. In January 1925 a Home Office Departmental Committee on the Treatment of Young Offenders (the Molony Committee) was established with a broad remit to investigate the treatment of 'offenders' under the age of 21, together with children and young people who as a result of deprivation were in need of 'protection and training'. The Committee reported:

> . . . there is little or no difference in character and needs between the neglected and the delinquent child. It is often a mere accident whether he is brought before the court because he is wandering or beyond control or because he has committed some offence. (Home Office, 1927: 6)

The emphasis was clearly placed on welfare and the need to either *reclaim* the deprived child (the victim) or *reform* the depraved child (the threat).

Welfare priorities were further consolidated through the Children and Young Persons Act 1933 which endorsed the principal recommendations of the Molony Committee. A specially selected panel of magistrates would preside over juvenile proceedings; the age of criminal responsibility was raised from 7 to 8; the juvenile court would adjudicate over civil and criminal matters; and all such adjudications should always 'have regard for the welfare of the child'. Similarly, the 1933 Act abolished the distinction between Reformatory and Industrial Schools renaming them Approved Schools, that is 'schools approved by the secretary of state'.

Further to the Second World War (1939–45) the inherent tensions and contradictions between 'welfare' and 'justice' policy priorities re-surfaced. The post-war Labour government, under the leadership of Clement Attlee (1945–51), engaged with an ambitious and wide-ranging legislative programme which included a Criminal Justice Bill in 1947. The Bill, and the subsequent Criminal Justice Act 1948, contained mixed provisions. On the one hand it placed a number of restrictions on the use of custodial detention for children and young people. In this sense it was consistent with the welfarist spirit of other key elements of social policy underpinning post-war reconstruction and the development of the Welfare State (The Family Allowances Act 1945; The National Health Service Act 1946; The National Insurance Act 1946; The National Assistance Act 1948; and The Children Act 1948). On the other hand, however, it bowed to pressure from the Magistrates Association for a new custodial sentence for children and young people whose behaviour was thought to be too challenging for the Approved Schools. This was provided by the Detention Centre Order designed to deliver a short but rigorous custodial experience to 'the type of offender' – to borrow the words of the Home Secretary, Chuter Ede – 'to whom it is necessary to give a short but sharp reminder that he is getting into ways that will inevitably lead him into disaster' (cited in Newburn, 1995: 132).

Indeed, the political management of the 'welfare–justice' tensions were particularly problematic for the Attlee administration as Harris and Webb (1987: 20) have noted: 'on the one hand it sought to hold on to criminal justice as part of its social reform policies, but on the other those very same policies rendered crime less explicable and less justifiable'. Equally, the political context was further complicated by the competing interests of the developing 'professional' constituencies. Social workers, probation officers, teachers, police officers, magistrates, prison officers and various residential institutions each competed for power and influence. Similarly, the academic 'experts' from psychology, sociology and criminology tussled both within their disciplines, and between them, in the course of debating their various aetiological accounts and proffering their respective policy prescriptions in respect of juvenile crime. The complexities of the welfare–justice relation were thus compounded by the 'professionalisation' of the Welfare State, within which the burgeoning 'welfare' and 'justice' bureaucracies were minded to protect their interests, expand their authority and extend their reach.

THE ASCENDANCY OF 'WELFARE' AND 'WELFARISM'

... the late 1960s ... have been seen as the high-water mark of reform in the field of juvenile delinquency; they represented, apparently, the triumph of 'welfare' as the dominant ideology. (Blagg and Smith, 1989: 99)

No defence can be offered . . . against the empirical reality that welfare oriented disposals can be unduly harsh; nor can it be contended seriously that crime is a disease to be cured. (Harris, 1982: 258)

By the mid- to late 1950s the Home Office was being pressed both by liberal child welfare 'experts' (increasingly concerned with the relation between family breakdown and juvenile crime), and by the Magistrates Association (whose interests inevitably rested with the role of the courts in balancing 'welfare' and 'justice'), to undertake a review of the juvenile justice process. Accordingly, in 1956 the Home Office, under the instructions of the Conservative Government (1951–64), established a departmental committee (the Ingleby Committee) to address the key issues that were being raised. The Ingleby Report, which was presented in 1960, recommended that the sentencing powers of the courts should be extended but it also proposed that the age of criminal responsibility should be raised from 8 to 12. The Children and Young Persons Act 1963 struck a compromise and raised the age of criminal minority to 10.

The recommendations of the Ingleby Committee disappointed many who had anticipated more radical proposals to 'decriminalise' elements of the justice process and to establish instead a more unified family (and welfare) oriented service. Prior to its election in 1964, the Labour Party had established a Study Group which prepared a report entitled 'Crime: A Challenge to Us All', otherwise known as the Longford Report (after its Chair, Lord Longford). The observations and recommendations of the Longford Report went substantially further than those of the Ingleby Committee, proposing that child 'offenders' should be removed from the jurisdiction of the criminal courts altogether as offending manifested 'the child's need for skilled help and guidance' (Labour Party, 1964: 28). The Longford Report underpinned the Labour Party's 1965 White Paper 'The Child, the Family and the Young Offender'. The White Paper proposed the abolition of the juvenile court and its replacement with a non-judicial 'Family Council' which would be an integral element of a unified 'Family Service'.

Inevitably the radical proposals contained within the Longford Report and the 1965 White Paper sparked exactly the kind of inter-agency power struggles that we referred to above. In particular magistrates, legal professionals and the police ('natural' allies of the Conservative Party in Opposition since the 1964 election), strongly objected to what they saw to be a significant diminution of their power and influence and made the strongest representations to government. Consequently, and no doubt mindful of its small Parliamentary majority, the Labour administration compromised. The 1968 White Paper, 'Children in Trouble', diluted key elements of the previous proposals without totally dispensing with their underpinning principles, and in so doing managed to draw the competing political, administrative and professional constituencies into a manageable consensus. The juvenile court was to survive (the 'justice' constituency) but the power and influence of social workers (the 'welfare' constituency) was to be substantially extended. This settlement found legislative embodiment in the Children and Young Persons Act 1969.

However, the new consensus barely concealed resistance and antagonism to the more radical elements of the 1969 Act, not least that derived within the upper echelons of the Conservative Party. In 1970 it was indeed the Conservative Party who triumphed at the polls, and as a result the Children and Young Persons Act was only partially implemented. The new 'welfare'-oriented system, far from supplanting the old 'justice' system, was in effect rather clumsily grafted on to it and the result ultimately spelt disaster for children who came before the juvenile courts:

> If one compares the sections of the Act that were implemented and those that were not, the answer is obvious: a new system came in but the old one did not go out . . . the two systems came to some form of accommodation . . . the old system simply expands in order to make room for the newcomer . . . the two systems have, in effect, become vertically integrated, and an additional population of customer-clients has been identified in order to ensure that they both have plenty of work to do. (Thorpe et al., 1980: 22–3)

In other words, ostensibly benign welfarism effectively extended and intensified processes of state-managed social control. Social work was given legislative licence to 'assess', 'intervene', 'care' and 'treat' but such 'welfare' dispositions co-existed with the punitive armoury of the 'justice' system: the juvenile court, the Detention Centre, the Borstal. Well-meaning, but too often ill-considered, social work intervention engaged children in 'treatment' programmes in the belief that they would 'do good' and offset the likelihood of further delinquency. When such approaches 'failed', as they infrequently did, then children were exposed to equally interventionist 'justice' disposals. The net result of ostensible 'humanitarianism' and 'reliance on the experts' (however well-intentioned they might have been), produced a 'widening of the net', a 'blurring of boundaries' and ultimately a 'diversification of penality' (Harris and Webb, 1987: 161–6). The ultimate consequence was that throughout the 1970s there was a massive increase of children confined either to residential placements in 'care' homes, and/or to periods of custodial detention within penal institutions.

THE ASCENDANCY OF 'JUSTICE'

> I think there is now a fairly wide consensus about what the response to juvenile offending should be . . . formal intervention should be kept to a minimum, consistent with the circumstances and seriousness of each case. (John Patten, Conservative Minister 1988, cited in Goldson, 1997b: 126)

> If anything, I have become firmer in my belief that penal custody remains a profoundly unsatisfactory outcome for children. (Virginia Bottomley, Conservative Minister 1988, cited in Goldson, 1997b: 126)

By the end of the 1970s the concepts of 'welfare' and 'treatment' in respect of juvenile justice had become almost synonymous with excessive intervention and intensified control. It was now received wisdom that the road to care and custody had too often been paved by the unintended consequences of benign intentions. Moreover, the election of a Conservative government in 1979, under the leadership of Margaret Thatcher, generated additional concerns. Newburn (1997: 642) describes the 1979 Conservative manifesto as 'the most avowedly "law and order" manifesto in British political history': it 'promised, among many other measures, to strengthen sentencing powers with respect to juveniles'. Indeed, the 1980 White Paper 'Young Offenders' proposed the re-introduction of Detention Centres with tough regimes designed to deliver a 'short, sharp, shock' (not unlike the provisions of the Criminal Justice Act 1948 – see above), and William Whitelaw, the Home Secretary, warned that the children and young people 'who attend them will not ever want to go back' (cited in Newburn, 1997: 642).

It was against this antagonistic backdrop that support developed for an approach to juvenile crime which was essentially informed by a classical justice model and which emphasised that the intensity of intervention/ punishment should be proportionate to the seriousness of the child's crime (as distinct from responding to their perceived 'needs'); that the same intervention/punishment should be determinate in accordance with sentences fixed by the court (as distinct from the relatively indeterminate nature of 'welfare' interventions); that administrative/professional discretion based upon spurious 'assessments' and 'needs' should be curtailed; that equality of treatment should prevail within the justice process; and that children's legal rights should be protected by proper representation and due process. Such an approach consolidated around three fundamental principles: diversion, decriminalisation and decarceration, which formed the cornerstones of an innovatory and unified practice and which was supported, in the words of Rutherford (1995: 57), by 'one of the most remarkably progressive periods of juvenile justice policy'.

The legitimacy for this 'new orthodoxy' was rooted in a paradoxical coalescence and coincidence of four otherwise disparate (even contradictory) concerns. First, elements of academic research. Second, professional practice developments within juvenile justice (informed by the lessons of the 1970s). Third, specific policy objectives of Thatcherite Conservatism. Fourth, the stated imperatives of the police and the courts to reduce the incidence of juvenile crime. Each of these 'concerns' combined to form a delicately balanced consensus which was to guide juvenile justice policy and practice through the decade of the 1980s and into the 1990s.

Academic research provided a consistent stream of evidence demonstrating that most juvenile offending was petty, opportunistic and transitory and that the majority of children 'grow out of it'. Similarly, the academics argued persuasively that premature and over-zealous intervention not only hampered the process of growing out of crime but it also, by the formal application of criminal 'labels', served to stigmatise children, trigger negative social reaction to them, and thus compound the likelihood of further delinquency. Such evidence was embraced by juvenile justice practitioners who applied it to 'decriminalising' children's relatively 'normal' deviant behaviour by diverting them from the formal state welfare/justice apparatus. Equally, research also confirmed that institutional and/or custodial responses to children and young people were damaging, expensive and counter-productive. Practitioners seized upon this too and developed imaginative community-based 'alternatives' to care and custody schemes.

The symbiosis of research and practice at this time developed within the space created by its paradoxical compatibility with specific policy objectives of the Thatcher administration. Indeed, throughout the 1980s the Conservative Party was committed to 'rolling back the frontiers of the state' and relieving the Treasury of some of its more onerous public spending commitments. In this respect little could be more appealing than to divert petty child offenders from the formal juvenile justice process, and to manage more serious child offenders within their working-class communities, at a fraction of what it would cost to send them to court and custody respectively. As Pratt (1987: 429) observed: 'to reduce the custodial population on the grounds of cost effectiveness . . . led to a general support for alternatives to custody initiatives'. Moreover, all of this was supported by 'respectable' academic evidence which confirmed its effectiveness. The new 'justice'-based approach to juvenile crime offered both economy *and* efficiency which was music to the ears of the New Right, notwithstanding its Law and Order rhetoric. Thus the government was keen to ensure that policy development accommodated the new juvenile justice practice.

The Criminal Justice Act 1982 imposed some tighter criteria for custodial sentencing and introduced the Specified Activities Order whereby a programme of community-based activities could be specified in court as an alternative to custodial detention. In 1983 the Department for Health and Social Security released £15 million for voluntary agencies, working in partnership with local authorities, to establish and develop community-based 'alternative to custody' projects for juveniles. The Criminal Justice Act 1988 tightened the criteria for custodial sentencing further, and in 1989 the Children Act abolished the Criminal Care Order that had been provided to such disastrous effect by the Children and Young Persons Act 1969, and finally removed all civil care proceedings from the juvenile court thus separating 'welfare' and 'justice' jurisdictions. Finally, the Criminal Justice Act 1991 consolidated the diversionary, decriminalising and decarcerative priorities in relation to juvenile justice which had developed throughout the 1980s offering, via the establishment of the Youth Court, the prospect of extending such practices to include 17-year-olds. Further, the 1991 Act abolished prison custody for 14-year-old boys, provided for the similar abolition of penal remands for 15–17-year-olds (although this provision has never been implemented), and placed a duty on all those engaged within the criminal justice system to 'avoid discriminating against people on the grounds of race or sex or any other improper reason'. This was the first time that such a provision had ever appeared in criminal law and it implicitly signalled an acknowledgement of the institutionalised injustices within the 'justice' process together with a commitment to remove them. The combined effect of all of this produced a very dramatic increase in diversionary practices (Goldson, 2000: 42–5), and an equally impressive reduction in the numbers of children and young people being sent to custodial institutions (Goldson, 1999: 6).

However, the consensus that bound academics, practitioners (from across the broadest range of criminal justice agencies) and right-wing Conservative politicians was always fragile. Indeed, as subsequent events were to prove, its fragility was exposed once its political expedience had been exhausted. Despite the quite remarkable success of juvenile justice policy and practice throughout the 1980s and early part of the 1990s, once political priorities required a new strain of authoritarianism all that had been achieved was soon lost and a quite different consensus emerged.

PUNISHMENT, RETRIBUTION AND THE NEW CORRECTIONAL CONSENSUS

It is a fact well known to students of social policy that reforms of the system often take place not so much because of careful routine analysis by ministers and civil servants in the relevant Department of State . . . but because one or more individual incident(s) occurs, drawing public attention to . . . policy in a dramatic way which seems to demand change. (Bottoms and Stevenson, 1992: 23–4)

Crime is an emotional subject and visceral appeals by politicians to people's fears and resentments are difficult to counter. It is easy to seize the low ground in political debates about crime policy. When one candidate campaigns with . . . promises that newer, tougher policies will work, it is difficult for an opponent to explain that crime is a complicated problem, that real solutions must be long term, and that simplistic toughness does not reduce crime rates. This is why, as a result, candidates often compete to establish which is tougher in his [sic] views about crime. (Tonry, 1996: 179)

By the early part of the 1990s two burgeoning processes, and one extra-ordinary event, conjoined to underpin an authoritarian backlash to the juvenile justice policy and practice which had emerged and developed throughout the previous decade.

First, although Conservative governments during the 1980s had been content to tolerate the development of progressive diversionary and decarcerative practices, such tolerance only extended so far as it suited key elements of their wider political project. Indeed, whilst it would not be true to say that the juvenile justice policies of the 1980s were solely a cynical product of the drive to cut public expenditure, it is unlikely that they would have commanded such wide support had they not been so compatible with that objective. In other words, Tory antipathy to public expenditure provided a paradoxical benefit for children in trouble. However, the very same determination to cut spending on public services also had a catastrophic effect on working-class children's welfare. Child poverty expanded and intensified between 1979 and 1987 during which time the proportion of children living below 50 per cent of average income, and the number of children living in households dependent upon supplementary benefit and family income supplement, doubled. By the mid-1990s the prevalence of child poverty was higher in Britain than any other country in the European Union. Similarly, during this same period a combination of hardening ideology, marketisation and financial retrenchment meant that increasing numbers of children and young people were permanently excluded from schools, the youth and community service was pared back, and structural unemployment cut deep into youth labour markets (Goldson, 1997c). The misery, alienation and institutionalised exclusion that was an inevitable product of such neglect was crudely caricatured and ideologically exploited. Before long the same children who had benefited from the 'progressive' juvenile justice policies and practices (but who had simultaneously suffered from swingeing cuts in public services) were being conceptualised as a dangerous, immoral and dysfunctional 'underclass' necessitating discipline and control.

Second, the fortunes of the Conservative Party, particularly in the opinion polls, were beginning to wane. The triumphalist spirit of the Thatcher years had been replaced by a distinctly more subdued and less confident mood under John Major's stewardship. There were many within the influential Tory ranks who felt that the time was ripe for re-stating some traditional values and convictions. This dovetailed into a fermenting body of opinion that juvenile justice in particular, and penal liberalism in general, had gone too far. Both the media and the Police were beginning to regularly draw attention to car crime, youth disorder, children offending whilst on court bail, and children who they described as 'persistent offenders'. The Police had always been rather reticent (if not reluctant) partners during the consensus decade of the 1980s, and they now began to distance themselves from it. A crude, reductionist assimilation of disparate behaviours amongst children was assembled and, in virtually no time, the fragility of the consensus which bound together more than ten years of effective juvenile justice policy and practice developments was exposed.

Third, in February 1993 an extraordinary event was to cement the authoritarian backlash. The murder of a 2-year-old child, James Bulger, and the subsequent conviction of two 10-year-old children, was shamefully hijacked to serve political interest. The atypicality of the case was disregarded and instead it was portrayed as the ultimate expression of child lawlessness. Within days of the toddler's death the Prime Minister, John

Major, was proclaiming that the time had come for 'society to condemn a little more and understand a little less', and the Home Secretary, Kenneth Clarke, referred to the scourge of 'really persistent nasty little juveniles'. Three months later and after a Cabinet re-shuffle, Michael Howard made his first public pronouncement as the new Home Secretary. Howard referred to 'a self-centred arrogant group of young hoodlums . . . who are adult in everything except years' and who 'will no longer be able to use age as an excuse for immunity from effective punishment . . . they will find themselves behind bars' (cited in Goldson, 1997b: 130).

By 1993 the combined effect of waning political fortunes, rumbling reactionary concerns and an extreme incident had dramatic effect. Child offenders became the new 'enemy within'. Moral panic and demonisation was mobilised with unprecedented impact. The language of punishment and retribution could be heard everywhere as juvenile crime was effectively (re)politicised. Moreover, this was more than symbolic gesture: it cut to the very core of state policy formation (Goldson, 2001).

Within months of the implementation of the Criminal Justice Act 1991 (October 1992) the Criminal Justice Act 1993 was hastily drafted to introduce measures which had particularly unfavourable implications for child offenders. Moreover, the specific sections of the Criminal Justice and Public Order Act 1994 that related to children, introduced a fierce tone of punishment and retribution. Such provisions included the introduction of new privately run Secure Training Centres (children's jails) for the incarceration of 12–14-year-olds (which reversed a trend in juvenile justice policy dating back to the 1908 Children Act), and the doubling of the maximum sentence of detention in Young Offender Institutions for 15–17-year-olds. However, the new mood of 'Law and Orderism' was not the sole preserve of the Conservative Party. The cadres and spin-doctors from the re-styled New Labour project were equally keen to seize the authoritarian moment, and the glue binding a cross-party correctional consensus began to set. Michael Howard argued that to take account of children's disadvantaged backgrounds in analyses of juvenile crime was to 'take the criminals' side' and to succumb to 'excuses' from 'bleeding heart' social workers and probation officers who are a 'relic from the 1970s'. New Labour, in its first official detailed statement with regard to juvenile crime when it was in Opposition, observed that:

> . . . punishment is important as a means of expressing society's condemnation of misbehaviour. . . . Young offenders need to be held to account for their actions . . . all this is common sense . . . ultimately the welfare needs of the young offender cannot outweigh the needs of the community to be protected from the adverse consequences of his or her offending behaviour. The government seems to have lost sight of this guiding principle. We intend to restore it, changing the law if necessary. (Cited in Goldson, 1999: 9)

Indeed, the correctional consensus survived the potentially disrupting impact of the 1997 General Election. The return of a (New) Labour government, following eighteen years of unbroken Conservative rule, represented continuity as distinct from change with regard to the imperatives of punishment and retribution underpinning juvenile justice policy. New Labour had pledged to be 'tough on crime' and within months of the May 1997 election the government produced a raft of 'consultative' documentation, soon followed by a White Paper, rather ominously entitled *No More Excuses: A New Approach to Tackling Youth Crime in England and Wales*. New legislation soon ensued. The Crime and Disorder Bill commenced its passage through Parliament in December 1997 and the Youth Justice and Criminal Evidence Bill was introduced in the House of Lords on 3 December 1998. The first Bill received Royal Assent on 31 July 1998 and the second on 27 July 1999. The Crime and Disorder Act 1998 is an extraordinarily wide-ranging and intrusive piece of legislation which is substantially weighted towards 'tackling' youth crime. Part 1 of the Youth Justice and Criminal Evidence Act 1999 provides for programmes of early intervention targeted at children at first conviction, and in this sense it is reminiscent of the interventionist priorities which underpinned the Children and Young Persons Act 1969 with such disastrous effect.

It is beyond the remit of this chapter to subject the latest policy developments with regard to children and crime to detailed scrutiny (see Goldson, 1999, 2000; Muncie, 1999; Pitts, 2001). However, there is little evidence to suggest that the mood of 'toughness', and the punitive and retributive priorities that characterise contemporary responses to children in trouble, will be immediately surpassed. Conversely, there is ample evidence to confirm that the current direction of policy will continue to swell the population of incarcerative institutions for children.

The numbers of imprisoned 15-, 16- and 17-year-olds almost doubled in the five years between June 1993 and June 1998. During the same period the number of 15–17-year-old boys as a proportion of the total population sentenced to custody more than doubled, and the corresponding figure for girls more than trebled. On 31 March 2000, 1,708 children and young people were serving sentences in prisons in England and Wales and many others were remanded in similar institutions whilst awaiting trial or sentence. Indeed, the most recent official statistics evidence the fact that in England and Wales the number of prisoners, including children and young people, expressed as a rate per 100,000 of the population, is the highest in Western Europe with one single exception. At the time of writing, the *complete* statistical details with specific regard to children and young people held in penal and secure institutions (including the Secure Training Centres referred to above, and other locked institutions) are yet to be published. Notwithstanding this, informed impression is such to suggest a continuing and increased reliance on custodial responses, the extent and precise nature of which has even exceeded official expectation (Goldson and Peters, 2000). However, New Labour is not to be deterred and has recently announced a £250 million 'reform plan' to 'buy 400 new places in the independent sector' (private jails) for the purposes of incarcerating children (Youth Justice Board, 2001). There can be no clearer expression of punitive and retributive intent.

CONCLUSION: WHICH CHILDREN, WHAT JUSTICE?

> In difficult times, it is tempting to avert the gaze from problems whose remedy will require a profound reorganisation of social and economic life and to fasten one's eyes, instead, on the promise that the continuity of things as they are can be somehow enforced by the imposition of social order and discipline 'from above' ... the construction of this 'Law and Order' consensus, the forging of the disciplinary common sense, is one of the most troubling features ... we must speak, not only of the tendency towards the authoritarian state, but rather of the production of an *authoritarian populism*. (Hall, 1982: 3–4, original emphasis)

Since childhood was institutionalised, since children were conceptually 'born', adult ambivalence has prevailed. Childhood is conceived as an ambiguous state, and children (at least some children) are variously understood as 'victims' who need protection, nurturing and care, or 'threats' who require correction, discipline and control. Herein lies the 'welfare–justice' relation which, as we have seen, has applied to juvenile justice policy for the best part of two centuries. Within this broad framework, 'children', 'crime', 'welfare' and 'justice' are dynamic constructs which are subject to constant definition and re-definition, construction and re-construction, invention and re-invention, and classification and re-classification. Such processes are influenced (if not determined) by socio-economic and political priorities and can only be understood within such contexts. There are also complex sets of (often competing) interests which impact upon the determination of policy and practice and a chapter such as this can do little more than offer a schematic overview.

What remains relatively constant within such dynamic processes, however, is the constituency of children who are located at the centre of the state's gaze, together with the overriding imperative to subject such children to control and regulation however that is nuanced. In this sense we may want to question the extent to which it is even legitimate to refer to juvenile *justice* when the 'justice' apparatus both emanates from, and presides over, a system which consistently produces and re-produces such flagrant *injustices*. It is neither coincidence nor accident that working-class children have always comprised the fodder of the juvenile 'justice' system, the very same system that routinely dispenses gendered and racialised injustices. Indeed, we may care to ponder whether *juvenile justice* can indeed ever be delivered without first securing *social justice*. Such questions are difficult and discomforting but to 'avert the gaze from problems whose remedy will require a profound reorganisation of social and economic life', and 'to fasten one's eyes, instead, on the promise that the continuity of things as they are can be somehow enforced by the imposition of social order and discipline "from above"' apparently leaves us with little alternative to 'authoritarian populism' and correctional consensus.

KEY TEXTS

Goldson, B. (ed.) (1999) *Youth Justice: Contemporary Policy and Practice*. Aldershot: Ashgate.
Goldson, B. (ed.) (2000) *The New Youth Justice*. Lyme Regis: Russell House.
Muncie, J. (1999) *Youth and Crime: A Critical Introduction*. London: Sage.

TEN

Child Abuse and Child Protection

BRIAN CORBY

INTRODUCTION

In the following chapter consideration will be given to how child protection policy and practice in Britain has historically been (and still is) influenced by a range of often contradictory ideas about childhood, paternalism, state intervention into family life, parents' rights and children's rights. It will aim to demonstrate how the interplay of these concepts has influenced child protection policy and practice in a way that has been both beneficial and harmful to children. It will conclude with an analysis of the current child protection scene and consider ways of understanding and responding to child abuse issues which are most likely to achieve improved outcomes for children, parents and society as a whole.

Before turning to these considerations, it is important to try and achieve some clarity about the concepts we are using. All are contested ideas with a variety of meanings.

Childhood

As has already been noted (Lavalette and Cunningham, this volume), there is a great deal of academic controversy over the historical development of the notion of childhood with particular disagreements between those taking a biological essentialist line (Pollock, 1983) and social constructionists (Ariès, 1962). For the former, the law of survival of the fittest rules, and it is clear that, in all species (animal and human) the young depend on adults for survival. Hence, childhood is a biological given determining the behaviours of children and parents. In contrast, social constructionists argue that childhood represents a way of thinking about the young which is determined by social and economic values. Ariès took this to an extreme in his work by arguing that until the sixteenth century there was no concept of children being different from adults because of their age and there was no need to treat them differently. Most social constructionists take a less extreme view, placing more emphasis on how notions of childhood and of ways of treating children are by no means fixed and can change rapidly in response to social and economic shifts. They are also more aware of how ideas about childhood can be used to control and shape children's experiences.

Paternalism

In the field of childhood studies, the notion of paternalism has tended to be negatively viewed in that it implies a disregard of children's freedoms and rights to self-determination. However, it should be noted that paternalism and childhood are concepts that are inextricably linked. The notion of paternalism cannot logically exist without a notion of childhood and vice versa. While there are obvious dysfunctions associated with the way in which paternalism can be (and has been) used, we need to be reminded of the fact that some degree of paternalism is necessary for children's survival and may have a considerable influence on children's future life-chances. Both philosophers (Scarre, 1980) and attachment theorists (Bowlby, 1971) have cogently argued this case.

State interventionism

The role of the state in intervening in families is a key issue for child protectionists. It is generally accepted in 'developed' societies that outside intervention is justified when children are considered to be at risk of serious harm within their families. However, the issues are rarely clear-cut, and in Britain there has traditionally been much circumspection about intervening into families. This is reflected in our legal system, the over-riding principle of which is that unless families (i.e. parents) consent, courts must decide about the rights and wrongs of state intervention. The only exception to this is in the case of emergencies where children are considered to be at immediate risk of significant harm. The extent and degree of state intervention into families is therefore highly contestable and this to some degree accounts for the 'fits and starts' nature of our responses to child abuse, and in particular for the swings between the more family-supportive and more directly child-protective approaches to safeguarding children which are outlined below. It should be noted that different countries do have different emphases in this respect. In France, for instance, where it should be noted that voluntary intervention into family life is also preferred, the scales of justice are more weighted against parental challenges to statutory authority than here (Lucock et al., 1996).

Parents' rights

Parents' rights with regard to the determination of their children's welfare and development are, as indicated above, largely supported in law.

However, where harm to children is apparent, these rights become challengeable. Nevertheless, even in these circumstances, there is considerable reluctance to dispense with parents' rights completely, except in the most extreme circumstances where adoption may be the ultimate outcome of intervention. As will be seen, currently there is considerable focus on preserving parents' rights in the process of child protection intervention, and of supporting parents in cases where they are struggling to provide adequate care for their children.

Linked to the concept of parents' rights is the notion of *parental responsibility*, which was introduced by the Children Act 1989. This concept emphasises parental duties and obligations rather than their rights. While to some degree this may work to enhance parental care it can also be used by the state to reduce its responsibility to ensure that deprived parents have the means of providing adequate support and care for their children (see Eekelaar, 1991).

Children's rights

Often deriving their theoretical underpinnings from social constructionist perspectives, children's rights advocates take a political stance on issues relating to children. The main tenets of their arguments are that societal views about children are essentially drawn from an adult perspective and that, therefore, they fail to do justice to children's own views. As a consequence they reinforce the notions of 'passive' children, thereby increasing their vulnerability to and their dependence on adults. The assertion of the rights of children, based on acknowledgement of their subjective view of the world and their ability to make key decisions for themselves, is seen as a key requirement for improving children's current and later life experiences.

It will be argued in what follows that of all the areas of policy and practice concerning children, it is in the field of child protection where the debates and controversies between and around the perspectives briefly outlined above are most acutely tested.

CHILD ABUSE: AN OVERVIEW

Physical and sexual abuse of children: early developments

The protection of children in Britain is closely associated with developments that took place in the 1960s and 1970s following the 'discovery' of baby battering by Henry Kempe and his colleagues in the USA (Kempe et al., 1962). Of course, the abuse of children and subsequent attempts to protect them has a much longer history than that (see Behlmer, 1982).

However, what was distinctive about Kempe's contribution was the emphasis placed on the cross-class nature of child abuse and its psychological and emotional causes. Previously, child protection concerns had centred around neglect of and cruelty to children in poor and 'disorganised' families. Intra-familial physical abuse of children dominated child protection concerns in Britain until the mid-1980s, though, despite Kempe's theorising, the focus of state concern remained on the children of the poor (see Creighton and Noyes, 1989).

In the mid-1980s sexual abuse of children within families became a key concern of child protection workers in Britain, again drawing from the American experience. As with physical abuse, emotional/psychological causal factors were emphasised by American theorists, including Kempe again (see Kempe and Kempe, 1978) and Giaretto (1981). Another key contribution with a different aetiological explanation came from feminist theorists (Russell, 1986) and activists (Rush, 1980), who identified male power, hegemony and socialisation as the key causal factors of such abuse. Such theorists also argued that sexual abuse of children was a cross-class phenomenon, and was not confined to families in that females were vulnerable to such abuse in many different types of setting outside the family (e.g. on the streets and at work). The British response was, nevertheless, to focus on intra-familial sexual abuse and, as with physical abuse, the focus of attention was largely on poor families (see Sharland et al., 1996).

Neglect

Neglect of children within families has a more varied history. It has always been associated with poverty and was indeed the main focus of state intervention to protect children prior to the modern 'discovery' of child abuse. Until the mid-1990s, however, concerns about neglect were relatively muted for a variety of reasons (see Wolock and Horowitz, 1984), not least because physical and sexual abuse of children dominated the attention of child protection agencies.

Emotional/psychological abuse

In the 1980s, again originating in the USA, child protection practitioners and researchers started to look at emotional/psychological abuse as a separate form of child mistreatment (as opposed to its manifestation as a consequence of physical and sexual abuse and neglect). Hard to define specifically, this form of abuse included being exposed to family violence, being humiliated, verbally abused and treated in a cold and indifferent way by parents (Garbarino and Vondra, 1987). In England and Wales such abuse was increasingly cited as a reason for child protection registration in the 1980s and 1990s.

The above-mentioned forms of child abuse still constitute the main causes for concern and reasons for child protective intervention in Britain, but the 1990s have seen a widening of concern to include other forms of abuse and in particular abuse of children outside the family.

Extra-familial abuse

The main 'new' forms of abuse include institutional abuse (see Stanley, 1999), organised abuse (Bibby, 1996), ritual abuse (La Fontaine, 1994), bullying (Smith and Sharp, 1994) and child prostitution (Barnardos, 1998). In addition there is considerable concern about children as abusers (both physical and sexual) (Erooga and Masson, 1999). In general terms, there has been a shift from exclusive concern about abuse of children by adults in families, to all forms of ill-treatment of children by all sorts (and ages) of abuser in a wide range of settings and situations. There is also now particular emphasis on the psychological damage incurred by all forms of abuse which has led to greater awareness of children's needs. In what follows, consideration will be given to how the concepts of childhood, paternalism, parents' and children's rights, together with the key issue of state intervention in family life, have influenced and helped shape some of the policy and practice developments outlined above.

PHYSICAL ABUSE, CHILDHOOD AND PATERNALISM

Physical abuse of children, as already noted, was the first of the forms of abuse recognised in recent times. Why it came to prominence within child protection when it did and in the way that it did are matters open to a good deal of speculation. Professional interests (Pfohl, 1977) and political reasons (Parton, 1985) have been put forward, but overriding these explanations are more general ones associated with shifts in thinking about childhood in affluent and so-called advanced societies. In the USA, Canada, Australia, New Zealand and Northern Europe, where standards of living were rising dramatically for the majority of their populations in the latter part of the twentieth century, concerns about child health and development gained far more prominence than before. Generally, the number of children born to each family was reducing and as a result children became more greatly prized than in previous generations. In more general terms, as the work of Beck (1992) has shown, the inhabitants of these societies developed expectations of being able to control risks and to live relatively risk-free lives. Factors such as these led to the belief that childhood should primarily be a safe time for children to explore and develop in secure surroundings. In such a climate the notion of children being physically ill-treated or neglected by their parents came to be seen as particularly unacceptable and requiring of external intervention. Until the late 1980s in Britain and many of the other countries referred to above, the response to these concerns was a relatively narrow one. The bigger picture of families in poverty and under stress was largely overlooked. Focus was firmly fixed on targeting specifically identified families (largely from the poorer sections of society) for child protection interventions, an approach that was backed by considerable political and public support. Indeed child protection professionals, particularly in Britain, were subjected to constant criticism for being insufficiently interventionist in cases where children were subsequently seriously or fatally abused (see Corby et al., 1998).

These developments did not arise from a children's rights perspective in its broadest sense, though there was a notion of children having the right to be protected from abuse. Rather, this was a period of increased state paternalism (see Fox Harding, 1991) driven by a largely adult perspective on the notion of childhood, i.e. that of a protected time preceding the rigours of being an adult. To some extent this was a period when parental rights and authority were being challenged with little apparent resistance. However, it should be noted that this model of child protection was essentially a conservative one in terms of family structures. It tended to pathologise only those families where child abuse took place (largely poorer families). There was no broader critique of the nuclear family as a potentially dangerous place for children. This was despite the fact that also at this time evidence was emerging of violent treatment of children within families being far more widespread than was reflected in official child protection statistics and activity (see Gelles and Cornell, 1985).

SEXUAL ABUSE, FEMINISM, PARENTS' AND CHILDREN'S RIGHTS

However, concerns about intra-familial sexual abuse, from the mid-1980s onwards, did lead to more questioning of family structures. As noted earlier, one of the driving forces behind the response to such abuse was a feminist analysis which laid the blame for abuse on gendered power imbalances both in the wider society and within the family. Research studies were also showing the incidence of intra-familial child sexual abuse to be much higher than previously thought possible (Baker and Duncan, 1985) – a further threat to the notion of the 'safe conventional family'. Armed with this knowledge, child protection professionals (particularly social workers) tackled families where sexual abuse was alleged in the same way as they did physical abuse, that is by direct protective intervention. Where the approach differed from physical abuse investigations was in relation to the need to draw evidence verbally from the child. In physical abuse and neglect cases, evidence of maltreatment was largely derived from the judgements of doctors about the cause of bruising, fractures and developmental delays. In sexual abuse cases where physical evidence was much less likely to be available, reliance had to be placed on the child's oral testimony. This was the case until the development of the Reflex Anal Dilatation test pioneered by two paediatricians in Leeds (Hobbs and Wynne, 1986). This test purported to provide evidence of anal abuse of children and was used in the Cleveland area in early 1987 (see Campbell, 1988). By the summer of that year, 121 children were in state care suspected of having been sexually abused, a rate of admission far exceeding anything that had gone before. Because of disputes between agencies in Cleveland about the rights and wrongs of the forms of action being taken to protect children, the child protection system effectively broke down.

The inquiry that ensued (Butler-Sloss, 1988) did not pass judgment on whether or not the children brought into care had been sexually abused. It was highly critical of the lack of inter-agency collaboration, and it called for caution in the use of unproven physical tests of sexual abuse. Key critic-isms, however, were reserved for the way in which child protection workers treated both parents and children in the process of the investi-gations that they carried out. Parents were considered not to have been reasonably informed of the reasons for their children being removed from their care and inadequately consulted about subsequent practices and procedures. Children were considered to have been subjected to too much and too intensive interviewing. Put simply, in contrast to the criticisms made about them in relation to physical abuse and neglect, child protection workers were seen to be insensitive and over-intrusive.

Cleveland was a watershed in thinking about, and responding to, child abuse in Britain. The state paternalism that had been at the heart of child protection in the 1970s and 1980s was now being seriously questioned. External political shifts to the right were emphasising family autonomy and questioning state intervention into family life. At the same time there was much questioning of professional authority and autonomy. Feminist writers, such as Campbell (1988), argued that the reaction at Cleveland was caused by patriarchal defence of the family from outside intervention.

Some of the recommendations of Cleveland were almost immediately incorporated into the Children Act 1989 and the associated child protection guidelines (Department of Health, 1991). The rights of parents to be properly informed of action to be taken (for example, by participating at child protection conferences), to be more fully involved in the decision-making process, and to be able to make legal challenges against key decisions (for example, in relation to emergency protection orders and contact) were affirmed. Similarly, children of sufficient age and under-standing were empowered to be more fully involved in decision-making (by also participating at child protection conferences), and to be granted greater rights of self-determination (for example, by being given the right to refuse medical examinations if they so wished).

ORGANISED AND RITUAL ABUSE, PARENTS AND CHILDREN'S RIGHTS

In the late 1980s and early 1990s there was a stream of concern about organised and ritual abuse, stemming largely from increased knowledge and awareness of child sexual abuse. The term 'organised abuse' includes intra-familial abuse (that is, abuse of children by more than one adult often across extended families and neighbourhood networks) and extra-familial abuse (particularly paedophile rings). This type of abuse is far less common than abuse by individuals but persists as a serious concern (see Bibby, 1996). Ritual abuse of children is a term largely associated with Satanic worship. Concerns about such abuse stemmed from literature drawn from the United States. There has been much controversy about this form of abuse – about its nature, extent and, indeed, its existence. Research commissioned by the Department of Health found that there was virtually no hard evidence that ritual abuse of children had taken place anywhere in Britain (La Fontaine, 1994). Nevertheless, the most publicised of the suspected ritual abuse cases, that in the Orkney Islands, resulted in an important inquiry which, like Cleveland, made a significant contribution to the development of child protection policy throughout Britain (Clyde, 1992). This report highlighted practices that were similar to those found in Cleveland five years earlier: summary removal of children from their parents with a minimum of explanation and communication about future plans, denial of contact, and repeated and intensive interviewing of children.

Later that year, central government issued a memorandum for good practice in interviewing children where serious child abuse was suspected (Home Office and the Department of Health, 1992). It recommended joint police and social work interviews of children conducted in a way which would first avoid the need for repeated interviews, and second produce evidence of sufficient standard to be used in court proceedings.

These developments, and those following on from Cleveland, could be seen as meeting both the interests and rights of parents and children, by both facilitating child protection and the rights of service-users in the process. However, what has happened could also be interpreted differently. We simply do not have sufficient information from service-users about whether they feel empowered by some of these measures. There was a large body of consumer study research commissioned by the Department of Health following Cleveland, which reported in 1995. However, its focus was not on responses to new developments, but more on their views of being on the receiving end of earlier forms of practice (Department of Health, 1995a). There is some information about service-users' views on participation at child protection conferences. The findings are varied. Some studies report a sense of greater involvement in the process (Thoburn et al., 1995). Others suggest that it is the style that has changed and not the substance and that service-users do not feel particularly empowered by participation policies (Corby et al., 1996). We have no information about service-users' views about joint police and social worker interviews. What we do know is that their success rate as measured in terms of successful prosecutions is very low (Social Services Inspectorate, 1994). Some analysts of the child protection field have argued that the new developments have had dysfunctional effects on children and child protection. They have pointed to a diminution of activity in response to child sexual abuse suspicions and allegations following Cleveland (see Corby, 1998). They have also concluded that joint interviews have hindered opportunities for children to disclose abuse rather than enhanced them (Westcott, 1999).

INSTITUTIONAL ABUSE

Alongside the developments already outlined in the 1990s there arose massive concern about abuse of children in residential settings. The last decade of the twentieth century saw a spate of inquiries and police investigations into such abuse, whereas, prior to this, there had been little evidence of concern (see Corby et al., 2001). Four main types of abuse have been identified: first, sexual abuse (carried out by individual care workers acting in secret); second, physical and emotional abuse (sometimes as a feature of the official regime and sometimes carried out covertly by individuals); third, the failure of a regime to protect a child from harm outside the home; and, fourth, failure to protect a child within the home from bullying from fellow residents. Key concerns have included: the failure of authorities to enable residents to make proper complaints; the failure to listen to complaints from residents and staff; the failure to respond protectively once complaints have been made; and the failure of inspection and other monitoring mechanisms to detect abusive regimes. Additionally, most inquiry reports have raised concerns about poor recruitment practices, low levels of qualification and training among residential workers, and lack of outside scrutiny and management of residential homes.

The growth of interest in the maltreatment of children in residential settings is clearly linked to the way in which concerns about the abuse of children living in their own homes have developed since the 1960s. Greater awareness about the risks to children within families, and about their needs for protection from physical and sexual abuse, have provided the conditions from which to consider the situation of children in care. Increased concern about the treatment of children in residential care is also linked to the shifts in relation to the value placed on childhood considered earlier. In some ways the outcries of concern about the safety of children *outside* their families are more acceptable to society in that they are less of a threat to mainstream family ideology. Certainly the ambivalence and uncertainty surrounding the investigation of intra-familial child abuse is not to be found in recent attempts to uncover institutional abuse. It is notable, for instance, that the notion of children's rights is more unequivocally accepted in this sphere than in relation to abuse of children within the family. One of the dysfunctional results of all the activity seen in the 1990s, however, is the discrediting of residential care generally as a resource for children separated from their families.

CURRENT THINKING ABOUT CHILD ABUSE AND FAMILY SUPPORT

The second half of the 1990s has witnessed some major transformations in thinking about, and responding to, child maltreatment. As noted earlier, by 1995 there was much confusion about the best way to deal with intra-familial child abuse in the wake of the Cleveland and Orkney inquiries, and research published in that year pointed to a need for greater emphasis on the broader welfare needs of children coming into child protection systems (Department of Health, 1995a). While the importance of maintaining an effective response to serious abuse cases was stressed, it was argued that most cases which came to child protection professionals' notice were not of that ilk. Many children (and their families) referred, had more general needs which frequently went unmet by welfare workers because of their narrow focus on child protection. As a consequence, there has been much emphasis placed by central government on creating a shift to ensure that there is more systematic assessment of all children referred to agencies as 'in need' and that child protection concerns are seen within a context of supporting families to address these needs (Department of Health, 2000a, 2000b). As yet it is too early to assess the impact of this change in policy.

REVIEWING DEVELOPMENTS

Much has happened in child protection work over the past thirty years and there have been many shifts in thinking about, and responding to, children generally during this period. Paradoxically, however, the net outcome of these shifts and developments is that there is much similarity between thinking about child protection assessment and intervention now and in the mid-1960s, particularly as far as abuse of children within families is concerned. We have returned to the more supportive, preventive approach to working with children and families that was characteristic of Children's Departments prior to their demise in 1970. Of course there are some differences. Welfare workers in the 1960s were not as aware of child abuse as we are today, and the prizing of childhood which, it is argued, lay at the heart of the rediscovery of child abuse, has continued and accelerated. Nevertheless, little progress has been made in terms of reducing child deaths (National Society for the Prevention of Cruelty to Children, 1999), and the numbers of children on protection registers (see Department of Health, 2000c), and the extent of undiscovered abuse, according to recent surveys (Cawson et al., 2001), remains high.

There have been relatively few major shifts in general thinking about relationships between children, parents and the state and their application to child protection practice. As noted above, concerns about abuse of children and the need to make childhood a better protected time have maintained the momentum that was gathered in the 1960s, but little else has changed to any great extent. There is still considerable ambivalence about state intervention into families, an ambivalence that, arguably, lies at the heart of current developments in adopting more family supportive methods of tackling child abuse and the rejection of more overtly protective approaches. There have been only minor concessions to children's rights in the process of dealing with child abuse allegations – for example, in relation to attendance at child protection conferences. Some of the measures adopted to enhance these rights, such as the Memorandum of Good Practice (Home Office and Department of Health, 1992) have arguably reduced the chances of more effective intervention, certainly in the case of sexual abuse. There has been some progress in relation to the rights of parents to be properly informed of issues of process in child protection investigations, rights which were certainly diminished in the late 1970s and through most of the 1980s. Some key new concepts relating to parental rights have been introduced, including those of parental responsibility and parental participation. These developments could be seen as enhancing parental rights in the child protection process, but they could also be seen as mechanisms for coercing parental involvement (see Corby et al., 1996).

By contrast, developments in relation to abuse of children outside the family have been more dramatic. Awareness of the risk to children of abuse outside the family is much greater than before, and children's rights to protection in residential care have been fully aired in inquiry and other reports (see Utting, 1997; Waterhouse, 2000). Better avenues of complaint have been opened up through Section 26 of the Children Act 1989, and by the appointment of Children's Rights Officers in England and Wales and a Children's Commissioner for Wales. New inspection procedures and whistle-blowing legislation are currently being promoted. Greater attention has been given to protecting children from organised abuse and child prostitution. One explanation of the contrasting developments in relation to extra-familial child abuse is that in many ways it is easier for the state to enhance children's rights to protection outside the family because there is no clash of interests between those of parents and children.

THE BROADER PICTURE

Most of the debate so far has been based on a notion that there is a fair degree of consensus about the nature and causes of child abuse, namely that it is a dysfunctional product of adult–child (and sometimes child–child) relationships. Children are seen as victims of vulnerable, stressed, inadequate and sometimes cruel and immoral adults who abuse their power and authority in a variety of ways. Similarly, most of the responses to child abuse derive from an agreed and relatively narrow perspective that there is need for a case-by-case approach involving childcare professional working as far as possible with children and families to assess and find solutions to problems by relieving stress, changing attitudes and behaviours, and in extreme cases by removing children from the family home. By and large, however, child protection policy-makers and practitioners have paid far less attention to the broader picture, i.e. the part played by social, cultural, economic and political factors on the causes of child abuse, and the way in which it is framed and responded to. For instance, the contribution of poverty and stress to child abuse is relatively neglected because of the political implications of taking such a stance.

Poverty and child abuse

Gil (1970), in the USA, was one of the first child abuse writers to raise the notion that the state might carry responsibility for child abuse in general because of the lack of adequate health, welfare and education services provided in poor neighbourhoods. Wolock and Horowitz (1984) have since argued that neglect of children has gained less attention in the USA than other forms of abuse because its causation has greater links with poverty, the extent of which the state is anxious to downplay. It is clear that poverty alone is not a sufficient explanation of the cause of child abuse. Most commentators would consider it important to take into account the emotional deficits of parents as well as the deprived circumstances in which they were living in order to understand why serious abuse and neglect takes place (Stevenson, 1998). Nevertheless, the bulk of officially registered child abuse cases are from poor families living in deprived neighbourhoods with low incomes, high lone-parent rates and a variety of stress factors including illnesses, disability and bereavements (Department of Health, 1995a).

Child poverty rates in Britain rose dramatically between the early 1980s and the mid-1990s, reaching a peak of about 4 million in the early 1990s (see Kumar, 1993). The current government's approach to child poverty is to raise the minimum wage, to encourage more parents to work and to improve daycare provision for children. How far these changes will impact on child protection work is questionable. The main thrusts of New Labour policy in this respect have been to place greater emphasis on systematic assessment of children's needs and on the teaching of parenting skills. So far, there has been little in the way of additional resources for families where children are deemed to be in need (Tunstill, 1997).

Children's rights and punishment

Similarly, there has been little focus on strengthening the position of children *vis-à-vis* adults by means of establishing broader and more far-reaching children's rights. A key opportunity has been lost in relation to use of physical punishment of children by their parents (see Freeman, 1999). In 1999 the European Court of Human Rights overturned a ruling made in the English courts that it had been lawful for a step-father to beat his 9-year-old son with a garden cane. This has led the UK government to consult with relevant bodies about the best way forward in relation to this issue (Department of Health, 2000d). However, the government has already made it clear that it will not follow the line of a large number of European countries which have already initiated a ban on all parental use of physical punishment. It is likely that it will remain lawful to smack children in England and Wales. For those advocating the development of children's rights as a means of combating child abuse, the continuing existence of parents' rights to hit children sets totally the wrong tone.

Gender, domestic violence and child abuse

Another key area to address at the broader level relates to gender and child abuse. While men are not alone in abusing children, they are more heavily implicated in sexual abuse (in over 95 per cent of all known offences) and, given the fact that they are likely to spend far less time in direct contact with children than women, they figure relatively highly in serious physical abuse cases. The impact of domestic violence (mainly a male activity) on children's emotional development is starting to be more fully acknowledged in research about child abuse (see Cleaver et al., 1999). By and large, however, the role of men and male socialisation at a more general level has not been as fully considered as it might have been (see Hearn, 1990). Only in the past few years has there been official policy progress in this area. The new *Working Together* guidelines (Department of Health, 2000b) highlight the issue of domestic violence and its impact on children's emotional development. In legislative terms, following the implementation of the Children Act 1989, and, more recently, of the Family Reform Act 1996, there are now greater opportunities for removing those suspected of abusing children (largely male) from the family home pending investigations. These developments are important ones that pose some key questions about how we view parents' rights. We have tended to see such rights as a joint matter in child protection work. It is clearly time to reconsider that and pay even more attention to protecting children by taking away the rights of one parent which may often be a male parent. On the more positive preventive side, we need to do far more to prepare young males for parenthood and sexual relationships than is currently the case.

More than intervention

Finally, in consideration of broader issues, it should be noted that in all the history of child protection work, the main focus of state intervention into families has been about how to investigate and initiate child protection work. Considerably less emphasis has been placed on preventive issues (see above) and on therapeutic and supportive work following on from investigations (see Oates and Bross, 1995). This arguably reflects state ambivalence about intervening into families in the first place, which as we have seen has dominated concerns throughout much of the 1990s (there may also be a resource issue here in that such services are relatively expensive). Yet our knowledge of the intermediate and longer-term consequences of child abuse (which has vastly increased over the past thirty years) suggests that we should be paying much more attention than we do to the kind of work that is carried out after early intervention (see Beitchmann et al., 1991, 1992). We now know that there are some well-established links between child abuse and mental illness (Read, 1998), violence (Lewis et al., 1989), low self-esteem (Howe, 1995) and parenting capacities (Egeland, 1988), for example. From this point of view, child protection work is as much a health as a policing issue. Recent developments in child protection policy, as noted above, have been more in the areas of prevention and initial assessments and not in the area of providing therapeutic and ongoing supportive services.

CONCLUDING COMMENTS

This chapter has reviewed the way in which thinking about child abuse and child protection has developed and changed over a period of almost forty years. It has examined how views about parents' and children's rights and the legitimacy of state intervention into family life have influenced these developments. This period has seen, first, a much more intrusive approach into families in order to protect children and, second, a shift back towards a more supportive approach. It has been argued that in the period between the early 1960s and the late 1980s, in the wake of growing affluence and smaller families, a new evaluation of childhood took place. This led to more intrusive intervention into family life to protect children deemed to be at risk of abuse. The 1990s saw a shift away from this approach towards a more family-supportive response to concerns about children increasingly described as 'in need'. At the same time much greater attention was placed on the mistreatment and abuse of children outside the family (particularly those living in residential homes and schools). It has been argued that a key catalyst in this change of emphasis was the 'discovery' of sexual abuse in the 1980s culminating in the Cleveland and Orkney inquiries. Events there led to a re-evaluation of the impact of state intervention into families. Feminist writers in particular explained this reaction by arguing that the 'discovery' of intra-familial abuse on the scale suggested by research was a threat to supporters of the nuclear family which in their view served mainly male interests.

It has also been argued that the return to a family-supportive approach has largely been welcomed by those who feel that the best way to reduce risks to children is to help parents who are often operating in difficult and deprived circumstances. Those advocating greater reliance on achieving these goals through strengthening the rights of children are more sceptical. Cutting across the parent–child debate is the feminist perspective which rejects the generic notion of parents and is greatly concerned by the lack of emphasis on gender issues in the shift back towards a family supportive approach.

Finally, it has been argued that, with the exception of the analysis put forward by feminist writers and a small number of radical commentators who have highlighted the impact of social exclusion on parenting and child mistreatment, the focus of attention of child protection policy in England and Wales has until recently been a narrow one. It has highlighted individual pathology as the key cause of child abuse and concentrated on developing systems and methods to tackle this problem at an individual level. In addition, it has placed particular emphasis on detection and intervention at the early stages and has been less focused on what happens afterwards in terms of provision of ongoing supportive and therapeutic resources. As a consequence, broader concerns have been neglected, namely the issue of child poverty, children's rights in general, male violence and its link to forms of socialisation, and dealing with the consequences of abuse. Clearly some of these issues are beyond the direct influence of child protection professionals and lie more squarely in the province of politicians, and it could, therefore, be argued that social workers and others in this field are best advised to focus on the immediate problems at the individual level. It is my view, however, that even on a case-to-case basis awareness and understanding of the political under-pinnings of child abuse situations are likely to enhance the quality of practitioners' interventions. More importantly, taking the longer view, it is more broad-based social change in relation to the enhancement of children's rights, the role of men in the family and an end to social exclusion that is most likely to have any real impact on the problem of child abuse that we currently face.

KEY TEXTS

Corby, B. (2000) *Child Abuse: Towards a Knowledge Base*, 2nd edn. Milton Keynes: Open University Press.

Parton, N. (ed.) (1997) *Child Protection and Family Support: Tensions, Contradictions and Possibilities*. London: Routledge.

Parton, N., Thorpe, D. and Wattam, C. (1996) *Child Protection, Risk and the Moral Order*. Basingstoke: Macmillan.

ELEVEN

Sex Education as Regulation

DEENA HAYDON AND PHIL SCRATON

INTRODUCTION

Ours is a moral cause, best expressed through how we see our families and our children. . . . Strong families cherished by a strong community. That is our national moral purpose. (Tony Blair, Labour Party Conference, September 1999)

In outlining his mid-term agenda for 'social justice', Prime Minister Tony Blair proclaimed the 'liberty to live in a free society' must be 'founded on rights and responsibilities'. The familiar theme was 'moral renewal'. He contrasted the potential of two babies born 'side by side' to different mothers. One to a mother with no job, no family and no male partner: 'for this child individual potential hangs by a thread'. The other to a 'prosperous home', extended family and employed father: 'Expectations are sky high, opportunities truly limitless'. In this crudely sketched world of polar opposites, Blair reconstructed the contrasting fortunes of each child as a morality tale. Seemingly ignoring their material contexts, he held up the 'family child' as an exemplar of the 'new moral order' central to New Labour's project.

This 1999 conference address came hard on the heels of a media-hyped moral panic concerning pre-teen pregnancy. Responding to disclosure that two 12-year-old girls had become mothers, Blair was 'appalled' and stated his conviction that this was a 'matter of anxiety and concern to anyone who believes in the future of this country'. Young people, he told the *Observer* (5 September 1999), had to be made aware of the 'undesirability of having sex at the age of 12' and parents had to 'take responsibility for their children. Twelve-year-old kids should not be on the streets at night'. What was necessary was a 'new national moral purpose for this new generation'.

Significant here was the uncomplicated, seemingly commonsense, presentation of 'moral purpose' as the goal and 'moral renewal' as the process – closely aligned with a view of childhood derived exclusively within heterosexual parenting and extended familial relations. Lone motherhood was condemned not because of material poverty but on the presumption of moral impoverishment. Pre-teen motherhood was explained not by a lack of understanding about sex and reproduction, or the abuse of power by male partners, but by weak parental responsibility and societal moral vacuum.

Placing himself at the eye of the storm over pre-teen pregnancy, the Prime Minister emphasised the sanctity of the family. He affirmed parental responsibility for children's behaviour, movements and decisions; for their moral awareness of 'right' and 'wrong'. These were the priorities for moral renewal which would encourage abstinence, keep children and young people off the streets and prevent them from having sex. Remarkably, given enlightened health and education initiatives and evidence from abroad, there was no mention of the effectiveness of sensitively delivered sex education. Instead, the issues were pushed back into the private domain; to the indiscriminate responses of parental discretion. This has been the persistent dynamic underpinning public outrage and political opportunism relating to 'revelations' about school nurses responding to sex-related questions in primary classrooms, head teachers and health professionals stating their support for provision of contraception to 'under-age' girls, or discussion about 'sexuality' within the school curriculum.

Whose responsibility should it be to provide sex/sexuality education? What is the relationship between state or parental responsibilities and children's rights to information, confidentiality, self-expression? What should be the content and context of sex/sexuality education? These are the questions with which this chapter is concerned. It is about the social construction of childhood and the politics of sex and sexuality. Moving from the historical context to theoretical perspectives about childhood, sex and sexuality, it analyses shifts in policy and concludes by considering the implications of establishing a positive children's rights agenda for sex and sexuality education.

SEX EDUCATION: THE LEGACY OF SOCIAL HYGIENE

'Preparation for adult life' has been an enduring objective of state education, with official policy reinforcing gendered roles and responsibilities according to age and class. Within this political and ideological context, school-based sex education – defined by legislation, policies and non-statutory guidance – has developed. More broadly, sex education has its roots in tensions between the purist and social hygienist movements at the turn of the nineteenth century. Purist medical and moral discourses promoted chastity and marital continence as antidotes to the assumed moral degeneration and sexual promiscuity of the poor, seeking regulation through legislation (e.g., the criminalisation of prostitutes). In contrast, social hygienists argued that sexual instincts were positive, evolutionary forces when geared to reproduction within a moral context. Female and male sexualities were polarized to conform with 'natural' biological and social roles. Female promiscuity was considered a threat to boys, and girls were expected to help men act responsibly by behaving in appropriately feminine ways and refusing familiarity. However, key social hygienists identified motherhood – pregnancy, childbirth and lactation – as positive dimensions of women's sexual, sensual and spiritual experiences. Eugenicism promoted marriage and fatherhood as a duty to maintain patriarchy and 'the race'.

Calls for sex education within elementary schools came after the First World War, alongside demands for sex reform and the relaxation of moral standards. Feminists were concerned to raise the consciousness of young women and challenge male immorality. Keen to expand their work into education, health professionals advocated sex education. While parents were considered responsible for the moral education of their children, assumptions about moral ineptitude led to demands for state intervention. Despite political differences in their reasons for proposing its implementation, social hygienists advocated regulation of sexual behaviour through sex education as an alternative to legislation. Working-class children would thus be prepared for work and parenthood through the incorporation of physical and health education into the school curriculum. Yet, the campaign for school-based sex education was resisted by successive governments until the 1940s. Mort (1987: 202) suggests this was because sex was perceived to be 'aligned with "the personal", with private domestic life, and hence only tangentially related to formal politics'.

In contrast to the neglect of sex education provision in schools, government documents reinforced sex differences and gender stereotypes in discussion about preparing children for adulthood. The 1926 Hadow Report emphasised housecraft (cookery, laundry, housewifery) for girls in accordance with the 'household duties which devolve on most women'. A health education handbook, published in 1928 by the Ministry of Education and revised in 1933, proposed that teachers should help pupils understand the struggle of modern communities against 'ingrained personal habits' and 'the thraldom of social custom, convention and vested interests, that threaten even the existence of mankind' (Ministry of Education, 1940: 9).

Further revised in 1940, this handbook confirmed that the 'practice and study of health should constitute an essential part of any organized system of public education' (ibid.: 8). Physical health and fitness were not only ends in themselves but a 'means to promote the mental and moral health and character of the child' (ibid.: 36). Education was concerned with 'moulding' children's feelings to 'forms that are acceptable when judged by cultural standards' (ibid.: 37). The objectives of health education were clarified (formation of healthy habits; development of right attitudes to health; knowledge about healthy ways of living). 'Health training' – via subjects such as physical training, organised games, biology, housecraft, and mothercraft for girls – and 'health studies' were advocated.

Providing a framework for future policy, the handbook acknowledged that effective planning involved: active co-operation and consultation with pupils; knowledge of pupils' home circumstances; consultation with all school staff and collaboration with health agencies. The intention was to initiate younger pupils into healthy habits and enable older pupils to practically apply health principles. For girls, 'Mothercraft and Infant Care' was a priority: 'vital . . . both for the individual and for the state' (ibid.: 63). In the early 1940s sex education was confirmed as a school responsibility – providing accurate and adequate knowledge of sexual physiology, as the mechanism of reproduction, while emphasising the emotional and psychological aspects since these were the most significant for most young people (Board of Education, 1943). Reflecting social hygienist principles, it was suggested that instruction should prioritise understanding and controlling sexual impulse and emotion, leading to mutual respect and adequate preparation for marriage.

Differential preparation for adulthood persisted throughout the 1950s and 1960s. For example, the 1959 Crowther Report stated that, in the final two years of compulsory education, 'boys thoughts turn most often to career, and only secondly to marriage and the family', while the converse was true for girls. It concluded: 'if it is sound educational policy to take account of *natural* interests, there is a clear case for a curriculum which respects the different roles they play' (emphasis added). Crowther noted social changes – unsupervised association between teenage girls and boys and the 'virtual disappearance of many of the old rules of right and wrong' – which had raised 'the problem of sexual ethics'. The report argued that teachers and youth workers were 'well placed to bring to attention the personal bewilderment and disaster [rise in teenage pregnancy] to which this public indecision over moral issues often leads the young'.

In 1963 the Newsom Report also assumed different interests and destinations for secondary-aged girls and boys. Affirming 'traditional' values, it emphasized: 'boys and girls should be offered firm guidance on sexual morality based on chastity before marriage and fidelity within it'. Four years later, the Plowden Report on primary education advocated that children's direct questions about sex should be answered. Although the 'proper people' to provide information were parents, each school 'should have a definite policy which, in consultation with parents, covers all children'. In 1968 a new handbook for health education was published. This related sexual relationships to parenthood; the production of dependent children and responsibility for their upbringing.

Defining the purpose and content of sex education almost a decade later, *Health Education in Schools* (Department of Education and Science, 1977) encouraged an approach beyond factual instruction. It advocated children's involvement in evaluating evidence, considering solutions and making decisions about personal and social health-related behaviour. Biology was perceived 'a necessity but not a sufficient basis for health education' (ibid.: 19). Considering broader social and political contexts, the report detailed six issues central to sex and health education. First, the availability of contraception on prescription raised sensitive questions about doctor–patient confidentiality. For young, unmarried girls (possibly still at school) this was a vital issue. Further, the contraceptive pill was no safeguard against the consequences of unpremeditated sex. Second, during the 1960s there had developed unparalleled freedom of speech, publication and action – the rise of the so-called 'permissive society' – thus schools could 'no longer avoid their responsibilities in sex education because information, often misleading, is thrust at children out of school' (ibid.: 112). Third, easier divorce had resulted in a rise in one-parent families, with implications for teaching about family relationships. Fourth, the development of a multi-racial society – with different attitudes, religious beliefs and social customs – required tolerance and understanding by teachers. Fifth, abortion laws generated a moral dilemma which young people may find offensive while conceding 'that it is sometimes the least of several evils'. Finally, discussion about 'sexuality in the handicapped' had led to increased acceptance of sexual practices within stable relationships, and occasionally marriage, 'which may have much to do with love but nothing to do with creation' (ibid.: 112).

According to the report, there was little evidence to support public anxiety about increasingly irresponsible sexual behaviour amongst young people. Births to under-16s remained rare. While sexual activity was only part of young people's morality it was so important that it could 'lead to a sacramental relationship of profound significance, or, at the other extreme, to the broken home, ruined children's lives or destroyed careers' (ibid.: 115). In this context, however controversial, sex education was considered 'inextricably' linked to the 'physical, emotional, and mental development of children' and the prospect of parenthood. Although parents had the main responsibility for sex education, it was the concern of all schools to address the moral dilemmas and decisions faced by children.

Appropriate knowledge in sex education was connected to stages in children's development, which were not necessarily age-related. Boys and girls required preparation for the biological and emotional consequences of puberty and the report recommended that boys should understand the distress and tiredness experienced by girls through menstruation. Both sexes had to realise that ejaculation was not always controllable, and girls had to be made aware that they could 'inadvertently' arouse sexual reactions which boys might neither understand nor be able to control. While acknowledging emotional and interpersonal contexts, the biological determinism implicit in the report's discussion of puberty failed to develop a more subtle consideration of the crucial issues of self-control and personal responsibility.

What the report did achieve was recognition that sexual intercourse could be enjoyable and include more complex activities than suggested by elementary accounts of reproduction. Knowledge of reproduction, it argued, could replace ignorance with facts, myths with realities, while challenging feelings of inadequacy. Contrasting 'innocence' with 'promiscuity', however, the report warned against creating anxieties in children who, in contrast with some of their peers, demonstrated little interest in the opposite sex, preferring to pursue their 'hobbies' or 'interests'. While addressing the issue of differential growth and development, the report adopted a tone of moral righteousness; such children should not feel 'forced into patterns of precocious experimentation which are an affront to their *innate* sense of modesty and decency' (ibid.: 117, emphasis added).

On specific issues, the report was more reflective. For example, masturbation – formerly defined as self-abuse – was presented as an 'inevitable', 'transient' and 'innocuous' part of children's developing self-awareness. Contraception was likely to be a familiar subject and should be discussed in terms of its purposes and morality. While 'saying no' remained the most frequent and certain way of girls avoiding unwanted pregnancy, all children should understand and have confidence in appropriate professional services. VD awareness, relating sexually transmitted diseases to sexual activity, including homosexuality, should be considered in secondary schools. The report also considered 'sexual deviations', stating that their consideration should be confined to response to direct questions. Male and female homosexuality were to be dealt with only if the issues arose, but there should be no 'speculations' presented about the 'complex and imperfectly understood causes of these relationships'. Fears that having close, same-sex friendships might suggest an inability to form heterosexual relationships should be allayed. Once again, despite broader social and cultural shifts, homosexuality and sexual diversity were contextualised as 'sexual deviation', with any possibility of sexuality education dismissed as inappropriate.

THE CONTEMPORARY POLITICS OF SEX AND SEXUALITY EDUCATION

The New Right agenda

Following the election of the New Right Thatcher government in 1979, the contemporary aims of education, and responsibility for establishing content, were defined. Secretaries of State were not expected to determine in detail what schools taught or how. It was anticipated that local education authorities (LEAs) would interpret and implement national policies and objectives according to local circumstances and needs. Schools were responsible for articulating aims, objectives and a curriculum relevant to pupils' future employment and responsibilities (Department of Education and Science, 1980, 1981). There was a consensus that educational aims should evolve to reflect changes in social attitudes and values, new employment patterns and innovations in learning; focused on developing mind, body and spirit. Public and professional debate implied support for a 'core' curriculum, including preparation for adult and working life. In addition to the arts and humanities, this was expected to include moral and health education, preparation for parenthood, family life and societal participation.

While moral education sought to promote integrity, considerate behaviour and understanding of the relationship between actions and beliefs, health education was concerned with preparation for personal, social and family responsibilities. In helping children make 'informed choices' about health matters, it was recognised that pupils would need to be aware of associated moral issues and value-judgements. The demands and duties of parenthood and family life were specified as central concerns. Sex education, requiring parental consultation, was recognised as one of the most sensitive elements within health education.

Despite regular publication of guidance, sex education provision was ad hoc until the 1986 Education (No. 2) Act placed responsibility on the governing bodies of county, controlled and maintained special schools. Given the discretion to decide whether or not sex education should be included in the secular curriculum, they were required to write and maintain a policy statement (outlining organisation and content of provision, or confirming the decision not to provide sex education). For voluntary aided and special agreement schools, it was anticipated that non-statutory Circular 11/87 (Department of Education and Science, 1987) would be considered. This affirmed the 'widely accepted view' that schools had a responsibility to offer pupils some education about sexual matters to ensure their health was not impaired. Parents were defined as the key figures in helping children cope with growing up and preparing them for the challenges and responsibilities associated with sexual maturity. Teaching was expected to complement and support the role of parents, although governing bodies could reject parents' requests for withdrawal of their children from sex education.

The 1986 Act and its associated guidance reflected and reinforced the New Right's reactionary position on morality, sexuality and contraceptive advice for young people. The Act specified that sex education should encourage pupils 'to have due regard to moral considerations and the value of family life'. Defining a 'moral framework', the Circular stated that sex education should 'objectively' present facts, enabling children to understand different sexual attitudes and behaviours; know what was legal; and make informed, responsible decisions about personal attitudes. The values of self-restraint, dignity, respect for self and others were prioritised in the context of familial heterosexuality. Recognising the physical, moral and emotional risks of promiscuous or casual sexual behaviour, pupils were expected to appreciate the benefits of stable, married, family life and the responsibilities of parenthood. Primary school sex education was expected to centre on the physical and emotional aspects of growing up, together with a basic understanding of human reproduction. Circular 11/87 emphasised the importance of matching provision to maturity and answering pupils' questions sensitively. At secondary level, physical aspects of sexual behaviour were encompassed in biology while sex education was subsumed within personal and social education (PSE) or health education.

These legislative and policy developments did not occur in a vacuum. Apart from the New Right agenda, there was a broader public debate concerning the morality of providing contraception and abortion to young people. In 1981 Victoria Gillick, guided by her religious beliefs and moral conviction, demanded guarantees from her local authority that girls under 16 would be refused contraception and abortion without parental knowledge and consent. This demand was rejected and Gillick mounted a legal campaign claiming that prescription of contraceptives to under-16s promoted, encouraged and facilitated unlawful sexual intercourse. The House of Lords rejected Gillick's argument in 1986, ruling that a doctor's intention would be protection from pregnancy rather than promotion of under-age sexual intercourse. The so-called 'Gillick ruling' stated that, although unusual, prescription of contraception by a doctor to a girl under 16 without parental consent was permissible provided that: it was in the girl's best interests; she understood the advice; she could not be persuaded to tell her parents; without advice or treatment her health would suffer; or she would continue to be sexually active.

The ruling, however, was negatively interpreted in Circular 11/87, which stated that its medical context had 'no parallel in school education'. Provision of advice on sexual matters without parental knowledge or consent would constitute 'inappropriate exercise of a teacher's professional duties' which 'could . . . amount to a criminal offence'. Teachers approached by pupils for advice were recommended to direct them to their parents and to warn pupils of the risks involved in behaviour likely to lead to physical/moral danger or breach of the law. It was within this prohibitive context that the Circular recommended provision of 'balanced', factual information about 'sensitive issues' such as contraception and abortion.

While the Gillick case progressed, another public outcry emerged over sexuality. The second Thatcher administration had turned its attention towards reorganising and disempowering local government, particularly the Greater London Council. A prime target was local government support for gay and lesbian initiatives. In May 1986 it was widely reported that Islington's children were being exposed to a 'vile book', and that 'gay porn books' were now available in schools. In reality, a teacher's centre held one resource copy of *Jenny Lives With Eric and Martin*. Regardless of reality, Baroness Cox used the 1987 Education Bill to connect wider public concerns over HIV/AIDS to the 'promotion of gay issues'. As well as misrepresenting HIV as a 'gay plague', the discourse mirrored nineteenth-century purist ideology: 'The denigration of the physical body, relentlessly manifested in AIDS, was cruelly mobilized as testimony to the degeneration of the social body. Biological contagion was promoted as synonymous with social contagion' (Corteen and Scraton, 1997: 92). Consistent with the government's public awareness campaign, Circular 11/87 argued that schools had 'a clear responsibility' to warn pupils of the health risks of casual, promiscuous sexual behaviour, whether heterosexual or homosexual, and the dangers of drug abuse. All schools, whatever their policy on sex education, were expected to consider behaviour risking HIV infection and risk-reduction strategies.

While not directly linked to HIV/AIDS in the Circular, a negative conception of homosexuality was articulated, stressing that for many people 'homosexual practice is not morally acceptable' and deeply offensive. It stated there was 'no place in any school in any circumstances' for teaching which advocated homosexual behaviour, presented homosexuality as the 'norm', or encouraged homosexual experimentation by pupils. Implying that open discussion of homosexuality constituted its promotion and provided a forum for predatory gay teachers to exploit impressionable young men, the Circular warned: 'encouraging or procuring homosexual acts by pupils who are under the age of consent is a criminal offence'. No such warning was directed to predatory heterosexual men! The debate over homosexuality reached an extreme when the Prime Minister, Margaret Thatcher, railed that children were being taught they had an 'inalienable right' to be gay. In a concerted backlash, premised on the assumption that heterosexuality was under threat, Section 28 of the 1988 Local Government Act prohibited local authorities from 'intentionally promoting homosexuality or publishing material with that intention and from promoting the teaching in any maintained school of homosexuality as a pretended family relationship'. While distinct from the actions of governing bodies and teaching staff, Section 28 (as it became known) inhibited discussion of sexual diversity in the classroom. Thus, another, untested, legal requirement – with no direct application to schools – became a vehicle for teachers' self-regulation.

State intervention in education increased significantly during the late 1980s. The 1988 Education Reform Act gave the Secretary of State for Education over 400 new powers, and the introduction of a National Curriculum undermined the role of LEAs and schools in determining appropriate curriculum content. The Act confirmed the purposes of education as provision of a broad, balanced curriculum promoting the spiritual, moral, cultural, mental and physical development of pupils, and preparing them for the opportunities, responsibilities and experiences of adult life. Regarding sex education, the statutory Science curriculum focused on human reproduction and a 'scientific' approach to the body as a 'system'.

During the early 1990s, government policies were inconsistent. In education, while the National Curriculum emphasised knowledge about biological 'facts', guidance concerning the non-statutory, cross-curricular theme Health Education (incorporating sex education) prioritised personal development, skills and attitudes. In this, major objectives included: quality of life; physical, social and mental well-being; information about healthy and risky behaviour; development of skills to help use knowledge effectively, resist pressure, respect others' needs. The intention was enabling pupils to maintain personal safety, manage relationships and make positive choices (National Curriculum Council, 1990). Health policy included the 1992 'Health of the Nation' strategy, which identified HIV/AIDS and sexual health as one of five key areas. Targets were established for reducing HIV/sexually transmitted disease (STD) and 'unwanted pregnancies'/conceptions amongst under-16s. *The Key Area Handbook on HIV/AIDS and Sexual Health* (Department of Health, 1995b) confirmed Sex Education Forum (1992) recommendations that sex education should be integrated into the learning process, begin in childhood, and provided for all children and young people. It acknowledged that biological information alone was not adequate in enabling people to act responsibly should they decide to become sexually active. Development of interpersonal skills, and a sense of self-worth, were also necessary.

Education legislation, however, conflicted with the health agenda. While primary school governors retained responsibility for determining whether to provide sex education, the 1993 Education Act made sex education in secondary schools mandatory. Education about HIV/AIDS and other STDs was removed from the Science curriculum at Key Stage 3 (11–14-year-olds) and placed within sex education. However, the Act established the right of parents to withdraw their children from sex education without having to account for their decision or specify alternative provision. Replacing previous guidance, Circular 5/94 (Department for Education, 1994) illustrated well the influence of the government's moral fundamentalism. Sex education, it stated, 'must not be value free'. Knowledge about loving relationships, human reproduction and the 'nature' of sexuality were confirmed as the purposes, within a moral framework promoting loyalty and fidelity as additional values of importance. Noting that many children came from backgrounds deficient in such values, teachers were expected to help pupils 'whatever their circumstances, to raise their sights'.

While teachers, health professionals and advisory groups were advocating provision of accurate information, improved interpersonal skills and increased self-confidence, popular discourses claimed that children were given 'too much information, too soon'. In response to the revelation that a school nurse had answered a question about oral sex during a primary school sex education lesson, the Shadow Education Secretary, David Blunkett, denounced such 'crass and inappropriate provision' (*Guardian*, 26 April 1994). Secretary of State for Education, John Patten, was 'incensed', questions were raised in Parliament and the nurse was impelled into hiding. Concurrently, the Health Education Authority booklet for young people, *Your Pocket Guide to Sex*, was dismissed by Health Minister, Brian Mawhinney, as 'smutty' and pulped. In response, Circular 5/94 emphasised that sex education provision should take account of children's capacity to absorb sensitive information, and the extent to which it was essential for them to have such information at that point in their development.

The right of withdrawal of their children from sex education confirmed parents as arbiters of children's access to knowledge and understanding about sex and relationships. Circular 5/94 also recommended that explicit questions raised by a child during class discussion should first be discussed by the teacher with the child's parents. If agreed, the matter could be handled by the teacher but outside the classroom situation. Confirming previous guidance about provision of contraceptive advice to under-16s, the Circular warned ominously that the legal position of a teacher giving advice had never been tested in a court. Further, a teacher who believed that a pupil had engaged in, or was thinking about, risky or unlawful behaviour was now expected to inform the head teacher. If the pupil was under the age of consent the parents were to be informed, preferably by the pupil. The head teacher was expected to check this had been done.

Although making no direct reference to sexual diversity in terms of provision, the Circular included a paragraph about Section 28 in a section clarifying legal issues. This was unnecessary as the legislation applied to local authorities rather than governing bodies or schools. Its inclusion reinforced concerns about discussing homosexuality in the classroom and re-affirmed self-censorship by teachers and governors. Circular 5/94 coincided with highly publicised and homophobic reaction to the Parliamentary debate concerning reduction of the age of consent for homosexual relations, in which political responses and the tabloid press condemned homosexuality as unnatural, abnormal and perverse. Children and young people, they again argued, had to be protected from the 'contagion' of homosexuality.

New Labour, new agenda?

Since its election in 1997, the Labour government has engaged in an alignment of education and health policies regarding sex education. It developed a non-statutory Personal, Social and Health Education (PSHE) framework incorporating sex education (QCA, 1999). This stressed development of personal confidence and responsibility, a healthy lifestyle, positive relationships and respect for others. The 1999 'Saving Lives: Our Healthier Nation' strategy identified schools as key settings for health promotion. It initiated local programmes, based on health and education partnerships, to provide accessible information for children and young people and equip them with the skills to make informed decisions. The 'Healthy Schools' programme (jointly led by the Department for Education and Employment and Department of Health) incorporated the theme of Sex and Relationships Education (SRE).

Circular 5/94 was replaced by SRE guidance (Department for Education and Employment, 2000), which emphasised lifelong learning about physical, moral and emotional development. It stressed the significance of marriage for family life, stable and loving relationships, respect, love and care, and the teaching of sex, sexuality and sexual health. Challenging popular assumptions, the guidance stated that effective SRE does not encourage sexual experimentation. Recognising the conflicting and confusing pressures experienced by children and young people, it noted that SRE should enable development of self-confidence, knowledge and skills to cope with such pressures. The guidance supported the central role of parents in policy development and planning. But the participatory role of pupils in effective policy and practice implementation was also recognised. A planned SRE programme was expected to identify learning outcomes appropriate to pupils' age, ability, gender, level of maturity and be based on assessment of their needs (Department for Education and Employment, 1999).

The SRE guidance specified content according to distinct phases of schooling. Early years education should consider relationships; focusing on friendship, bullying and self-esteem. In the final year of primary school, content should include changes relating to puberty, reproduction, and discussion about children's anxieties – recognising differential development and adjusting teaching methods accordingly. Addressing previous criticism of school sex education, the guidance stated that SRE programmes should focus equally on boys and girls at both primary and secondary levels. Also significant was recognition of the need for culturally appropriate and inclusive provision; requiring development of content and delivery in consultation with parents and pupils.

The guidance re-affirmed secondary school sex education within the context of promoting self-esteem and responsibility for actions – particularly regarding sexual activity and parenthood – arguing that young people should be aware of risk-taking behaviour, peer pressure and the arguments for delaying sexual activity. Connecting provision to government strategies for reducing teenage pregnancies, HIV/AIDS and other STDs, the guidance proposed that trained staff should provide information about different types of contraception (including emergency contraception) and their effectiveness, as well as where confidential advice, counselling or treatment could be obtained. Teaching about safe sex and the prevention of HIV, AIDS and sexually transmitted infections (STIs) were established as high priorities. The clear intention of the SRE guidance was to provide children and young people with information, opportunities to explore dilemmas and develop communication/assertiveness skills. While respecting religious convictions, the emphasis should be on preparation for the responsibilities and challenges of adult life; including the need to negotiate relationships, avoid pressure to engage in unwanted/unprotected sex, and be effective service users.

The guidance did not define a moral framework. It sought, through provision of SRE within the PSHE framework, to respond to young people's well-documented requests for greater emphasis on feelings, relationships and values within school-based sex education. The 1986 requirement concerning sex education provision in the context of moral considerations and the value of family life remained statutory. However, the guidance noted government recognition that strong, mutually supportive relationships exist outside marriage, and that children should not be stigmatised because of their home circumstances. Recommendations concerning confidentiality were also more permissive – based on meeting pupils' needs. Given that effective SRE encourages understanding about what constitutes appropriate sexual behaviour, the guidance acknowledged that it could lead to disclosure of child protection issues. Therefore, teachers would need to have a clear understanding of schoolchild protection policy and procedures. The guidance stressed that teachers are not legally bound to inform parents or the head teacher of disclosure, unless specifically requested by the head teacher. But pupils should be aware that unconditional confidentiality cannot be guaranteed. They should be assured, however, that their 'best interests' will obtain, and informed about sources of confidential help. Although health professionals working in schools have to abide by school policies, the guidance confirmed that they are bound by their professional codes of conduct to maintain confidentiality and can provide advice or information to pupils on health-related matters (including contraception) outside the classroom context.

The Labour government's initial determination to repeal Section 28 met with considerable opposition. Within the guidance Section 28 was not mentioned, but the right of young people – whatever their developing sexuality – to experience SRE relevant and sensitive to their needs was affirmed. Homophobic bullying was singled out as a major issue for schools to tackle. However, having noted that teachers should deal with sexual orientation honestly and sensitively, the guidance stated: 'there should be no direct promotion of sexual orientation'. This reinforced the implication that 'sexual orientation' applies solely to homosexuality.

CHALLENGING CONSTRUCTIONS OF CHILDHOOD, SEX AND SEXUALITY

The preceding overview of twentieth-century sex education policy demonstrates that – despite the rejection of a focus on biology within health education and growing commitment to personal and social education – particular constructions of childhood, sex and sexuality have prevailed. These include: childhood innocence and vulnerability; childhood as a prolonged period of preparation for (gendered) adult roles and responsibilities; the normalisation and promotion of heterosexuality, marriage, parenthood and the family; the link between heterosexual sex and reproduction; the marginalisation of alternative sexualities as 'unnatural' and 'aberrant'.

Throughout this period, influenced by the work of Piaget, the professional training of generations of child welfare, education and health practitioners has connected biological age to physical growth, intellectual maturity, social competence and emotional awareness. The key assumption is that children develop – biologically, psychologically and emotionally – in clearly defined stages. On this basis professionals monitor, assess, measure and classify children's progression, from birth towards the final stage of 'mature' adulthood. They track the 'natural' growth and development of the 'normal' child. Intervention occurs when a child's progress is assessed as 'abnormal' – either above or below the defined 'norms' for their age or stage of development.

What this model ignores is the significance of social, cultural and economic factors for personal development, experiences and opportunities. Children and young people are socialised within families, communities, religions, cultures and schools. In these contexts, the boundaries between 'acceptable' and 'non-acceptable' behaviour are drawn. Behaviour labelled 'deviant' or 'anti-social' in one context might be tolerated, even encouraged, in another. Wherever the lines are drawn, however, adults set the limits. It is assumed that, without adult guidance, sound parenting and the interventions of practitioners, children would lack discipline and self-control. This is a negative view of children as lacking the capacity to make appropriate moral decisions about their lives. It presumes that, left to their own perceptions, interpretations and actions, children would deviate from rules and conventions, thus threatening social stability.

Consequently, children and young people are identified as requiring both protection and regulation. They are expected to be cared for yet controlled, inquisitive yet confined, free-spirited yet disciplined. This places adults – parents, relations, professionals – as the primary definers; giving them immense influence and power over the children for whom they are responsible. Nowhere is this more apparent than in interventions around sex and sexuality. With moral 'awareness' and sexual experience presumed to be related to age and physical development, a tension exists between maintaining and prolonging the questionable notion of childhood 'innocence' and the imposition of a state of 'ignorance'. Although socialised by gender from birth, children are regarded as asexual – devoid of sexual feelings – until puberty at the earliest. While children and young people are exposed routinely to highly sexualised imagery they are expected to conform to gendered stereotypes and abstain from sexual relations.

Their awareness of sex differences develops within the context of norms and expectations that promote heterosexual relations, marriage and the family. Experiences of what it is to be a boy/man or girl/woman permeate all aspects of their lives and reinforce these social and cultural expectations. The 'family and education institutions', writes Evans (1994: 3), are required to 'preserve [children's] innocence and purity en route to adulthood', in an idealised world which fails to recognise the tensions around gender divisions and male dominance.

Yet prolonging childhood beyond puberty, far from protecting children leaves them vulnerable. It amounts to 'protective exclusion' based on their 'alleged lack of responsibility, capability and competence' (Qvortrup, 1997:

86). What is considered 'appropriate' information and knowledge concerning their physical change and development, their understanding of sex and sexuality, becomes a 'private' matter for families. With sex and sexuality (specifically regarding physical contact and experimentation) defined as the exclusive preserve of adults, the presumption often is that children do not need to know about that with which they should not be involved. Yet research demonstrates that young children have an active curiosity and a (sometimes partial) awareness of sex and sexuality (Farrell, 1978; Goldman and Goldman, 1982; Jackson, 1982; Allen, 1987). Their capacity to understand sexual feelings, desires and concerns, and to explore emotions, is rarely appreciated or accommodated by parents. As with childhood, the defining discourse is biological; with adults perceiving children's sexual development as determined by physicality.

While 'biology' provides the physical context and capacity for sexual activity, it provides no understanding of social, political and cultural contexts and their moral imperatives. Any 'sense of naturalness' is located not in 'biological facts' but in 'socially constructed definitions of what is sexual' (Jackson, 1982: 18). Children and young people are instructed within a framework founded on denial and abstinence. Their informal (peers, family, media) and formal (education, religion) access to sexual knowledge and information, tied to heterosexuality and reproduction, 'denies their immediate feelings and emotions, their pleasures or desires' (Corteen and Scraton, 1997: 85). It provides 'one possible, and permissible, version of their future – marriage and parenthood', with any sexual expression other than heterosexuality 'rejected as deviant or perverse' (ibid.). This prolonged period of childhood, informed by biological instruction alongside personal denial and abstinence, is a rejection of different and diverse sexual experiences (see Epstein and Johnson, 1998).

Surrounded by sexual fantasy and sexualised imagery, young people experience and participate (passively if not actively) in intimate relations far removed from marriage and reproduction. In terms of heterosexual relations, however, the messages remain unequivocal. The predatory and dominating behaviour associated with masculinity and the passive and submissive behaviour associated with femininity are presented as derived in 'nature'. This is an ideological construction, regardless of its pervasiveness across cultures, in which women's sexuality is dictated by and responsive to male sexuality both in role and in style. Men who fail to 'live up' to the expectations of masculinity soon find their heterosexuality scrutinised and questioned.

For all the claims that the 'gender gap' has closed, particularly in education, there has been minimal change in the subordination of girls and young women in heterosexual relations (see Coppock et al., 1995). As Lees (1993: 132–3) shows, the 'legitimacy of naturalness' through which girls 'reconcile the discrepancy between their knowledge of marriage and the universal expectation that [it is] their natural destiny' becomes their defining context. Their sexuality becomes fully established – and active –

through marriage; in response to male desire and biological reproduction. For girls and young women being sexually active prior to marriage, initiating rather than abstaining, provokes condemnation – their reputations publicly denounced.

The contradictions are obvious. Constantly reminded to emphasise their femininity, to respond to and excite the male gaze, girls and young women are negatively labelled should they be confident, assertive or sexually active. For boys and young men, any deviation from the expectations and public manifestations of heterosexual masculinity leads to marginalisation at best, violence at worst. Open declarations of self-doubt or vulnerability are used as indicators of weakness. This does not suggest that girls and boys are totally determined into gendered and sexual roles and expectations. What it identifies is the strength of the social forces and expectations which underpin and reinforce heterosexuality. The socio-cultural pressures that make heterosexuality 'compulsory' are supported by, and supportive of, the fantasies and realities of exploitation, misogyny and homophobia.

Some of these issues have been addressed, at least in part, by the SRE guidance and greater integration of health and education objectives. The social and cultural contexts of children's experiences are recognised in guidance which prioritises participation of children and young people in the development of school policy and practice; provision of accurate information and advice about sources of counselling and treatment regarding sexual matters; respect for confidentiality, and targeting homophobic bullying in schools. Shifting SRE from the biology curriculum to PSHE acknowledges that reproduction is a social process as well as a physical act. And recognising that sex education should be provided from the early years onwards promotes its integration into the routine of school provision.

Still, however, the issue of morality remains. Tony Blair's comments on moral renewal, childhood and the family indicate that reactionary ideology has not been exorcised by more enlightened policy changes. There remains a political reticence to address all aspects of sexual relations, including the power bases of age, gender and sexuality. In addition, rights established by ratification of the UN Convention on the Rights of the Child (for example, the rights to seek, receive and impart information and ideas – Article 13 – and to the highest attainable standard of health – Article 24 – as well as the principle of the 'best interests of the child' as a primary consideration in all actions concerning the child – Article 3) are undermined by the fact that PSHE remains a non-statutory element of the curriculum. Despite UN Committee disapproval (UN Committee, 1995), Labour's retention of parental right of withdrawal from sex education contravenes the right of children to express their views on all matters affecting them and to have their views taken seriously – Article 12 (see also Haydon, 2001).

Research with children and young people has consistently demonstrated an overwhelming demand for sex and sexuality education, help and advice. Reliance on the private domain of the idealised family as the primary site for information and instruction has been exposed as woefully inadequate. Statutory sex and sexuality education – inclusive and responsive to children's experiences, views and needs – has the capacity to effectively challenge the myths surrounding childhood, sex and sexuality, and the exploitative relations that many young people (particularly girls and young women) endure. Such a curriculum would not only inform children's futures, but also deal with the confusion, concerns and struggles of their daily lives.

ACKNOWLEDGEMENT

With thanks to the Young People, Rights and Justice Research Group in the Centre for Studies in Crime and Social Justice, Edge Hill University College.

KEY TEXTS

Epstein, D. and Johnson, R. (1998) *Schooling Sexualities*. Buckingham: Open University Press.

Evans, D. (1994) 'Falling angels? The material construction of children as sexual citizens?', *International Journal of Children's Rights*, 2: 1–33.

Haydon, D. (2001) 'Children's rights to sex and sexuality education', in B. Franklin (ed.), *The Handbook of Children's Rights: Comparative Policy and Practice*, 2nd edn. London: Routledge.

TWELVE

Children, Politics and Collective Action: School Strikes in Britain

STEPHEN CUNNINGHAM AND MICHAEL LAVALETTE

INTRODUCTION: CHILDREN, YOUNG PEOPLE AND POLITICS

We start with a very obvious question: *Why have a chapter dealing with children, young people and politics when children's and young people's direct involvement with the major political parties in Britain is in dramatic decline?* In the General Election of 2001 in Britain, large numbers of young people refused to vote. The youth organisations of the major political parties are all a mere shell of their former selves. The conclusion would seem to be that children and young people are not interested in politics.

Further, while there is some academic interest in children's rights and child advocacy work, there is very little attention given to the role of children's participation in collective action – the various forms of protest from marches, strikes, occupations and demonstrations which are seen to be the preserve of (a minority) of adult 'activists'. *Why look at children and collective action?*

There are four specific responses to these questions. The first is simply to note that disillusionment or uninterest in parliamentary politics and mainstream political parties is not confined to young people, nor is it evidence of uninterest in a range of political issues and movements. The large numbers of young people active in a range of political and social campaigns (such as the various Third World debt, environmental and anti-racist campaigns, and the anti-capitalist movement) emphasises that children and young people continue to be politically engaged. Thus, by 'politics' we do not limit ourselves to the world of 'official parliamentary' debates and issues but include concern, interest and involvement in a wide range of social, environmental and political campaigns. It may date us but this vision of politics was neatly summed up by the late 1970's New Wave group the Tom Robinson Band who, on their *Power in the Darkness* album cover, proclaimed their own youthful political engagement in the following way:

Politics isn't party political broadcasts and general elections, it's yer kid sister who can't get an abortion, yer best mate getting paki-bashed, or sent down for possessing one joint of marijuana . . . it's everyday life . . . for everyone who hasn't got a cushy job or rich parents. (Tom Robinson, 1978)

The second response is that the issue of children and politics – generally discussed in terms of children's rights – is an important area of academic controversy (see Lavalette, 1999a). Much that is positive within this debate is a concern to emphasise children's role as *active subjects*, capable of understanding and engaging with the social world – a contrast to previously dominant perspectives on children which treated them as *passive objects*, incapable of rational thought or active participation in politics. It is clear that children and young people do attempt to shape and change their world in various ways – studying how and why they do so are important and interesting questions.

Third, the dominant perspective within the rights debate focuses on children as *individual actors* but this has been at the expense of looking at children's involvement in collective action, as potential *collective actors*. The 'rights debate' tends to treat 'children' and 'young people' as single, unified social categories – leading to notions that all children are the same and have the same individual rights and interests, regardless of social barriers or privileges. But as we noted in Chapter 2 and as other chapters have emphasised, children are divided by a range of social phenomena and have different, often antagonistic, interests – children's involvement in collective action emphasises this fact much more clearly than abstract discussion of 'rights'. Our focus in this chapter is on working-class children's involvement in a particular form of collective action – school strikes – in the pursuit of rational, class-specific goals.

Finally, amongst the non-governmental organisation (NGO) community, there is a growing interest in rising levels of 'activism' amongst 'Third World' children, particularly working children. This 'activism' is invariably portrayed as a novel development. For example, UNICEF (1997: 9) suggests that it is 'only recently' that children have 'themselves . . . formed organisations to demand access to education, . . . and improved working conditions'. Children, it points out, are now 'becoming increasingly active participants in studying their own reality, coming to conclusions and making suggestions with regard to their schools, their family–work responsibilities, facilities for leisure or earning money'. Some NGOs have described how this 'activism' has spread to involve children in 'advanced' capitalist societies (Save the Children, 1999; 8/6/2000; 22/3/2000). However, whilst much of the literature concerning the 'politicisation' of children is welcome, it invariably fails to acknowledge a long, but 'hidden' tradition of political organisation and protest among working-class children in the 'advanced' economies.

These four reasons are our initial response to the questions 'why children, young people and politics?' and 'why collective action?'. But we want to argue something else as well, that children's involvement in collective action is far more likely at certain periods – during heightened waves of protest.

Theorists of social movements often note that history has been marked by various 'waves' of protest: there are periods in history when mass protest and various forms of collective action spread across the globe, bringing with them a vision and a hope that it is possible to establish a better world; and there are periods when nothing seems to happen and protest seems futile (Harman, 1988; Tarrow, 1994). According to Tarrow, protest waves:

> are characterized by heightened conflict: not only in industrial relations, but in the streets; not only there, but in villages and schools. In such periods, the magnitude of conflictual collective action of many kinds rises appreciably above what is typical. . . . What is most distinctive about such periods is . . . that the demonstration effect of collective action on the part of a small group . . . triggers a variety of processes of diffusion, extension, imitation and reaction among groups that are normally quiescent. (1994: 155/6)

As previous chapters have indicated, children and young people operate from a particularly disadvantaged position within a range of social locations – the family, the school and the informal workplace for example. These locations afford them little in the way of what Alex Callinicos (1987) terms 'structural capacities', that offer an obvious collective forum for the expression of their collective power. While they may rebel as individuals (running away from home or playing truant for example), while they may join demonstrations, riots and rebellions in their locality, it is, in the 'advanced economies', the school strike that represents the clearest expression of a collective, class-specific response to grievance from working-class children. It is therefore a highly political event, which involves children challenging and questioning their social position and the legitimacy of the school authorities, the local state and the imposition of a range of bourgeois norms and values. Such challenges are far more likely during a heightened wave of protest, when children gain the confidence to join the rebellious upsurge and try and shape their own futures. In what follows we look at four periods when children, influenced by heightened levels of social conflict, entered school strikes to raise their particular demands as working-class children.

CHILDREN'S STRIKES AND 'NEW UNIONISM'

In a recent history of the 'second wave of unionisation', Charlton (1999) describes the rapid birth and spread of 'new unionism' at the end of the nineteenth century. Conservative craft-based trade societies were eclipsed by the emergence and consolidation of new, 'general' trade unions that were more prepared to take militant industrial action in the pursuit of their members' interests (Charlton, 1999). In March 1889, Will Thorne led his newly organised union of gasworkers in London to a historic victory, securing a reduction in the basic working day from twelve hours to eight. Encouraged by this success, Ben Tillet, Tom Mann and John Burns led London's dockworkers to victory in a bitter dispute over pay and conditions. Throughout Britain – in Clydeside, Teesside, Humberside, Merseyside and South Wales – dockworkers, gasworkers, miners and other sections of workers sought to replicate the success of their counterparts in the capital (Pelling, 1963; Browne, 1979, Charlton, 1999). The year 1889 was, in short, one of unprecedented and intense industrial conflict.

However, 1889 was also the year of another unusual and original form of strike activity – the school strike. In the early autumn of 1889 contemporaries witnessed what has been described as the first nationwide 'children's rebellion' (Taylor, 1994: 89). In September and October Britain found itself in the grip of a series of pupil protests. The first outbreak occurred in Hawick, in the Scottish Borders, on 25 September. According to an account of the dispute in the *Hawick Express*, children from two Board schools 'went on strike, marched in processional order . . . causing considerable commotion'. They demanded 'shorter hours, fewer and easier lessons, and better teachers' (cited in Taylor, 1994: 91). Within days, the strike movement had spread to Glasgow and Aberdeen, and had begun to attract the interest of national newspapers. On 26 September, *The Times* commented on the breakdown in discipline and the 'very shocking' demands presented by the children. Like many other contemporary accounts of the strike, its report was entirely bereft of sympathy for the children's cause, locating the blame for the dispute with their parents' 'hotheaded' and 'irresponsible' embrace of militant 'New Unionism':

> Of course, the whole thing is frivolous, and a speedy collapse is inevitable; but the incident, though ludicrous enough, may serve to show the parents of the strikers how dangerous is the example which they set their own children. (*The Times*, 30/9/1889)

The Times's portrayal of the strike as 'frivolous' and 'ludicrous' was part of the attempt to undermine the rationale for the children's actions, to dismiss the very notion that they could form or articulate legitimate political demands. It also suggests a simplistic notion that children unquestionably follow, sheep-like, their parents' actions.

The 'speedy collapse' predicted by *The Times* failed to materialise and by 7 October its correspondents were reporting that the school strike movement had spread to England. As the dispute gathered pace, striking children throughout Britain articulated a series of basic and consistent demands – free education, less rote learning and the abolition of corporal punishment. These demands were motivated by genuine grievances. For example, the call for free education was, at the time, a 'key issue' for the labour movement across Britain; indeed the Trades Union Congress had been committed to the introduction of a free national system of education since 1885 (Simon, 1965).

The demand for the abolition of corporal punishment was also based on genuine complaints. As Thompson (1975: 32–3) has shown, 'one of the most recurrent themes from the late nineteenth and early twentieth century childhoods is that of the savagery of school teachers towards their pupils'. Children were regularly caned, 'not only for being late or for talking in class, but for not getting their answers right, for not speaking correctly, even for coughing'.

Children's complaints about the excessive use of rote learning methods also appear to have been well founded. As Simon (1965) points out, the regimes found in the schools that catered for working-class children were stultifying and deadening. Moreover, this aspect of elementary schooling was not incidental, as R.H. Tawney put it, elementary schools 'were intended in the main to produce an orderly, civil obedient population, with sufficient education to understand a command' (cited in Simon, 1965: 119). To this end, the school curriculum, with its emphasis on 'drill' and reading, writing and arithmetic, was designed to crush rather than enhance initiative, and to develop habits of obedience, docility and passivity (Simon, 1965: 118).

The strikes, therefore, were based on a genuine set of grievances about the nature and content of working-class education. But by striking, the children were challenging the authority of schools, local government and, indeed, some central pillars of bourgeois thought about the role of children in society. What was the response to the strikes?

Initially, the authorities responded by isolating, and administering ad hoc beatings to children considered to be directing the protests. However, in many cases, teachers' threats of physical punishment failed to act as a sufficient deterrent. Indeed, such tactics frequently appeared to strengthen the resolve of the strikers, and led to teachers themselves becoming the targets of threats and violence. For instance, in Holyhead 'some of the teachers were . . . subjected to rough treatment by their pupils, who armed themselves with sticks and cabbage stalks', and cases of personal violence towards teachers were also reported in Liverpool and Cardiff (*The Preston Guardian*, 19/10/1889; *The Times*, 9/10/1889). However, the strikers reserved the most serious acts of intimidation and violence for children refusing to participate in the dispute. In Workington, forty children 'armed themselves with sticks and made an effort to prevent other boys going into the school, and in several instances parents had to interfere to protect their boys'. In other areas much larger groups of children gathered in an attempt to prevent 'blacklegs' from entering schools. In Clerkenwell, a 'very riotous' group of up to 300 strikers 'armed with sticks and stones . . . molested the scholars as they came out' (*The Preston Guardian*, 19/10/1889). In Islington, 500 children armed with sticks and stones laid siege to St Mathias's school, informing 'blacklegs' that they would 'bash their heads in' if they refused to join the strike (*The Times*, 14/10/1889). In such cases, the authorities invariably turned to the police for assistance. The following request for police help, made by the headmaster of Single-Street School on 9 October, was far from unique:

> I write to report an interference with our scholars by the boys of some neighbouring schools, and to ask your protection. At midday a crowd of boys armed with sticks and stones came to the schools and called upon our boys to 'come out on strike'. Those that refused to do so were called 'blacklegs' and had brickbats and stones flung at them. Many of the boys were hurt, and one has gone to hospital.

Following the headmaster's plea, two policemen were posted at the gates of Single-Street School to 'protect . . . children and entrances, and prevent brutal intimidation' (*The Times*, 11/10/1889). In fact, the posting of constables at school entrances became a fairly commonplace occurrence throughout the length and breadth of Britain during the three-week-long dispute, and there can be little doubt that without the use of the police the authorities would have struggled to contain the strike movement.

However, the presence of police officers could do little to ensure that those involved in the strike returned to school. Here, the education authorities turned to the courts for support. For instance in West Hartlepool the School Board applied for and obtained summonses against the parents of 250 children who were absenting themselves from school (*The Lancashire Evening Post*, 10/10/1889). In other towns and cities, children were placed before the courts and punished severely for their parts in the strike. Thus, Lambeth Police Court ignored the pleas for clemency made by 14-year-old Elijah Goodey's father, and remanded the boy to the workhouse for one week. According to the magistrate, the sentence would 'act as an example to the other disorderly lads, who appear to have joined together to defy the school authorities and the police' (*The Times*, 12/10/1889). More commonly strikers coming before the courts faced fines and/or 'binding over' orders. The latter invariably stipulated that any future misconduct would result in either a flogging or imprisonment.

Thus the state responded with a fair degree of brutality, directed especially against 'local leaders' of the movement. The coercion gradually produced a return to school after a three-week period of resistance. The 'children's rebellion', it seemed, had been defeated, without any of the demands being met. The strike, though, should not be seen as entirely inconsequential, for within two years a significant step towards the implementation of one of the protesters' key demands – free education for all – had been made. In 1891 the then Conservative government reversed its previous implacable opposition to free schooling and passed the Free Education Act. Although this did not introduce universal free education (this was not achieved until 1902), it gave School Boards the ability to admit children freely into their schools. Of course, any suggestion that the reversal of policy was a result of the 'children's rebellion' alone would be naïve. As Simon (1965: 131) points out, the opposition Liberal Party had committed itself to the abolition of school fees and hence there were pressing electoral reasons for the Conservative government to do likewise. However, at the very least the 1889 school strikes focused attention on this issue and served to reinforce already existing pressures for free education.

The 'children's rebellion' of 1889 erupted in areas such as Clydeside, Merseyside, South Wales and London's East End, where New Unionism was gaining strength and where there had been recent outbreaks of industrial unrest among adult workers. There was 'a clear correlation between the location of major school strikes and areas of militant "New Union" activity' (Taylor, 1994: 96). However, the school strikes were not, as publications such as *The Times* frequently alleged, isolated acts of copycat hooliganism. As *The Preston Guardian* (12/10/1889) acknowledged, those participating in the rebellion were 'not merely playing at strike', they were 'in dead earnest' and inspired by more serious motives than the infantile foolishness attributed to them by journalists. Thus, whilst children did emulate many of the tactics of the New Union movement – wildcat strikes, demonstrations, picketing, processions, streamers and banners – they did so in the pursuit of a range of genuine grievances.

THE GREAT UNREST

Our second example is drawn from 1911 and any discussion of the school strike movement of that year must begin by acknowledging the remarkable parallels that existed between the political and industrial climates of 1889 and 1911. For like 1889, 1911 was marked by a period of unprecedented militant industrial unrest. The number of disputes reported to the Labour Department of the Board of Trade had increased from 399 in 1908 to 903 in 1911. In 1909 the number of people directly involved in industrial disputes was only 170,000; by 1911 this had risen to 831,000. The number of strike days during the same period increased from 2,560,000 to 38,142,000 (Williams, *c.* 1950). However, statistics alone fail to convey the revolutionary fervour gripping Britain. The French historian Elie Halevy has used the term 'domestic anarchy' to describe the events of 1911, whilst the British historian George Dangerfield has argued that the 'Workers Rebellion' of that year marked the beginning of *The Strange Death of Liberal England*. Certainly, the summer of 1911 was awash with rumours and fears of revolutionary upheaval. Troops were dispatched to twenty-seven different towns and cities and General Officers commanding Britain's army garrisons were instructed by the Home Office to use their own discretion in deciding whether to use firepower to maintain law and order (Dangerfield, 1964: 268). Throughout the length and breadth of Britain fierce battles subsequently erupted between strikers, their families and the police and armed forces. In Liverpool on 15 August barricades and street bonfires were used to hamper the progress of police and soldiers, and according to one contemporary source, 'the whole area was for a time in a state of siege'. Two days later, when the War Office had finally managed to gain control of the city, two strikers were shot dead by the army (cited in Cliff and Gluckstein, 1996: 47). On 18 August two more strikers were killed by troops in Llanelly, South Wales, and four more died there later in the day (and many more were injured) when railway trucks that had been set on fire exploded (Dangerfield, 1964: 268–9).

Against this background, school strikes exploded onto the scene once more. It is perhaps no coincidence that the first two areas to be affected by the school strike movement of September 1911 were Llanelly and Liverpool. The strikes started in Llanelly on 5 September, when boys at Bigyn Council School walked out after one of their number had been beaten by a teacher for passing a piece of paper around in class. Children from two other elementary schools joined the strike a day later (*The Times*, 7/9/1911). On 8 September children in Liverpool struck, 'parading the district and calling upon other schools, asking the scholars to come out in sympathy' (*The Times*, 9/9/1911). The Liverpool strikers put forward a range of basic demands – the abolition of the cane, the abolition of home lessons, an extra half-day holiday and the payment of monitors (elder children chosen by head teachers to deliver basic instruction to younger pupils). Children in the sixty or so other major towns and cities affected by the school strike movement that swept across Britain over the next three weeks subsequently adopted many of these demands.

As had been the case in 1889, the possibility that the grievances presented by the protesters were genuine was rejected outright by contemporary accounts of the strike. Once again, blame for the disruption was placed on the 'hot-headed' and 'foolish' example set by militant mothers and fathers. This claim was invariably 'substantiated' by an acknowledgement of the fact that the most serious strikes appeared to occur in areas that had been most affected by Syndicalist strike activity, and by references to the 'astonishing similarity' of the tactics used by child and adult strikers.

There can, of course, be little doubt that many of the children participating in the strike movement will have been influenced by the wider industrial conflict occurring at the time. In addition, commentators were quite right to point out the close correspondence between the tactics used by child and adult strikers. However, there is an alternative explanation for this behaviour than that advanced by contemporary newspaper accounts. For instance, children themselves sometimes played an important, albeit 'hidden', part in 'adult' disputes, and it was through this participation and not through 'childhood imitation' that they learned and internalised strategies of working-class resistance. For example, children's involvement in the year-long miners' strike that affected the Rhondda Valley between 1910 and 1911 was significant. As the following communiqué from the Home Office official J.F. Moylon to his superiors in London highlights, children also played a significant part in protests against strike-breakers. Indeed, according to Moylon, the impact of their actions was 'more serious' than the illegal harassment of blacklegs by adult strikers:

> More serious still [than illegal picketing] are assaults on officials and 'blacklegs' and their families and attacks on their houses. Cases of actual assault are, so far, not numerous, but window smashing is common. The procedure is for a crowd largely composed of women and children to gather round the official's house and stone it. The men in the crowd usually stand by and look on. . . . During the last two days a new plan of painting 'B' or 'Bl' or 'Scab' on a 'blackleg's' house has been adopted. (Home Office, 1911: 34)

Like their counterparts in South Wales, children in other parts of the country will inevitably have participated in similar demonstrations. It is, therefore, not surprising that protesters involved in the school strike movement sometimes resorted to similar tactics to those used during the 'Workers' Rebellion'. This is not to suggest that all the protests were characterised by violent behaviour. However, on occasions strikers did resort to physical force. In Birkenhead, police protection was needed for teachers, and School Board officers were 'stoned and compelled to abandon their work' (cited in Marson, 1973: 16). In Liverpool, gangs of strikers smashed street lamps and school windows, and 'loyal scholars were beaten with sticks' (*The Times*, 9/11/1911). And in Dundee, on the evening of 14 September, around 1,500 children were involved in an assault on up to nine school buildings, attacking teachers and breaking at least 100 windows (cited in Marson, 1973: 21).

Similar if less spectacular scenes were replicated across Britain's towns and cities, and as was the case in 1889, police officers had to be stationed at school gates (see *The Times*, 12/9/1911). Again, contemporary commentators saw this as evidence to support their assertion that the strikes were an expression of the 'perverse' and 'wilful' nature of delinquent working-class children. However, as Humphries (1981) has argued, attacks on teachers, school buildings, pupil blacklegs and the police had a profound instrumental value. They helped in the recruitment of children to the cause, they assisted in the maintenance of pupil solidarity and were necessary in order to counter the coercive strike-breaking methods of the school authorities and the police.

Irrespective of the strategies adopted by the strikers, it is clear that many of the demands they made were justified. Certainly, complaints about the excessive use of corporal punishment were well founded: canings for the most minor of 'offences', such as 'going unwashed', 'untidiness' and 'dirty habits', were a routine, everyday occurrence (Humphries, 1981; Musgrave, 1977; Thompson, 1975). Nor were children's demands for the abolition of homework and for additional holidays unreasonable, given the gloomy, overcrowded conditions of most working-class homes, and the pressure on working-class children to contribute to the family purse by working outside school hours (Lavalette, 1994, 1999b; Cunningham, 1999; Stack and McKechnie, this volume). Likewise, calls for the payment of 'monitors' were also, no doubt, justifiable. In understaffed, overcrowded elementary schools, the assistance of monitors was crucial for both the instruction of younger children and the maintenance of discipline, and the call for a penny per week 'compensation' for carrying out monitorial duties was hardly unreasonable. Finally, that the children's strike movement was not simply an expression of delinquent-led, anti-social adolescent rebellious-ness is evident from the fact that parents in some areas gave it their active support. In Hull 'women incited the children to follow the "strikers" example' (*The Times*, 13/9/1911), in Leeds 'some of the mothers . . . showed open sympathy' (*The Times*, 14/9/1911) and in Birkenhead pupils had 'the open connivance at least of their parents' (*Liverpool Daily Post and Mercury*, 14/9/1911, cited in Marson, 1973: 16).

Once again the strike movement of 1911 started to subside after three weeks and the children faced immense brutality on their return to the classroom. *The Lancashire Daily Post* (14/9/1911), attributed the disruption to the proliferation of 'humane methods' of teaching and 'ridiculous restrictions concerning the use of the cane', a sentiment that held con-siderable sway. In the aftermath the school authorities in Lancaster responded with 'severe punishment being inflicted by the masters', while in Sunderland, 'truants' returning to school were 'soundly birched' (*The Times*, 16/9/1911).

But the school strikes of 1911 should not be seen as a complete failure. On a practical level evidence suggests that the incidence of corporal punishment in schools fell and continued to fall in the years following the strike (Musgrave, 1977). While as Humphries (1981: 120) notes, the strike represented a welcome 'expression of the resistance of the local working class community to the abuse of fundamental rights by the authoritarian and bureaucratic organization of state schooling'.

As in 1889, children showed that they had not been overwhelmed by the stultifying, sometimes brutalising regimes found in elementary schools, and that they were, against all the odds, prepared to engage in collective acts of resistance in order to improve their educational environment.

GLORIOUS SUMMER

The school strikes of 1889 and 1911 might be thought to be an interesting quirk of a bygone era but this is not the case, as two more recent examples confirm. The first relates to the strikes of 1972. Like 1889 and 1911, this was a year of unprecedented economic dislocation and trade union militancy (Darlington and Lyddon, 2001). The number of strike-days climbed from 10,980,000 in 1970 to 23,909,000 in 1972, a figure higher than that for any other year since the General Strike of 1926. According to one Labour historian, Royden Harrison, the labour unrest of 1972 'was far more massive and incomparably more successful' than even the Syndicalist-inspired industrial militancy of 1911 (cited in Cliff and Gluckstein, 1996: 309).

It was in this climate that a new school strike movement emerged in May 1972. In some respects, it bore a number of similarities to its predecessors. Like their counterparts in 1889 and 1911, the children who marched out of school in 1972 were protesting at the authoritarian, sometimes brutalising, nature of state schooling. However, unlike 1889 and 1911, the mass walkouts of 1972 were not ad hoc, 'spontaneous' eruptions of dissent. On the contrary, they constituted a premeditated, highly organised attempt to enshrine a series of basic rights into a formal school children's 'charter'. Thus, whereas the earlier 'children's rebellions' had no formal leadership or strategy, the 1972 school strike movement was spearheaded by a London-based Schools Action Union (SAU). The SAU was founded in January 1969 by a small group of London schoolboys who had been inspired by the success of the student unrest in France a year earlier. Ultimately, it would prove to be a very effective campaigning body. Through its well-circulated pamphlets and newsletters, it articulated (and organised protests around) a number of basic demands, including an end to corporal punishment and detentions, greater children's participation in the running of schools, the abolition of school uniforms, better school meals and the reintroduction of free school milk (which had been stopped for primary school children by Education Secretary Margaret Thatcher in 1970) (*The Times*, 15/5/72). Between 1969 and 1972, the SAU consolidated its support base among school children and organised a number of small-scale demonstrations in London (see *The Times*, 3/3/1969, 24/7/1969, 29/7/1969, 10/2/1970). However, the most significant confrontation between it and the school authorities occurred in the capital in May 1972, when it organised two one-day strikes.

As had been the case in the past, the child protesters received little sympathy in the media. For the *Lancashire Evening Post* (18/5/1972), 'the idea of pupil power' was 'just about the most outrageous affront to common sense our zany world has ever come up with'. *The Times* (17/5/1972) also rejected children's calls for a greater say in their education. There must, it argued, 'be something of an authoritarian structure in a school', and a few agitators should not be allowed to 'disrupt the purposes of the place to which everyone else subscribes'. Most newspapers also drew attention to SAU's use of the symbols and language of other contemporary adult 'left-wing' protest movements, and like 1889 and 1911, the close correspondence between the strategies and slogans used by child and adult protesters was interpreted as clear evidence of 'childhood imitation'. Children, it was argued, were naïvely copying the irresponsible actions of adult militants.

The Times (17/5/1972) also sought to link the agitation to the actions of certain left-wing groups who, it alleged, were seeking to turn schools into 'seminaries of revolution' by encouraging children into 'organised truancy, deliberate breaches of school discipline and possibly of the law'. However, it is clear from contemporary accounts of SAU's meetings and demonstrations that its organisational and decision-making structures were organised by school children themselves.

The catalyst for the May 1972 disruptions appears to have been a strike at Rutherford Comprehensive School in London. Children demanded the abolition of caning and school uniforms, and the introduction of lunchtime passes. Within a matter of days, the headmaster announced that the phasing out of caning and school uniforms was being considered, and that school passes may be granted (*The Times*, 11/5/1972). Encouraged by this success, SAU co-ordinated a series of minor protests at individual schools in the South of England, and organised a strike and a mass rally in Hyde Park on 10 May. The Inner London Education Authority (ILEA) initially adopted an uncompromising response to SAU's threat to disrupt schooling, announcing that it was advising head teachers to treat those who absented themselves from school as truants. It also stated that it was writing to at least 3,000 parents, reminding them that they were breaking the law if their children failed to attend classes. However, the protest went ahead and was attended by up to 1,500 striking London school children (*The Times*, 10/5/1972). After hearing speeches from SAU leaders, the children marched on mass to London's County Hall, where Dr Eric Briault (a senior figure in the ILEA) was handed a letter of protest. It stated:

> For the past five days school students from an increasing number of schools in London have been rising up and saying a determined 'no' to being pushed around like dumb animals. The days when they would passively accept being beaten, and locked up on the sole authority of the head was over. (Cited in *The Times*, 10/5/1972)

Simon Steyne (16), one of the children who led the march to County Hall, stated that the 'only thing' he had learned from the ILEA's dismissive reaction to SAU's demands was the need to 'be more militant' (*The Times*, 10/5/1972). Sixty SAU delegates subsequently met to discuss the situation on Sunday 14 May, whereupon it was decided to call a further one-day 'General Strike' and a march to Trafalgar Square on Wednesday the 17th (*The Times*, 15/5/1972).

The growing campaign met with some initial successes, including a significant change in approach from the ILEA. In its advice to schools likely to be affected by the planned Trafalgar Square demonstration, the ILEA recommended that schools take 'a broadly liberal attitude' and advised head teachers 'to make a clear distinction between taking normal and proper steps to deal with breaches of discipline, including truancy, and giving due consideration to the legitimate views of pupils, some of whom may have been involved in recent events' (cited in *The Times*, 10/5/1972). On 17 May, up to 2,500 children participated in the demonstration and marched to Trafalgar Square, but when the demonstrators reached their destination, they were greeted by a large contingent of police officers, who refused to allow them access to the Square. Fighting subsequently broke out between the protesters and the police, and fourteen children and ten young adults were taken into custody, including most of SAU's Executive.

The following day pictures of the fighting and arrests were emblazoned across the newspapers. But rather than prompting a 'backlash' against SAU, the publicity given to its activities seemed to have two unintended effects. First, it stimulated similar protests elsewhere (for details of these see *The Lancashire Evening Post*, 22/5/1972; *The Times*, 23/5/1972, 24/5/1972). Secondly, it prompted a serious national debate about the merits of the children's demands. It soon became evident that not all adults were prepared to condemn the tactics adopted by the SAU or the reforms it was advocating. Indeed, some saw the school strike movement as a welcome development. As one correspondent to *The Times* (20/5/1972) argued, children were simply 'taking seriously the rhetoric about "social responsibility" so often thrust at them and despite more or less frenzied threats . . . demonstrating their intention to bring about badly needed changes in our schools':

> To judge from some of the adults' cries of outrage one might think that the demonstrating pupils wanted to tear down all the schools and shoot all the teachers. Instead they were simply demanding an end to canings, freedom to wear ordinary clothes, and greater democracy in the running of school affairs. . . . Our schools must change, and it is very heartening that the people most directly concerned, schoolchildren themselves, are showing their determination to change them.

The National Council for Civil Liberties (NCCL) also entered the debate on the side of SAU, directing its criticism at the media's entirely negative response to the children's demands. The press, it argued, had sought to construct an 'elaborate conspiracy theory' around the demonstrations, without mentioning the merits of the reforms children were calling for:

> Some of the aims of this particular demonstration correspond closely with the NCCL's call for the end to corporal punishment, the right of children to determine their personal appearance and for participation by pupils in the running of their schools. These aims seem modest enough in terms of a pronouncement by the General Secretary of the NUT [National Union of Teachers] to the effect that 'when it comes to civil rights, children are the most underprivileged group in the whole community'.

Children, the NCCL argued, had a 'constructive contribution' to make in the debate over the future shape of education in Britain, and instead of 'pouring scorn' on their attempts to air their grievances, commentators and policy-makers should be 'listening carefully to what the aggrieved party has to say' (*The Times*, Correspondence, 27/5/1972).

SAU's demand for an end to physical punishment was unsuccessful. Corporal punishment remained a feature of British schooling well into the 1980s, despite the fact that it had been abolished in Poland (in 1783), Holland, France, Finland (all in the nineteenth century) and later Belgium, Germany, Italy, Norway, Sweden and Denmark (all before 1970). But in other respects the protests that gripped Britain's schools in 1972 had some success. On an ideological level, the movement gave impetus to the growing interest in children's rights from some academics and policy-makers (Hall and Adams, 1971; NCCL, 1971).

On a more practical level, a number of local councils outside London decided to concede some of the demands: Labour-controlled Wolver-hampton Council announced that it intended to allow one pupil aged between 11 and 15 on each of the governing bodies of the town's thirty secondary schools (*The Times*, 23/5/1972); Brighton's Conservative-controlled local authority proposed that two pupil representatives sit on the governing councils of each of the town's fourteen schools (*The Times*, 24/5/1972); and eventually, even the ILEA came to formally acknowledge the merits of SAU's demands, releasing a statement which said that 'it was important to give careful consideration to the views of pupils and to give them opportunities to participate in decisions which affect them in schools through schools councils or similar means' (cited in *The Times*, 17/5/1972).

THE GREAT MINERS' STRIKE, UNEMPLOYMENT AND YOUTH TRAINING

Our final case-study is slightly different to the previous three. It comes, not from a period of working-class advance, but on the back of the defeat of the miners' strike of 1984/5. The strike officially ended on 5 March 1985 when miners across the country marched back to work; three days before this, however, pupils at a comprehensive school in the pit village of Armthorpe, Yorkshire, rioted, padlocked the school gates and formed a 150-strong picket line in front of the school. Bricks were thrown through the school windows, fences were torn down and pupils attempting to gain entry to the school were harassed (*The Times*, 2/5/1985).

Armthorpe had become accustomed to violent confrontations. The pit villages of Yorkshire had been under police siege for much of the previous year and its population had fiercely resisted the persistent police harass-ment it had been subjected to during the dispute. As the following com-ments made by a witness concerning a 'police riot' that took place in the battle-hardened village illustrate, children were not 'insulated' from the aggressive tactics adopted by the police:

> The village was cordoned off for two days while the police tried to break the miners' picket line. Two children appeared on a television news programme to describe how they had seen police smash a local man's head against a lamp-post. (Cited in *The Times*, 2/5/1985)

Were, then, the children who walked out of Armthorpe Comprehensive School in March 1985 simply copying scenes they had seen played out time and again by adults? Their headmaster believed that they were. Children, he stated, 'had dropped the game of cops and robbers in favour of police and pickets'. However, others within the school offered an alternative explanation. 'The strike', the head tutor for year three pupils stated, 'was really about unemployment, and, I suppose, if I really think about it, that the school perpetuates middle-class values in a working-class society'. The school's deputy head supported this analysis: 'It's becoming harder', he explained, 'to make the pupils see the importance of school work. I just signed off three boys and said to them all "just make sure you keep trying to find a job" . . . [but] . . . they almost all face disappointment – and unemployment benefits' (cited in *The Times*, 2/5/1985). In short, it seemed that the disruption at Armthorpe Comprehensive School resulted from a realisation on the part of pupils of the desperately insecure future they faced on leaving school – a situation made worse by the threat hanging over the mining industry at the end of the strike.

Given contemporary economic and social conditions, the children were right to be concerned. At the time, the unemployment rate for 16-year-olds was 23 per cent. A further 45 per cent were enrolled on the Conservative government's Youth Training Scheme (YTS), meaning that 68 per cent of school leavers were without a proper job (*Hansard*, 16/5/1985, Vol. 79, Col. 555).

The same concerns about mass unemployment that underpinned the isolated protest at Armthorpe Comprehensive School in March influenced the decision made by 200 schoolchild delegates at the Labour Party's Young Socialists (LPYSs) Easter Conference to call for a half-day nation-wide school strike to take place on 25 April. The delegates were opposed not only to the economic policies that had created mass youth unem-ployment, but also to the Conservative government's main method of dealing with it – YTS. YTS was introduced in 1983, ostensibly to provide young unemployed people with opportunities to gain 'training' and 'work experience'. The wages of the 'trainees' (in 1985, just £26 per week – about half the average for regular youth employment) were paid entirely by the state. Theoretically, participation on the YTS was voluntary and 16–18-year-olds could remain on Supplementary Benefit if they chose to do so. However, as Conservative ministers gradually tightened the social security system during the 1980s, the pressure applied on young people to enrol on the YTS increased. The clear aim was to 'encourage' participation through subtle coercion (Vincent, 1991). In most cases the 'training' provided on YTS was largely irrelevant to the needs of the 'trainee' and the 'oppor-tunities' on offer did little to open up avenues to permanent full-time work (Hill, 1983). Critics argued that YTS was motivated principally by a desire to exert a degree of control over young unemployed people and to remove them from politically damaging unemployment statistics (Lee, 1992).

The decisive factor that led schoolchild delegates at the LPYS's con-ference to call for a nationwide half-day school strike against the YTS was the government's announcement that participation would in future be compulsory, and that the duration of 'training placements' would be extended from twelve to twenty-four months. The Labour MP Dave Nellist subsequently explained to Parliament why those involved in the demonstration had felt compelled to undertake action of this kind:

> The 25 April strike was not anti-school, anti-teacher or anti-parent. It opposed YTS conscription and the Government who have destroyed the hopes of a generation of school leavers, 500,000 of whom have not worked since they left school under the Tory Government. . . . In 1974, 5 per cent of 16-year-olds not in full-time education were unemployed. That figure rose to 23 per cent last year.

The children's strikes of April 1985 did, therefore, differ quite significantly from the movements discussed above. Rather than being focused narrowly on the organisation of state schooling, the 1985 protests had at their heart much wider structural concerns. Thus, the children involved in the mass walkouts of 1985 were rebelling against what they perceived to be the failure of the neo-liberal-inspired Conservative government's economic and social policies.

Despite media and government attempts to discredit the proposed strike the half-day demonstration went ahead as planned on 25 April. Estimates vary as to the number of children ultimately involved. *The Times* (26/4/ 1985) claimed that backing was 'minimal' in most towns and cities, whereas the strike's supporters argued that 250,000 took part in the demonstration (*Hansard*, 16/5/1985, Vol. 79, Col. 554; *The Lancashire Evening Post*, 2/5/1985). Given that at least 4,000 children participated in Liverpool alone, and a further 1,000 in Manchester, Glasgow and Cardiff, it seems likely that support for the strike was considerably stronger than *The Times* was prepared to acknowledge. For the most part, the demonstrations passed without incident. Typically, the strikers marched peacefully to pre-arranged meeting points, whereupon they listened to speeches from their peers denouncing the Conservative government's record on youth unemployment. However, in some areas, disturbances did occur. For instance, at Caerphilly, Mid Glamorgan, '300 children . . . ran through the streets throwing stones, and at Reading, Berkshire, 41 children were arrested for throwing stones and trampling through gardens' (*The Times*, 26/4/1985).

As in the past, the national and local media were entirely unsupportive of the action taken by the schoolchildren. The editorial in the *Lancashire Evening Post* (24/4/1986) typify the attitude adopted by most sections of the press towards the protest:

> Children over 14 are now being asked to spearhead the attack on the Government's Youth Training Scheme – by going on strike. It is a monstrous suggestion and youngsters should pay no heed to this advice. . . . They can best demonstrate their good sense by striving at school to obtain the necessary qualifications possible to equip them outside. . . . Alas, in 1985 no-one has a divine right to a job.

The *Evening Post*'s editorial was in-tune with the Conservative government's thoughts on the subject. Prime Minister Margaret Thatcher condemned the strike outright, claiming that children were being manipulated by unscrupulous 'far-left' political groupings:

> I totally deplore and condemn this thoroughly mischievous attempt by left-wing groups . . . to hide behind children in expressing any concerns they may feel about the Youth Training Scheme. (Cited in *The Times*, 25/4/1985)

Once again, the possibility that children might have had something to say about an issue that directly affected them, and that they might actually harbour genuine concerns about the extent of youth unemployment, was ignored. According to the government, children were simply being 'led astray' by militants.

Were suggestions of 'manipulation' and 'political interference' at all justifiable in 1985? As evidence to support their claims, critics of the strike pointed to adult involvement in the organisation of the demonstration. In fact, many of those involved in co-ordinating the 1985 protests were *not* schoolchildren themselves. Indeed, the strike was spearheaded and funded by the Youth Trade Union Rights Campaign (YTURC), a Labour Party and trade union-financed body committed to securing decent conditions for young workers on government training schemes. YTURC was made up mainly of LPYS activists, many of whom were former YTS 'trainees' themselves. At the previous year's Labour Party Conference YTURC had been instrumental in securing the passage of a motion calling for a minimum YTS allowance of £55, the right for 'trainees' to join trade unions, and for the right to a job at the end of the scheme (*Hansard*, 16/5/1985, Vol. 79, Cols 555–6). However, although Government spokespersons and the media claimed that YTURC's contribution to the children's strikes provided conclusive proof of a 'left-wing' conspiracy, its involvement stemmed from far less sinister considerations. As *The Times Educational Supplement* (3/5/1985) subsequently acknowledged, pupils themselves approached YTURC asking it to assist in the setting up of regional strike committees. As one of the striking Liverpool schoolchildren stated, 'As far as we could see, YTURC was the only organised campaign group that was trying to do something about YTS. What else could we do really?' YTURC itself also dismissed claims that it was responsible for initiating the protest. 'School students', one of its members pointed out, 'have become aware of the need to fight back not because of a few leaflets handed out by the Youth Trade Union Rights Campaign, but because of the way their own brothers and sisters have been treated by this Government' (*The Lancashire Evening Post*, Correspondence, 2/5/1985).

Another noteworthy feature of the 1985 school strike was the strong degree of support it obtained from parents, local authorities and national politicians. In Preston, for example, parents were said to have been 'quite firmly' behind the strike, and headmasters received notes from them requesting leave of absence for their children to attend the demonstration that took place in the town centre. The leader of the town's Labour Party branch declared his approval of the youngsters' fight against the YTS, as did the chairman of the council's Education Committee (*The Lancashire Evening Post*, 26/4/1985). Liverpool's Labour-controlled City Council went further, giving an assurance that no child involved in the demonstration would be penalised or victimised (*The Times Educational Supplement*, 25/4/1985). The support and encouragement received from national politicians was also considerable: a significant number of backbench Labour MPs and at least four members of the Labour Party's National Executive Committee – Michael Meacher, Tony Benn, Eric Heffer and Dennis Skinner – supported the strikes (*The Times*, 25/4/1985).

How should we judge the movement's overall impact? If the success of the protest is to be measured in the narrow terms of whether it initiated a reorientation of the Conservative government's socio-economic objectives, and, more specifically, whether it led it to re-think its proposals for the YTS, then it must be seen as a failure. Mass youth and adult unemployment continued to be seen by Conservative ministers as a 'price worth paying' for 'economic stability' and little, if anything, was done to either prevent or alleviate it. With regard to the YTS, 16–18-year-olds were stripped of their right to social security benefits in 1988 when participation on the scheme became compulsory (Gazeley and Thane, 1998). However, in other respects the strike was a success. First, the ability of schoolchildren across the country to amass such a broad constituency of support for their cause must be seen as one of the major achievements of the 25 April strike. It showed that children's 'voices' were not ignored and that they could help inform and shape political debate in Britain. Second, the strike should also be seen as an ideological triumph. On the one hand, it showed that a significant proportion of working-class children had not been swept along in the 'Thatcherite tide', and that despite threats of disciplinary action and suspension from their schools, they were still prepared to vent their anger at what they felt were profoundly unjust policies. On the other hand, the strike demonstrated that an important step forward had occurred in relation to children's political awareness and activism. For unlike the 1889, 1911 and 1972 children's strikes, which were focused narrowly on the organisation of state education, the 25 April demonstration was motivated by much wider structural concerns. It was, in fact, just one of a number of occasions (albeit an important one) during the 1980s when children displayed an increased willingness to speak out and demand action on a range of national and international issues that concerned them.

CONCLUSION

This chapter is slightly different from others in the collection. Its purpose has been to focus on four occasions when children have entered collective action to protest against shared, class-specific grievances. In each case we have suggested that the grievances were well-founded and that the actions, led by children themselves, were an appropriate, rational response to their concerns. Further, on each occasion we have suggested the wider conflicts of the period have led some children to question a range of factors about their world and its priorities and, more specifically, that the inspiration for such activity has come from some children observing and learning the strategies and tactics of collective action from wider working-class mobilisations.

We could have discussed other examples. The heroic struggle of black schoolchildren in South Africa against apartheid, the children of Paris in 1968 who joined the protests of May that year, or the working-class youth of the 'Edelweiss Pirates' who fought running battles with the Hitler youth throughout the 1930s and early 1940s in Germany – we make no claims that children in Britain are unique in this process. But in Britain (as elsewhere) there is a hidden vibrant history of working-class children engaging in collective action to improve their world and stand up for their rights. These four examples are the tip of the iceberg, but they also offer, we suggest, a different slant on the struggle for children's rights.

KEY TEXT

Humphries, S. (1981) *Hooligans or Rebels? An Oral History of Working Class Childhood and Youth 1889–1939*. Oxford: Blackwell.

THIRTEEN

Childhood: Themes and Issues

JIM McKECHNIE

At this point in any book of this type it is common for the editors to offer the reader a 'conclusion'. However, we have decided to adopt a different approach for two reasons. First, we are of the opinion that the individual chapters speak for themselves. Second, since this text is aimed at critically evaluating the area of childhood studies we felt that it would be more relevant to leave the reader with some issues for consideration and discussion.

Throughout this book certain themes have emerged and these have been explicit or implicit in all of the chapters. Below we have highlighted, and stated our views, on a number of these themes. It is our contention that in evaluating any conceptualisation of childhood particular attention should be paid to how these issues are addressed.

HISTORICAL PERSPECTIVE

In a number of current texts it is argued that childhood is a phenomenon that is 'constructed and reconstructed'. Adopting such a position would lead one to question the validity of considering the experience of childhood in different times, given that childhood is continually reconstructed there is in effect no continuity.

Throughout the chapters in this text this position is challenged. We would argue that adopting an historical perspective has a number of advantages. First, it provides a comparative base. Second, by considering change over time it is possible to identify specific forces and the role they play in the construction of children's experiences. Third, a number of the chapters argue that there is evidence to support the view that there is some degree of continuity in childhood over time.

AGENCY

One of the central tenets within the new sociology of childhood is the need to acknowledge the 'agency' of children. Such an emphasis is to be welcomed and has parallels with the views of many psychologists. One of the challenges facing social scientists is in defining and demonstrating such 'agency'. However, there is an additional issue that needs to be addressed. If children, like adults, are viewed as playing an active role in constructing and determining their own lives does this mean that they have a free hand in such an enterprise? In considering childhood, and adulthood for that matter, it must be acknowledged that agency is constrained. It is constrained by individual experience and circumstances and by the social structures within a society.

That does not mean that we should view children as passive recipients of the society and culture around them. However, it does mean that we need to accept the fact that the society and its structures constrain agency. To paraphrase Marx, 'people make history, but not in circumstances of their own choosing'. A number of the chapters in this text argue that in areas of social policy the 'social control' of children has emerged as a key concern.

CLASS AND SOCIAL DIVISION

Any attempt to understand childhood must deal with the issue of social division. Two contrasting positions are emerging. First, within the new sociology of childhood it is suggested that while class, race and gender are important factors that affect children and childhood there is a stronger commonality experienced by all children irrespective of social division. This commonality is based on their status as children within society and encompasses such factors as the lack of power they have. The second, alternative, viewpoint is that social divisions are primary elements to our understanding of childhood. These social divisions are so important that they result in markedly different experiences of childhood. For example, a number of chapters in this text contrast the childhoods of the poor and the wealthy.

In understanding the different experience of childhood that children have, emphasis has been placed on *'children's voices'*. The idea of listening to the voices of children is embedded in the United Nations Convention on the Rights of the Child. The importance of children's voices has also been emphasised by the proponents of the new sociology of childhood. Such an emphasis is to be welcomed since ignoring the views of children devalues them as citizens and leads to poorer policy.

However, the issue for debate is not whether we should listen to children's voices but rather how are we to respond to such voices? Implicit in the new sociology of childhood is the view that 'children's voices' are in some way to be given privileged status within areas relating to childhood. It is our view that within research and policy-making children's voices should, and need to, be heard but that they should not be given a privileged status. Research findings will offer greater insights if a range of methods are used and policy decision-making will be more effective if a multiplicity of 'voices' are listened to. The challenge is to create the space for 'children's voices' and to change adult attitudes towards the value they place in what is said.

SOCIAL CONSTRUCTIONISM

For a number of years social scientists have been attempting to deal with the explanatory role of culture, or context, and incorporate this within a range of disciplines. Within the literature this has manifested itself as a choice between extremes of 'universalism' or 'relativism'. Social constructionism offers one position within this debate. From this perspective an emphasis is placed on the diversity that exists within and between cultures. Concepts such as gender, race and sexuality are socially constructed, as is childhood. The new sociology of childhood draws heavily on this perspective when it is argued that childhood is 'constructed and reconstructed'. However, the pressing question is to explain *how* concepts such as childhood are constructed and changed over time.

We would argue that the process of social construction does not exist in a vacuum. While social constructionism is attempting to explain diversity due to contextual or cultural variation, the process of social construction is in turn influenced by that context. Therefore, the concepts that are constructed, such as childhood, must be built under the influence of the dominant institutions and structures of that society. One of the most dominant structures is that of *the State*.

Throughout this book different authors have highlighted the impact of policy on children's lives. The implication is that any understanding of childhood, and the factors which influence its construction, must include an interpretation of the State's role in this process. If we accept that context plays a role in defining childhood we must also be able to consider the structures within that context. Implicit in this is an understanding that structures change over time, highlighting the need for the use of an historical perspective.

The themes outlined above tie the different chapters in this book together. As part of your review of the different chapters we would suggest that you, either individually or with your peers, identify where and how these themes emerge.

One of the primary aims of this text has been to offer a critical view of childhood studies. In the spirit of this aim we would urge that you seek out other texts on childhood and evaluate the positions adopted by other authors on the themes and issues identified above. Ultimately you may, or may not, agree with the views and positions taken by the authors within this book. What we hope is that, in seeking to clarify your own position on the issues and debates about childhood, you gain a clearer understanding of this growing academic area.

Bibliography

Allen, I. (1987) *Education in Sex and Personal Relationships*. London: Policy Studies Institute.

American Federation of Teachers (2000) *Small Class Size: Education Reform that Works*. Washington, DC: AFT.

Andrews, K. and Jacobs, J. (1990) *Punishing the Poor: Poverty Under Thatcher*. London: Macmillan.

Apple, M. and Whittey, G. (1999) Structuring the post-modern in education policy', in D. Hill, P. McLaren, M. Cole and G. Rikowski (eds), *Postmodernism and Education Theory*. London: Tufnall.

Ariès, P. (1962) *Centuries of Childhood*. Harmondsworth: Penguin.

Ascheson, D. (1998) *Independent Inquiry into Inequalities in Health*. London: Department of Health. http://www.doh.gov.uk/ih/ih.htm.

Atkinson, A.B. (1996) 'Seeking to explain the distribution of income', in J. Hills (ed.), *New Inequalities*. Cambridge: Cambridge University Press.

Baker, A. and Duncan, S. (1985) 'Child sexual abuse – a study of prevalence in Great Britain', *Child Abuse and Neglect*, 9: 457–67.

Ball, S.J. (1996) 'Performativity and fragmentation in "postmodern schooling"', unpublished paper quoted in R. Slee, G. Weiner and S. Tomlinson (eds) (1998) *School Effectiveness for Whom?* London: Falmer.

Barn, R. (1993) *Black Children in the Public Care System*. London: Batsford.

Barnardo's (1998) *Whose Daughter Next? Children Abused Through Prostitution*. London: Barnardo's.

Barter, C. (1996) *Nowhere to Hide*. London: Centrepoint.

Beck, U. (1992) *Risk Society: Towards a New Modernity*. London: Sage.

Becker, H.S. (1996) 'The epistemology of qualitative research', in R. Jessor, A. Colby and R. Shedder (eds), *Ethnography and Human Development*. Chicago: University of Chicago Press.

Becker, S., MacPherson, S. and Falkingham, F. (1987) 'Some local authority responses to poverty', *Local Government Studies*, 13: 35–48.

Behlmer, G. (1982) *Child Abuse and Moral Reform in England 1870–1908*. Stanford, CA: Stanford University Press.

Beitchman, J., Zucker, K., Hood, J., Da Costa, G. and Akman, D. (1991) 'A review of the short-term effects of child sexual abuse', *Child Abuse and Neglect*, 15: 537–56.

Beitchman, J., Zucker, K., Hood, J., Da Costa, G., Akman, D. and Cassavia, E. (1992) 'A review of the long-term effects of child sexual abuse', *Child Abuse and Neglect*, 16: 101–8.

Benzeval, M. (1997) 'Health', in A. Walker and C. Walker (eds), *Britain Divided: The Growth of Social Exclusion in the 1980s and 1990s*. London: Child Poverty Action Group.

Beresford, P., Green, D., Lister, R. and Woodard, K. (1999) *Poverty First Hand: Poor People Speak for Themselves*. London: Child Poverty Action Group.

Bibby, P. (ed.) (1996) *Organised Abuse: the Current Debate*. Aldershot: Aldgate.

Blagg, H and Smith, D. (1989) *Crime, Penal Policy and Social Work*. Harlow: Longman.

Board of Education (1943) *Sex Education in Schools and Youth Organisations*. London: HMSO.

Bolin-Hort, P. (1989) *Work, Family and the State: Child Labour and the Organisation of Production in the British Cotton Industry (1780–1920)*. Lund, Sweden: Lund University Press.

Bottoms, A. and Stevenson, S. (1992) 'What went wrong? Criminal justice policy in England and Wales 1945–70', in D. Downes (ed.), *Unravelling Criminal Justice*. London: Macmillan.

Bowlby, J. (1971) *Attachment and Loss. Vol. 1: Attachment*. Harmondsworth: Penguin.

Boyd, B. (1999) 'Scottish school pupils: characteristics and influences', in T. Bryce and W. Humes (eds), *Scottish Education*. Edinburgh: Edinburgh University Press.

Boyden, J., Ling, B. and Myers, W. (1998) *What Works for Working Children*. Smedjebacken: UNICEF/Radda Barnen.

Boyson, R. (1975) *The Crisis in Education*. London: Woburn.

Britain (2001) *Britain 2001 National Statistics*. London: The Stationery Office.

Browne, H. (1979) *The Rise of British Trade Unions: 1825–1914*. London: Longman.

Bryan, B., Dadzi, S. and Scafe, S. (1985) *The Heart of the Race: Black Women's Lives in Britain*. London: Virago.

Bryce, T. and Humes, W. (eds) (1999) *Scottish Education*. Edinburgh: Edinburgh University Press.

Bryman, A. (1988) *Quantity and Quality in Social Research*. London: Unwin Hyman.

Burt, C. (1925) *The Young Delinquent*. London: University of London Press.

Butler-Sloss, Lord Justice E. (1988) *Report of the Inquiry into Child Abuse in Cleveland 1987*, DHSS Cmnd 412. London: HMSO.

California Department of Education (2000) *Class Size Reduction*. California: California Department of Education.

Callinicos, A. (1983) *The Revolutionary Ideas of Marx*. London: Bookmarks.

Callinicos, A. (1987) *Making History*. Cambridge: Polity.

Callinicos, A. (1989) *Against Postmodernism: A Marxist Critique*. Cambridge: Polity.

Callinicos, A. (1993) *Race and Class*. London: Bookmarks.

Campbell, B. (1988) *Unofficial Secrets*. London: Virago.

Carpenter, M. (1851) *Reformatory Schools for the Children of the Perishing and Dangerous Classes and for Juvenile Offenders*. London: Gilpin.

Carpenter, M. (1853) *Juvenile Delinquents: Social Evils, Their Causes and Their Cure*. London: Cash.

Cawson, P., Wattam, C., Brooker, S. and Kelly, G. (2001) *Child Maltreatment in the United Kingdom: A Study of the Prevalence of Child Abuse and Neglect*. London: NSPCC.

Chapman, B. (2001) 'Young homeless people's experiences of social exclusion at the hands of the gatekeepers of Services'. Unpublished MA social work thesis, University of Liverpool.

Charlton, J. (1999) *It Just Went Like Tinder*. London: Redwoods.

Cleaver, H., Unell, I. and Aldgate, J. (1999) *Children's Needs–Parenting Capacity: the Impact of Parental Mental Illness, Problem Alcohol and Drug Use, and Domestic Violence on Children's Development*. London: The Stationery Office.

Cliff, T. and Gluckstein, D. (1996) *The Labour Party: A Marxist History*. London: Bookmarks.

Clyde, Lord (1992) *Report of the Inquiry into the Removal of Children from Orkney in February 1991*, HoC 195. London: HMSO.

Cohen, S. (1985) *Visions of Social Control*. Cambridge: Polity Press.

Cole, M. and Cole, S. (2001) *The Development of Children*, 4th edn. New York: Worth.

Cole, M. and Hill, D. (1999) 'Equality and secondary education: what are the conceptual issues?', in D. Hill and M. Cole (eds), *Promoting Equality in Secondary Schools*. London: Cassell.

Cole, M., Hill, D. and Rikowski, G. (1997) 'Between postmodernism and nowhere: the predicament of the postmodernist', *British Journal of Educational Studies*, 45: 187–200.

Coleman, S.R. and Mehlman, S.E. (1992) 'An empirical update (1969–1989) of D.L. Krantz's thesis that the experimental analysis of behavior is isolated', *Behavior Analyst*, 15: 43–9.

Coll, C.G. and Magnusson, K. (1999) 'Cultural influences on child development: are we ready for a paradigm shift?', in A.S. Masten (ed.), *Cultural Processes in Child Development: the Minnesota Symposia in Child Psychology*, Vol. 29. Mahwah, NJ: Lawrence Erlbaum.

Connell, R.W. (1987) *Gender and Power*. Cambridge: Polity Press.

Coolican, H. (1994) *Research Methods and Statistics in Psychology*, 2nd edn. London: Hodder and Stoughton.

Coppock, V., Haydon, D. and Richter, I. (1995) *The Illusions of 'Post-Feminism': New Women, Old Myths*. London: Taylor and Francis.

Corby, B. (1998) *Managing Child Sexual Abuse Cases*. London: Jessica Kingsley.

Corby, B., Doig, A. and Roberts V. (1998) 'Inquiries into child abuse', *Journal of Social Welfare and Family Law*, 20: 377–95.

Corby, B., Doig, A. and Roberts V. (2001) *Public Inquiries into Abuse of Children in Residential Care*. London: Jessica Kingsley.

Corby, B., Millar, M. and Young, L. (1996) 'Parental participation in child protection work: rethinking the rhetoric', *British Journal of Social Work*, 16: 457–92.

Cornwell, D. and Hobbs, S. (1984) 'Spontaneous play in childhood', *Psychological Record*, 36: 161–66.

Cornwell, D. and Hobbs, S. (1986) 'The identification of play, ERIC document ED 263 990', *Research in Education*, 21: 109.

Corsaro, W.A. (1997) *The Sociology of Childhood*. Thousand Oaks, CA: Pine Forge Press.

Corteen, K. and Scraton, P. (1997) 'Prolonging "childhood", manufacturing "innocence" and regulating sexuality', in P. Scraton (ed.), *'Childhood' in 'Crisis'?* London: UCL Press.

Creighton, S. and Noyes, P. (1989) *Child Abuse Trends in England and Wales 1983–1987*. London: NSPCC.

Cresswell, J.W. (1998) *Qualitative Inquiry and Research Design: Choosing among Five Traditions*. Thousand Oaks, CA: Sage.

Crosland, A. (1956) *The Future of Socialism*. London: Constable.

Cunningham, H. (1990) 'The employment and unemployment of children in England c. 1680–1851', *Past and Present*, 126: 116–50.

Cunningham, H. (1995) *Children and Childhood in Western Society since 1500*. London: Longman.

Cunningham, S. (1999) 'The problem that doesn't exist? Child labour in Britain 1918–1970', in M. Lavalette (ed.), *A Thing of the Past?: Child Labour in Britain in the Nineteenth and Twentieth Centuries*. Liverpool: Liverpool University Press.

Cunningham, S. (2000) 'Child labour in Britain 1900–1973'. Unpublished PhD, University of Central Lancashire.

Cunningham, H. and Viazzo, P.P. (eds) (1996) *Child Labour in Historical Perspective 1800–1985*. Florence: UNICEF International Child Development Centre.

Curtis Committee (1946) *Report of the Care of Children's Committee*, Home Office, Cmnd 6922. London: HMSO.

Dangerfield, G. (1964) *The Strange Death of Liberal England* [first published 1935]. New York: Capricorn Books.

Darlington, R. and Lyddon, D. (2001) *Glorious Summer: Class Struggle in Britain 1972*. London: Bookmarks.

Davies, E. (1972) 'Work out of school', *Education*, 10 November: I–IV.

Davies, N. (1997) *Dark Heart*. London: Chatto and Windus.

Davies, N. (2000) *The School Report*. London: Vintage.

Davin, A. (1982) 'Child labour, the working class family and domestic ideology in nineteenth century Britain', *Development and Change*, 13: 4.

Davin, A. (1990) 'When is a child not a child?', in H. Carr and L. Jamieson (eds), *The Politics of Everyday Life*. Basingstoke: Macmillan.

Davin, A. (1996) *Growing Up Poor*. London: Rivers Oram Press.

DeMause, L. (ed.) (1974) *The History of Childhood*. New York: Harper Row.

Denham, S.A. and Auerbach, S. (1995) 'Mother–child dialogue about emotions and pre-schoolers' emotional competence', *Genetic, Social and General Psychology Monographs*, 121: 311–37.

Denzin, N.K. and Lincoln, Y.S. (1994) *Handbook of Qualitative Research*. Thousand Oaks, CA: Sage.

Department for Education (1994) *Circular Number 5/94. Education Act 1993: Sex Education in School (6.5.94)*. London: DFE.

Department for Education and Employment (1998) '£75 million boosts radical Education Action Zones to raise standards', DfEE press release, 23 June 1998.

Department for Education and Employment (1999) *National Healthy School Standard Guidance.* Nottingham: DfEE.

Department for Education and Employment (2000) *Sex and Relationship Guidance.* Nottingham: DfEE.

Department of Education and Science (1968) *The Handbook of Health Education.* London: HSMO.

Department of Education and Science (1977) *Health Education in Schools.* London: HMSO.

Department of Education and Science (1980) *A Framework for the School Curriculum.* London: HMSO.

Department of Education and Science (1981) *The School Curriculum.* London: HMSO.

Department of Education and Science (1987) *Circular Number 11/87. Sex Education at School (25.9.87).* London: DES.

Department of Health (1991) *Working Together under the Children Act 1989: a Guide to Arrangements for Inter-agency Cooperation for the Protection of Children from Abuse.* London: HMSO.

Department of Health (1995a) *Child Protection: Messages from Research.* London: HMSO.

Department of Health (1995b) *The Key Area Handbook on HIV/AIDS and Sexual Health.* London: Department of Health.

Department of Health (2000a) *Framework for the Assessment of Children in Need and their Families.* London: Department of Health.

Department of Health (2000b) *Working Together to Safeguard Children: a Guide to Inter-agency Working to Safeguard and Promote the Welfare of Children.* London: Department of Health.

Department of Health (2000c) *Survey of Children and Young Persons on Child Protection Registers Year Ending 31st March 2000.* London: Department of Health.

Department of Health (2000d) *Protecting Children, Supporting Parents: a Consultation Document on the Punishment of Children.* London: Department of Health.

Department of Social Security (2000) *Households Below Average Income.* London: HMSO.

Dockrell, J. and Joffe, H. (1992) 'Methodological issues involved in the study of young people and HIV/AIDS: a social psychological view', *Health and Education Research*, 7: 509–16.

Donaldson, M. (1978) *Children's Minds.* London: Fontana.

Donzelot, J. (1979) *The Policing of Families.* London: Hutchinson.

Dunford, J. (1999) 'The comprehensive success story', *Forum*, 41: 28–30.

Educational Priorities Panel (2000) *Smaller is Better.* New York: EPP.

Eekelaar, J. (1991) 'Parental responsibility: state of nature or nature of the State?', *Journal of Social Welfare and Family Law*, 1: 37–50.

Egeland, B. (1988) 'Breaking the cycle of abuse: implications for prediction and intervention', in K. Browne, C. Davies and P. Stratton (eds), *Early Prediction and Prevention of Child Abuse.* Chichester: John Wiley.

Ensor, R.C.K. (1950) 'The problems of quantity and quality in the British population', *Eugenics Review*, 13: 128–35.

Epstein, D. and Johnson, R. (1998) *Schooling Sexualities.* Buckingham: Open University Press.

Erooga, M. and Masson, H. (eds) (1999) *Children and Young People who Sexually Abuse Others: Challenges and Responses.* London: Routledge.

Evans, D. (1994) 'Falling angels? The material construction of children as sexual citizens', *International Journal of Children's Rights*, 2: 1–33.

Farrell, C. (1978) *My Mother Said . . . the Way Young People Learned about Sex and Birth Control.* London: Routledge and Kegan Paul.

Ferguson, N., Davies, P., Evans, R. and Williams, P. (1971) 'The Plowden Report's recommendations for identifying children in need of extra help', *Educational Research*, 13: 210–13.

Field, F. (1974) *Unequal Britain.* London: Arrow.

Fimister, G. (ed.) (2001) *An End in Sight? Tackling Child Poverty in the UK.* London: Child Poverty Action Group.

Finlayson, D. (1972) 'Parental aspirations and the educational achievement of children', *Educational Research*, 14: 61–4.

Forder, A. (1966) *Social Casework and Social Administration.* London: Faber and Faber.

Fox Harding, L. (1991) *Perspectives in Child Care Policy*. Harlow: Longman.

France, A., Bendelow, G. and Williams, S. (2000) 'A "risky" business: researching the health beliefs of children and young people', in A. Lewis and G. Lindsay (eds), *Researching Children's Perspectives*. Buckingham: Open University Press.

Franklin, B. (ed.) (1995) *The Handbook of Children's Rights: Comparative Policy and Practice*. London: Routledge.

Freeman, M. (1999) 'Children are unbeatable', *Children and Society*, 13: 130–41.

Frend, R., Rafferty, Y. and Bramel, D. (1990) 'A puzzling misinterpretation of the Asch "conformity" study', *European Journal of Social Psychology*, 20: 29–44.

Freud, S. (1961) *Beyond the Pleasure Principle*. London: Hogarth Press.

Friman, F.C., Aklen, K.D., Kerwin, M.L.E. and Larzelere, R. (1993) 'Changes in modern psychology: a citation analysis of the Kuhnian displacement thesis', *American Psychologist*, 49: 658–64.

Fuller, P. (1979) 'Uncovering childhood', in M. Hoyles (ed.), *Changing Childhood*. London: Readers and Writers.

Garbarino, J. and Vondra, J. (1987) 'Psychological maltreatment: issues and perspectives', in M. Brassard, R. Germain and S. Hart (eds), *Psychological Maltreatment of Children and Youth*. Oxford: Pergamon Press.

Garbarino, J., Stott, M. and Faculty of Erikson Institute (1992) *What Children Can Tell Us*. San Francisco: Jossey-Bass.

Garland, D. (1985) *Punishment and Welfare: a History of Penal Strategies*. Aldershot: Gower.

Gazeley, I. and Thane, P. (1998) 'Patterns of visibility: unemployment in Britain during the nineteenth and twentieth centuries', in G. Lewis (ed.), *Forming Nation, Framing Welfare*. London: Routledge.

Gelles, R. and Cornell, C. (1985) *Intimate Violence in Families*. Beverly Hills, CA: Sage.

Gelsthorpe, L. and Morris, A. (1994) 'Juvenile justice 1945–1992', in M. Maguire, R. Morgan and R. Reiner (eds), *The Oxford Handbook of Criminology*. Oxford: Clarendon Press.

Giaretto, H. (1981) 'A comprehensive child sexual abuse treatment program', in P. Mrazek and C. Kempe (eds), *Sexually Abused Children and Their Families*. New York: Pergamon Press.

Gil, D. (1970) *Violence against Children*. Cambridge, MA: Harvard University Press.

Gillborn, D. and Mirza, H. (2000) *Educational Inequality – Mapping Race, Class and Gender: A Synthesis of Research Evidence*. London: OFSTED.

Gillborn, D. and Youdell, D. (2000) *Rationing Education*. London: Oxford University Press.

Goldman, R. and Goldman, J. (1982) *Children's Sexual Thinking*. London: Routledge and Kegan Paul.

Goldson, B. (1997a) '"Childhood": an introduction to historical and theoretical analyses', in P. Scraton (ed.), *'Childhood' in 'Crisis'?* London: UCL Press.

Goldson, B. (1997b) 'Children in trouble: state responses to juvenile crime', in P. Scraton (ed.), *'Childhood' in 'Crisis'?* London: UCL Press.

Goldson, B. (1997c) 'Locked out and locked up: state policy and the systemic exclusion of children "in need" in England and Wales', *Representing Children*, 10: 44–55.

Goldson, B. (2001) 'The demonisation of children: from the symbolic to the institutional', in P. Foley, J. Roche and S. Tucker (eds), *Children in Society: Contemporary Theory, Policy and Practice*. Basingstoke: Palgrave.

Goldson, B. (ed.) (1999) *Youth Justice: Contemporary Policy and Practice*. Aldershot: Ashgate.

Goldson, B. (ed.) (2000) *The New Youth Justice*. Lyme Regis: Russell House.

Goldson, B. and Peters, E. (2000) *Tough Justice: Responding to Children in Trouble*. London: The Children's Society.

Grieg A. and Taylor, J. (1999) *Doing Research with Children*. London: Sage.

Griffin, C. (1995) 'Feminism, social psychology and qualitative research', *The Psychologist*, 8: 119–21.

Guardian (2001) 'Labour cut education spending to 40-year low', The *Guardian*, 4 September 2001.

Hain, P. (1986) *Political Strikes: the State and Trade Unionism in Britain*. Harmondsworth: Penguin.

Halevy, E. (1924) *History of the English People in the 19th Century*. London: Fisher Unwin.

Halifax, N. (1988) *Out, Proud and Fighting* (pamphlet). London: Socialist Workers Party.

Hall, J. and Adams, P. (eds) (1971) *Children's Rights: Towards the Liberation of the Child*. London: Elek.

Hall, S. (1982) *Drifting into a Law and Order Society*. London: The Cobden Trust.

Hallan, S. and Ireson, J. (2001) 'Ability grouping in schools: practices and consequences'. Paper presented at the American Educational Research Conference, 2001.

Halsey, A.H. (1972) *Educational Priority. Vol. 1: Problems and Policies*. London: HMSO.

Hanawalt, B. (1993) *Growing Up in Medieval London*. New York: Oxford University Press.

Harker, R. (1971) 'Social class factors in a New Zealand comprehensive school', *Educational Research*, 13: 155–58.

Harman, C. (1988) *The Fire Last Time: 1968 and After*. London: Bookmarks.

Harris, R. (1982) 'Institutionalized ambivalence: social work and the Children and Young Persons Act 1969', *British Journal of Social Work*, 12: 247–63.

Harris, R. and Webb, D. (1987) *Welfare, Power and Juvenile Justice*. London: Tavistock.

Hart, B. and Risley, T.R. (1995) *Meaningful Differences in the Everyday Experience of Young American Children*. Baltimore: Paul H. Brookes.

Haydon, D. (2001) 'Children's rights to sex and sexuality education', in B. Franklin (ed.), *The Handbook of Children's Rights: Comparative Policy and Practice*, 2nd edn. London: Routledge.

Hearn, J. (1990) 'Child abuse and men's violence' in the Violence against Children Study Group, *Taking Child Abuse Seriously*. London: Unwin Hyman.

Hendrick, H. (1994) *Child Welfare: England 1872–1989*. London: Routledge.

Henriques, B. (1955) *The Home-Menders*. London: Harrap.

Henwood, K. and Pidgeon, N. (1995) 'Grounded theory and psychological research', *The Psychologist*, 8: 115–18.

HEROS (2000) *Class Size Research*. USA: HEROS.

Heyduk, R.G. and Fenigstein, A. (1984) 'Influential works and authors in psychology: a survey of eminent psychologists', *American Psychologist*, 40: 556–9.

Hibbett, A. and Beatson, M. (1995) 'Young people at work', *Employment Gazette*, 103: 169–77.

Hill, D., McLaren, P., Cole, M. and Rikowski, G. (eds) (1999) *Postmodernism in Educational Theory: Education and the Politics of Human Resistance*. London: Tufnell Press.

Hill, M. (1983) 'Government responses to unemployment', in M. Loney, D. Boswell and J. Clarke (eds), *Social Policy and Social Welfare*. Milton Keynes: Open University Press.

Hobbs, S. and McKechnie, J. (1997) *Child Employment in Britain: a Social and Psychological Analysis*. Edinburgh: The Stationery Office.

Hobbs, S. and McKechnie, J. (1999) 'Child employment: what happens in the workplace?' Paper presented at the Sites of Learning Conference, Centre for the Social Study of Childhood, University of Hull, 14–16 September 1999.

Hobbs, C. and Wynne, J. (1986) 'Buggery in childhood – a common syndrome of child abuse', *The Lancet*, ii: 792–6.

Hobbs, S., Lindsay, S. and McKechnie, J. (1996) 'The extent of child employment in Britain', *British Journal of Education and Work*, 9: 5–18.

Hobbs, S., McKechnie, J. and Lavalette, M. (1999) *Child Labor: a World History Companion*. Santa Barbara, CA ABC-Clio.

Hobsbawm, E.J. (1994) *Age of Empire 1875–1914*. London: Abacus.

Home Office (1911) *Colliery Strike Disturbances in South Wales: Correspondence and Report, November 1910*, Cmnd 5568. London: HMSO.

Home Office (1927) *Report of the Departmental Committee on the Treatment of Young Offenders*. London: HMSO.

Home Office and the Department of Health (1992) *Memorandum of Good Practice on Video-recorded Interviews with Child Witnesses for Criminal Proceedings*. London: HMSO.

Horrell, S. and Humphries, J. (1999) 'Child labour and British industrialization', in M. Lavalette (ed.), *A Thing of the Past? Child Labour in Britain in the Nineteenth and Twentieth Centuries*. Liverpool: Liverpool University Press.

Howe, D. (1994) 'Modernity, postmodernity and social work', *British Journal of Social Work*, 24: 5.

Howe, D. (1995) *Attachment Theory for Social Work Practice*. London: Macmillan.

Hughes, M. and Grieve, R. (1980) 'On asking children bizarre questions', *First Language*, 1: 149–60.

Humphries, S. (1981) *Hooligans or Rebels? An Oral History of Working Class Childhood and Youth 1889–1939*. Oxford: Blackwell.

Jackson, S. (1982) *Childhood and Sexuality*. London: Blackwell.

James, A. (1999) 'Researching children's social competence', in M. Woodhead, D. Faulkner and K. Littleton (eds), *Making Sense of Social Development*. London: Routledge.

James, A. and Prout, A. (eds) (1990) *Constructing and Reconstructing Childhood: Contemporary Issues in the Sociological Study of Childhood*. London: Falmer Press.

James, A. and Prout, A. (eds) (1997) *Constructing and Reconstructing Childhood: Contemporary Issues in the Sociological Study of Childhood*, 2nd edn. London: Falmer.

James, A., Jenks, C. and Prout, A. (1998) *Theorizing Childhood*. Cambridge: Polity Press.

Jeffs, T. and Smith, M.K (1996) '"Getting the dirtbags off the street": curfews and other solutions to juvenile crime', *Youth and Policy*, 53: 1–14.

Jessor, R. (1996) 'Ethnographic methods in contemporary perspective', in R. Jessor, A. Colby and R. Shedder (eds), *Ethnography and Human Development*. Chicago: University of Chicago Press.

Jolliffe, F., Patel, S., Sparks, Y. and Reardon, K. (1995) *Child Employment in Greenwich*. London: Borough of Greenwich, Education Social Work Service.

Jones, A. (1993) 'UK: anti-racist child protection', *Race and Class*, 35: 75–85.

Jones, C. (1984) *State Social Work and the Working Class*. London: Macmillan.

Jones, C. (2001) 'Voices from the front line: social workers and New Labour', *British Journal of Social Work*, 31: 547–62.

Jones, C. and Novak, T. (1999) *Poverty, Welfare and the Disciplinary State*. London: Routledge.

Keenan, M., Kerr, K.P. and Dillenburger, K. (eds) (2000) *Parents' Education as Autism Therapists: Applied Behaviour Analysis in Context*. London: Jessica Kingsley.

Kempe, C.H. and Kempe, R. (1978) *Child Abuse*. London: Fontana.

Kempe, C.H., Silverman, F., Steele, B., Droegemueller, W. and Silver, H. (1962) 'The battered child syndrome', *Journal of the American Medical Association*, 181: 17–24.

Krausen, R. (1973) 'The relationship of certain "pre-reading" skills to general ability and social class in nursery children', *Educational Research*, 15: 72–9.

Kumar, V. (1993) *Poverty and Inequality in the UK: the Effects on Children*. London: National Children's Bureau.

La Fontaine, J. (1994) *The Extent and Nature of Organised and Ritual Abuse: Research Findings*. London: HMSO.

Labour Party (1964) *Crime: A Challenge to Us All. Report of a Labour Party Study Group*. London: Labour Party.

Labour Party (1997) *New Labour: Because Britain Deserves Better*. London: Labour Party.

Labour Party (2001) *Ambitions for Britain: Labour's Manifesto 2001*. London: Labour Party.

Lampl, P. (n.d.) 'Special report: opening up elite education', The Sutton Trust.

Lancashire Daily Post, The: various dates.

Lancashire Evening Post, The: various dates.

Lavalette, M. (1994) *Child Employment in the Capitalist Labour Market*. Aldershot: Avebury.

Lavalette, M (1998) 'Child labour: historical, legislative and policy context', in B. Pettitt (ed.), *Children and Work in the UK – Refocusing the Debate*. London StC Fund/CPAG.

Lavalette, M. (ed.) (1999a) *A Thing of the Past? Child Labour in Britain in the Nineteenth and Twentieth Centuries*. Liverpool: Liverpool University Press.

Lavalette, M. (1999b) 'Theorizing children at work: family, state and relations of production in historical context', in M. Lavalette (ed.), *A Thing of the Past? Child Labour in Britain in the Nineteenth and Twentieth Centuries*. Liverpool: Liverpool University Press.

Lavalette, M., Hobbs, S., Lindsay, S. and McKechnie, J. (1995) 'Child employment in Britain: policy, myth and reality', *Youth and Policy*, 47: 1–15.

Lavalette, M., McKechnie, J. and Hobbs, S. (1991) *The Forgotten Workforce: Scottish Children at Work*. Glasgow: Scottish Low Pay Unit.

Lavalette, M., Mooney, G., Mynott, E., Evans, K. and Richardson, B. (2001) 'The woeful record of the House of Blair', *International Socialism*, 90: 77–102.

Lawson, J. and Silver, H. (1973) *A Social History of Education in England*. London: Methuen.

Leacock, E. (1981) *Myths of Male Dominance*. New York: Monthly Review Press.

Leahey, T.H. (1992) 'The mythical revolutions of American psychology', *American Psychologist*, 47: 308–18.

Lee, D. (1992) 'Poor work and poor institutions: training and the youth labour market', in P. Brown and R. Scase (eds), *Poor Work: Disadvantage and the Division of Labour*. Milton Keynes: Open University Press.

Lee, K. (1999) 'Doctors' report "Growing Up In Britain" highlights growing inequality in children's health', World Socialist website: http://www.wsws.org/articles/1999/pov-j16_prn.shtml.

Lees, S. (1993) *Sugar and Spice: Sexuality and Adolescent Girls*. Harmondsworth: Penguin.

Lewis, A. and Lindsay, G. (eds) (2000) *Researching Children's Perspectives*. Buckingham: Open University Press.

Lewis, D., Mallouh, C. and Webb, V. (1989) 'Child abuse, delinquency and violent criminality', in D. Cicchetti and V. Carlson (eds), *Child Maltreatment: Theory and Research on the Causes and Consequences of Child Abuse and Neglect*. Cambridge: Cambridge University Press.

Lindenmeyer, K. (1997) *'A Right To Childhood': The US Children's Bureau and Child Welfare 1912–1946*. Chicago: University of Illinois Press.

Liverpool Health Authority (2001) *Liverpool's Health 2001: The Annual Report of the Director of Public Health*. Liverpool: Liverpool Health Authority.

Lloyd-Smith, M. and Tarr, J. (1999) 'Researching children's perspectives: a sociological dimension', in A. Lewis and G. Lindsay (eds), *Researching Children's Perspectives*. Buckingham: Open University Press.

Long, R. (2001) 'Grim facts of life shame Glasgow', *Evening Times*, 15 March 2001.

Lovaas, O.I. (1993) 'Afterword', in C. Maurice (ed.), *Let Me Hear Your Voice: a Family's Triumph over Autism*. New York: Alfred A. Knopf.

Lovie, A.D. (1983) 'Attention and behaviourism – fact and fiction', *British Journal of Psychology*, 74, 301–10.

Lucock, B., Vogler, R. and Keating, H. (1996) 'Child protection in England and France – authority, legalism and social work practice', *Child and Family Law Quarterly*, 8: 297–312.

MacLennan, E. (1980) *Working Children*. London: Low Pay Unit.

MacLennan, E., Fitz, J. and Sullivan, J. (1985) *Working Children*. London: Low Pay unit.

Marson, D. (1973) *Children's Strikes in 1911*. Oxford: History Workshop, Ruskin Essays in Social History.

Martin, A.E. (1944) 'Child neglect: a problem of social administration', *Public Administration*, 22: 105–13.

Maurice, C. (1993) *Let Me Hear Your Voice: a Family's Triumph over Autism*. New York: Alfred A. Knopf.

May, M. (1973) 'Innocence and experience: the evolution of the concept of juvenile delinquency in the mid-nineteenth century', *Victorian Studies*, September.

McKechnie, J. and Hobbs, S. (eds) (1998) *Working Children: Reconsidering the Debates: Report of the International Working Group on Child Labour*. Amsterdam: Defence for Children International.

McKechnie, J. and Hobbs, S. (2000) 'Child employment: filling the research gaps', *Youth and Policy*, 66: 19–33.

McKechnie, J. and Hobbs, S. (2001) 'Work and education: are they compatible for children and adolescents?', in P. Mizen, C. Pole and A. Bolton (eds), *Hidden Hands: International Perspectives on Children's Work and Labour*. London: Routledge/Falmer.

McKechnie, J., Lavalette, M. and Hobbs, S. (2000) 'Child employment research in Britain', *Work, Employment and Society*, 14: 573–80.

McKechnie, J., Lindsay, S. and Hobbs, S. (1994) *Still Forgotten: Child Employment in Rural Scotland*. Glasgow: Scottish Low Pay Unit.

McMahon, W. and Marsh, T. (1999) *Filling the Gap: Free School Meals, Nutrition and Poverty*. London: Child Poverty Action Group.

McPherson, A. and Raab, C. (1988) *Governing Education: a Sociology of Policy since 1945*. Edinburgh: Edinburgh University Press.

Merrick, D. (1996) *Social Work and Child Abuse*. London: Routledge.

Middleton, S., Shropshire, J. and Croden, N. (1998) 'Earning your keep? Children's work and contributions to family budgets', in B. Pettitt (ed.), *Children and Work in the UK: Reassessing the Issues*. London: Child Poverty Action Group.

Millar, J. (1991) 'Bearing the cost', in S. Becker (ed.), *Windows of Opportunity: Public Policy and the Poor*. London: CPAG.

Ministry of Education (1940) *Health Education: Suggestions on Health Education for the Consideration of Teachers and Others concerned in the Health and Education of Children*. London: HMSO.

Ministry of Education/Central Advisory Council for Education (1959) *15 to 18* (Crowther Report). London: HMSO.

Ministry of Education/Central Advisory Council for Education (1963) *Half Our Future* (Newsom Report). London: HMSO.

Ministry of Education/Central Advisory Council for Education (1967) *Children in Their Primary Schools* (Plowden Report). London: HMSO.

Mizen, P. (1995) *The State, Young People and Youth Training*. London: Mansell.

Mizen, P., Bolton, A. and Cole, C. (1999) 'School age workers: the paid employment of children in Britain', *Work, Employment and Society*, 13: 1–16.

Moorehead, C. (1987) *School Age Workers in Britain Today*. London: Anti-Slavery Society.

Morgan, M. (1996) 'Qualitative research: a package deal?', *The Psychologist*, 9: 31–2.

Morris, J. (2000) *Having Someone Who Cares*. London: National Children's Bureau/Joseph Rowntree Foundation.

Morrison, J. (2001) 'Child guinea pigs to view "adult" film scenes', *Independent on Sunday*, 17 June 2001.

Morrow, V. (1994) 'Responsible children? Aspects of children's work and employment outside school in contemporary UK', in B. Mayall (ed.), *Children's Childhood: Observed and Experienced*. London: Falmer Press.

Morrow, V. and Richards, M. (1996) 'The ethics of social research with children: an overview', *Children and Society*, 10: 90–105.

Mort, F. (1987) *Dangerous Sexualities: Medico-Moral Politics in England since 1830*. London: Routledge and Kegan Paul.

Mortimore, P., Sammons, P., Stoll, L., Lewis, D. and Ecob, R. (1988) *School Matters*. London: Open Books.

Muncie, J. (1999) *Youth and Crime: a Critical Introduction*. London: Sage.

Musgrave, P.W. (1977) 'Corporal punishment in some English elementary schools, 1900–1939', *Research in Education*, No. 17, May.

Nandy, A. (1992) *Tradition, Tyranny and Utopias: Essays in the Politics of Awareness*. Delhi: Oxford University Press.

Nardinelli, C. (1990) *Child Labour and the Industrial Revolution*. Bloomington: Indiana University Press.

National Curriculum Council (1990) *Curriculum Guidance 5: Health Education*. York: National Curriculum Council.

National Society for the Prevention of Cruelty to Children (1999) *Out of Sight: NSPCC Report on Deaths from Abuse 1973–1998*. London: NSPCC.

NCCL (1971) *Children Have Rights*. London: NCCL.

Newburn, T. (1995) *Crime and Criminal Justice Policy*. Harlow: Longman.

Newburn, T. (1997) 'Youth, crime and justice', in M. Maguire, R. Morgan and R. Reiner (eds), *The Oxford Handbook of Criminology*, 2nd edn. Oxford: Clarendon Press.

Newstead, S.E. (1983) 'Perceived importance of famous psychologists', *Bulletin of the British Psychological Society*, 36: 239–41.

Nisbet, J. and Watt, J. (1995) *Educational Disadvantage in Scotland*. Edinburgh: Scottish Community Education Council.

Norcross, J.C. and Tomcho, T.J. (1994) 'Great books in psychology: three studies in search of a consensus', *Teaching of Psychology*, 21: 86–90.

Oakley, A. (1998) 'Experimentation in social science: the case of health promotion', *Social Sciences in Health*, 4: 73–89.

Oakley, A. (1999) 'People's ways of knowing: gender and methodology', in S. Hood, B. Mayall and S. Oliver (eds), *Critical Issues in Social Research*. Buckingham: Open University Press.

Oates, R. and Bross, D. (1995) 'What have we learned about treating child physical abuse? A literature review of the last decade', *Child Abuse and Neglect*, 19: 463–73.

O'Donnell, C. and White, L. (1999) *Hidden Danger: Injuries to Children at Work*. London: Low Pay Unit.

Oppenheim, C. and Harker, L. (1996) *Poverty: The Facts*. London: Child Poverty Action Group.

Pacione, M. (1997) 'The geography of educational disadvantage in Glasgow', *Applied Geography*, 17: 169–92.

Parton, N. (1985) *The Politics of Child Abuse*. Basingstoke: Macmillan.

Paul, D.B. and Blumenthal, A.L. (1989) 'On the trail of Little Albert', *Psychological Record*, 39: 547–53.

Pelling, H. (1963) *A History of British Trade Unionism*. Harmondsworth: Penguin.

PEP (1948) *Population Policy in Great Britain*. London: Political and Economic Planning.

Pettitt, B. (ed.) (1998) *Children and Work in the UK: Reassessing the Issues*. London: Save the Children.

Pfohl, S. (1977) 'The "discovery" of child abuse', *Social Problems*, 24: 310–23.

Phillips, A. (1999) *What Equalities Matter*. Cambridge: Polity Press.

Piaget, J. (1962) *Play, Dreams and Imitation in Childhood*. London: Routledge and Kegan Paul.

Piaget, J. (1972) *Psychology and Epistemology* [first published 1927]. Harmondsworth: Penguin.

Piaget, J. (1995) *Sociological Studies*. London: Routledge.

Pinchbeck, I. and Hewitt, M. (1973) *Children in English Society*, Vol. 2. London: Routledge and Kegan Paul.

Pitts, J. (2001) *The New Politics of Youth Crime: Discipline or Solidarity?* Basingstoke: Palgrave.

Place, U.T. (1956) 'Is consciousness a brain process?', *British Journal of Psychology*, 47: 44–50.

Pollock, L. (1983) *Forgotten Children: Parent–Child Relations from 1500 to 1900*. Cambridge: Cambridge University Press.

Pond, C. and Searle, A. (1991) *The Hidden Army: Children at Work in the 1990s*. London: Low Pay Unit.

Power, S. and Gewirtz, S. (2001) 'Reading EAZs', *Journal of Education Policy*, 16: 39–51.

Pratt, J. (1987) 'A revisionist history of intermediate treatment', *British Journal of Social Work*, 15: 417–36.

Prendergast, S. (1994) *This is the Time to Grow Up: Girls' Experiences of Menstruation in School*, 2nd edn. London: Family Planning Association.

Preston Guardian, The: various dates.

Prout, A. and James, A. (eds) (1990) *Constructing and Reconstructing Childhood*. London: Falmer.

Prout, A. and James, A. (eds) (1997) *Constructing and Reconstructing Childhood*, 2nd edn. London: Falmer.

QCA (1999) *The National Curriculum of England: Non-statutory Frameworks for Personal, Social and Health Education and Citizenship of Key Stages 1 and 2; Personal, Social and Health Education at Key Stages 3 and 4*. London: Qualifications and Curriculum Authority.

Qvortrup, J. (1990) 'A voice for children in statistical and social accounting: a plea for children's rights to be heard', in A. Prout and A. James (eds), *Constructing and Reconstructing Childhood*. London: Falmer.

Qvortrup, J. (1993) Nine theses about "childhood as a social phenomenon"', in J. Qvortrup (ed.), *Childhood as a Social Phenomenon: Lessons from an International Project. Eurosocial Report No. 47*. Vienna: European Centre for Social Welfare Policy and Research.

Qvortrup, J. (1994) 'Childhood matters: an introduction', in J. Qvortrup, M. Bardy, G. Sgritta, and H. WIntersberger (eds) *Childhood Matters: Social Theory, Practice and Politics*. Aldershot: Avebury.

Qvortrup, J. (1997) 'A voice for children in statistical and social accounting: a plea for children's rights to be heard', in A. James and A. Prout (eds) *Constructing and Reconstructing Childhood*. London: Farmer. pp. 85–116.

Read, J. (1998) 'Child abuse and severity of disturbance among adult psychiatric patients', *Child Abuse and Neglect*, 22: 359–68.

Rentoul, J. (1997) *The Rich Get Richer*. London: Unwin.

Rickford, F. (1995) 'Flying the flag', *Community Care*, 2–8 February: 22–24.

Rikowski, G. and Neary, M. (1997) 'Working children in Britain today', *Capital and Class*, 63: 23–35.

Rimmland, B. (1993) 'Foreword', in C. Maurice (ed.), *Let Me Hear Your Voice: a Family's Triumph over Autism*. New York: Alfred A. Knopf.

Ritchie, A. (1999) *Our Lives*. Edinburgh: Save the Children Scotland.

Robinson, P. (1976) *Education and Poverty*. London: Methuen.

Robin's Report (1963) *Higher Education*. London: HMSO.

Roker, D. (1991) 'Gaining "the edge": the education, training and employment of young people in private schools'. Paper presented at the ESRC 16–19 Initiative 'New Findings' Workshop, Harrogate.

Rose, S.A. and Blank, M. (1974) 'The potency of context in children's cognition: An illustration through conservation', *Child Development*, 45: 499–502.

Royal Commission (1949) *On Population*, Cmnd 7695. London: HMSO.

Rush, F. (1980) *The Best Kept Secret*. Englewood Cliffs, NJ: Prentice-Hall.

Russell, D. (1986) *The Secret Trauma: Incest in the Lives of Girls and Women*. New York: Basic Books.

Rutherford, A. (1995) 'Signposting the future of juvenile justice policy in England and Wales', in *Howard League for Penal Reform, Child Offenders UK and International Practice*. London: Howard League for Penal Reform.

Samelson, F. (1974) 'History, origin myth and ideology: discovery of social psychology', *Journal for the Theory of Social Behaviour*, 4: 217–31.

Save the Children (1999) Press release, *Youth Delegates Head for Durban Summit*. Save the Children. Internet reference: http://www.savethechildren.org.uk/pressrels/051199.html (accessed 20/2/2001).

Save the Children (22/3/2000) Press release, *Black Young People Say 'Stop and Listen'*. Save the Children. Internet Reference: http://www.savethechildren.org.uk/pressrels/220300.html (accessed 20/2/2001).

Save the Children (8/6/2000) Press release, *Welsh Traveller Children Speak Out*. Save the Children. Internet Reference: http://www.savethechildren.org.uk/pressrels/080600.html (accessed 20/2/2001).

Scarre, G. (1980) 'Children and paternalism', *Philosophy*, 55: 117–24.

Schorr, A. (1992) *The Personal Social Services: an Outside View*. York: Joseph Rowntree Foundation.

Scraton, P. (ed.) (1997) *'Childhood' in 'Crisis'?* London: UCL Press.

Seebohm Report (1968) *Report on the Personal and Allied Social Services*, Cmnd 3703. London: HMSO.

Sex Education Forum (1992) *A Framework for School Sex Education*. London: Sex Education Forum.

Sharland, E., Seal, H., Croucher, M., Aldgate, J. and Jones, D. (1996) *Professional Intervention into Child Sexual Abuse*. London: HMSO.

Shore, H. (1999) *Artful Dodgers: Youth and Crime in Early Nineteenth-Century London*. London: Royal Historical Society.

Simon, B. (1960) *Studies in the History of Education 1780–1870*. London: Lawrence and Wishart.

Simon, B. (1965) *Education and the Labour Movement 1870–1920*. London: Lawrence and Wishart.

Skinner, B.F. (1957) *Verbal Behavior*. New York: Appleton Century Croft.

Skinner, B.F. (1968) *The Technology of Teaching*. New York: Appleton Century Croft.

Slee, R. and Weiner, G. (1998) 'School: effectiveness for whom?', in R. Slee, G. Weiner and S. Tomlinson (eds), *School Effectiveness for Whom?* London: Falmer.

Smith, P. and Sharp, S. (1994) *School Bullying: Insights and Perspectives.* London: Routledge.

Social Services Inspectorate (1994) *The Child, the Court and the Video: a Study of the Implementation of the Memorandum of Good Practice on Video Interviewing of Child Witnesses.* London: Department of Health.

Social Trends (2000) *Social Trends 30.* London: Office for National Statistics.

Spooner, B. (1998) 'A tale of two schools in one city: Foxwood and Cross Green', in R. Slee, G. Weiner and S. Tomlinson (eds), *School Effectiveness for Whom?* London: Falmer.

Squibb, P. (1973) 'Education and class', *Educational Research*, 15: 194–208.

Stanley, N. (1999) 'The institutional abuse of children: an overview of policy and practice', in N. Stanley, J. Manthorpe and B. Penhale (eds), *Institutional Abuse: Perspectives across the Life Course.* London: Routledge.

Steinberg, L., Greenberger, E. and Ruggerio, M. (1982) 'Assessing job characteristics: When 'perceived' and 'objective' measures don't converge', *Psychological Report*, 50: 771–780.

Stephens, T. (1945) *Problem Families.* Liverpool and Manchester: Pacifist Service Units.

Stevenson, C. and Cooper, N. (1997) 'Qualitative and quantitative research', *The Psychologist*, 10: 159–60.

Stevenson, O. (1998) *Neglected Children: Issues and Dilemmas.* Oxford: Blackwell.

Stewart, J. (1995) 'Children, parents and the state: The Children Act, 1908', *Children and Society*, 9: 90–9.

Tarrow, S. (1994) *Power in Movement.* Cambridge: Cambridge University Press.

Taylor, T. (1994) 'As the cocks crow, the young ones learn: the school strikes of 1889 and the New Union Movement', *History of Education*, 23: 89–106.

Taylor, W. (1993) *Governments and Professional Education.* Buckingham: Open University Press.

TES (2001a) 'Setting can be harmful', *Times Educational Supplement*, 13 April 2001.

TES (2001b) 'Action zones frozen out', *Times Educational Supplement*, 5 January 2001.

TES (2001c) 'Cold water poured on hotbeds of innovation', *Times Educational Supplement*, 6 April 2001.

TES (2001d) 'Teacher leads dash to privatize', *Times Educational Supplement*, 21 September 2001.

Thane, P. (1982) *The Foundations of the Welfare State.* London: Longman.

The Psychologist (1995) Vol. 8, No. 3, 109–29.

The Psychologist (1997) Vol. 10, No. 4, 159–62.

The Psychologist (1998) Vol. 11, No. 10, 481–8.

Thoburn, J., Lewis, A. and Shemmings, D. (1995) *Paternalism or Partnership? Family Involvement in the Child Protection Process.* London: HMSO.

Thompson, P. (1975) 'The war with adults', *Oral History Journal*, 3: 29–39.

Thorne, B. (1987) '1986 Cheryl Miller Lecture: revisiting women and social change; Where are the children?', *Gender and Society*, 1: 85–109.

Thorpe, D.H., Smith, D., Green, C.J and Paley, J.H. (1980) *Out of Care: the Community Support of Juvenile Offenders.* London: George Allen and Unwin.

Times, The: various dates.

Tobias, J. (1972) *Crime and Industrial Society in the Nineteenth Century.* Harmondsworth: Penguin.

Tomlinson, S. (1998) 'A tale of one school in one city: Hackney Downs', in R. Slee, G. Weiner and S. Tomlinson (eds), *School Effectiveness for Whom?* London: Falmer.

Tonry, M. (1996) 'Racial politics, racial disparities, and the war on crime', in B. Hudson (ed.), *Race, Crime and Justice.* Aldershot: Dartmouth.

Tunstill, J. (1997) 'Implementing the family support clauses of the 1989 Children Act: legislative, professional and organisational obstacles', in N. Parton (ed.), *Child Protection and Family Support: Tensions, Contradictions and Possibilities.* London: Routledge.

UN Committee of the Rights of the Child (1995) *Concluding Observations of the Committee on the Rights of the Child: United Kingdom of Great Britain and Northern Ireland CRC/C/14*, Add. 34 (15 February). New York: United Nations.

UNESCO (2000) *Statistical Yearbook.* Paris: UNESCO.

UNICEF (1997) *Social Mobilisation and Child Labour: Background Paper to the Oslo Conference on Child Labour on 27–30th October 1997*. New York: UNICEF.

Utting, Sir W. (1997) *People Like Us: the Report of the Review of the Safeguards for Children Living Away from Home*. London: HMSO.

Valsiner, J. (2000) *Culture and Human Development*. London: Sage.

Vincent, J. (1991) 'The Conservatives diary: policies affecting poor families: June 1979–July 1991', in S. Becker (ed.), *Windows of Opportunity: Public Policy and the Poor*. London: CPAG.

Walker, R. (1999) 'Life-cycle trajectories', in *Persistent Poverty and Lifetime Inequality: The Evidence. CASE Report 5*. London: London School of Economics, Centre for Analysis of Social Exclusion.

Waterhouse, Sir R. (2000) *Lost in Care: Report of the Tribunal of Inquiry into the Abuse of Children in Care in the Former County Council Areas of Gwynedd and Clwyd since 1974*, HC 201. London: The Stationery Office.

Waterman, A.H., Blades, M. and Spencer, C. (2000) 'Do children try to answer nonsensical questions?', *British Journal of Developmental Psychology*, 18: 474–77.

Wedge, P. and Prosser, H. (1973) *Born to Fail?* London: Arrow.

Weeks, J. (1989) *Sex, Politics and Society: The Regulation of Sexuality since 1800*. London: Longman.

Wein, N. (1971) 'The education of disadvantaged children', *Educational Research*, 13: 12–19.

West, P. and Sweeting, H. (1996) 'Nae job, nae future: young people and health in a context of unemployment', *Health and Social Care in the Community*, 4: 50–62.

Westcott, H. (1999) 'Communication', in N. Parton and C. Wattam (eds), *Child Sexual Abuse: Responding to the Experiences of Children*. Chichester: John Wiley.

Whitney, B. (1999) 'Unenforced or unenforceable? A view from the professions', in M. Lavalette (ed.), *A Thing of the Past? Child Labour in Britain in the Nineteenth and Twentieth Centuries*. Liverpool: Liverpool University Press.

Wilkinson, R. (1994) *Unfair Shares: The Effects of Widening Income Differentials on the Welfare of the Young*. Ilford: Barnardo's.

Wilkinson, R. (1996) *Unhealthy Societies*. London: Routledge.

Williams, F. (c. 1950) *The Fifty Year March: The Rise of the Labour Party*. London: Odhams Press.

Wilson, A. (1980) 'The infancy of the history of childhood: an appraisal of Philippe Ariès', *History and Theory*, 19: 133–49.

Wilson, E. (1977) *Women and the Welfare State*. London: Tavistock.

Wolock, L. and Horowitz, B. (1984) 'Child maltreatment as a social problem: the neglect of neglect', *American Journal of Orthopsychiatry*, 54: 530–43.

Women's Group on Public Welfare (1943) *Our Towns*. Oxford: Oxford University Press.

Women's Group on Public Welfare (1948) *The Neglected Child and His Family*. Oxford: Oxford University Press.

Woodward, K. (2001) 'Feminist critiques of social policy', in M. Lavalette and A. Pratt (eds), *Social Policy: a Conceptual and Theoretical Introduction*, 2nd edn. London: Sage.

Wynn, M. (1970) *Family Policy*. London: Unwin.

Yamey, G. (1999) 'Study shows growing inequalities in health in Britain', *British Medical Journal*, 319: 1453.

Younghusband Report (1959) *The Report of the Working Party on Social Workers in the Local Authority Health and Welfare Services*. London: HMSO.

Youth Justice Board (2001) *Reform of the Juvenile Secure Estate: a Four Year Plan by the Youth Justice Board*. London: Youth Justice Board for England and Wales.

Index